Berkeley's Puzzle

Berkeley's Puzzle

What Does Experience Teach Us?

John Campbell
and Quassim Cassam

OXFORD
UNIVERSITY PRESS

OXFORD
UNIVERSITY PRESS

Great Clarendon Street, Oxford, OX2 6DP,
United Kingdom

Oxford University Press is a department of the University of Oxford.
It furthers the University's objective of excellence in research, scholarship,
and education by publishing worldwide. Oxford is a registered trade mark of
Oxford University Press in the UK and in certain other countries

Published in the United States of America by Oxford University Press
198 Madison Avenue, New York, NY 10016, United States of America

British Library Cataloguing in Publication Data

Data available

Library of Congress Control Number: 2014936669

ISBN 978-0-19-871625-9

Preface

The discussions that led to this book began when we were both graduate students, and they have taken many forms: sometimes published exchanges, more often comments on one another's talks, or hasty lunches at the Duke of Cambridge. Although we have both changed our minds many times we seem somehow never to have quite agreed. But it eventually seemed that the issues we were discussing had reached a fairly sharp form, and that it was time to give a full statement of where we were.

We have had a lot of help in preparing this book. Campbell's contribution was tried out in a series of graduate seminars at Berkeley, with wonderfully incisive comments from many graduate students, too many to be usefully listed by name, though they include Christopher Allen, Austin Andrews, Adam Bradley, Sophia Dandelet, Peter Epstein, James Hutchinson, Jackson Kernion, Antonia Peacocke, Janum Sethi, and Umrao Sethi. Discussions with Geoff Lee and Mike Martin were extremely helpful. Imogen Dickie gave an insightful, detailed set of comments on Campbell's first three chapters. Barry Stroud commented on all of Campbell's chapters and made a most helpful set of remarks at an APA symposium on the draft book. Despite, or because of, his strong disagreements, John Searle, with Klaus Strelau, provided time in his seminar for discussion of our approaches.

Cassam's contribution has benefited from discussions with friends and colleagues at Warwick. Early feedback from a discussion group run by Naomi Eilan was especially helpful. We had three readers from OUP: one anonymous, the others Michael Ayers and Howard Robinson, who provided trenchant critiques of our early draft.

Contents

1

The Historical Background

John Campbell

1. Berkeley's Puzzle

We ordinarily think that the world around us is independent of our minds. There
are many things that existed long before we did—rivers and rocks and mountains
and so on. More poignantly, it seems entirely possible that the rocks and mountains may last longer than the human species. The rocks and mountains are independent of us. They would have existed even if humans had never existed.

Berkeley's Puzzle is a problem about how we can so much as come to think about
mind-independent objects, like rocks and mountains, in the first place. The Puzzle
depends on two ideas. They are not difficult to articulate or understand. And they
each seem sensible enough. Many philosophers working today would accept one
or the other or both.

(1) It is because of sensory experience that we have knowledge of our sur-
    roundings. For example, it is in virtue of your visual experience of what is in
    front of you at the moment that you know what is there. Sensory experience
    is the foundation of both our knowledge that things are thus and so, and our
    knowledge of what things and properties are there in our environment.

(2) If we ask what sensory experience can contribute to our knowledge, the
    only answer is that it contributes knowledge of sensory experience itself.
    Consider the possibility of someone who does not have sensory expe-
    rience of some aspect of the world. (Perhaps they have some theoretical,
    or implicit, knowledge of it.) What does this person learn when they now
    experience that aspect of things? The compelling answer is that they learn
    something about what it is like to experience that aspect of the world. And
    that is all.

Yet put together, these two ideas imply that all we can have knowledge of is sensory experience itself. We can't have knowledge of mind-independent objects. We can't even form the conception of rocks and mountains as mind-independent.

The problem of the role of sensory experience in knowledge seemed particularly nasty in the seventeenth century. The picture provided by mathematical physics seemed both compelling and quite alien to the view of the world provided by our ordinary sensory experience. For example, as Koyré remarks, on Newton's view:

> Not only are the heavenly spaces empty and void, but even the so-called 'solid bodies' are full of void. The particles that compose them are by no means closely packed together, but are separated from one another by void space. The Newtonians, from Bentley on, took an enormous pride and pleasure in pointing out that 'matter' proper occupies a practically infinitesimal part of space.
>
> (Koyré 1965, p. 14, fn. 4)

Mathematical physics gave us a firm conception of 'matter'. But it seemed to show our surroundings to be unlike anything in sensory experience. How can experience be playing a role in giving us knowledge of our surroundings, when in fact physics seems to show our surroundings to be so alien?

The trouble is that physics seems to push sensory experience inside the head. And we now have the problem of explaining how this stuff inside the head can be playing any privileged or distinctive role in generating our knowledge of the world around us. We have a conception of the 'qualitative character' of our sensory experience, the way it is for you when you see a beach ball against a blue sky, for example. If mathematical physics is the whole truth about our surroundings, then the qualitative character of our sensory experience seems to have little to do with the qualitative character of our surroundings. This is a problem, because we ordinarily think of sensory experience as the foundation of our knowledge of our surroundings. What role is there for sensory experience in providing us with knowledge of what is going on around us?

The problem is particularly obvious in the case of colour. Colour does not seem to be in the world as described by physics. How then can colour experience be playing any role in giving us knowledge of our surroundings?

Before physics, you might have thought that the qualitative character of sensory experience is actually constituted by the qualitative character of the world. When you encounter the beach ball on the beach, for example, you are having an experience that you could not have had unless the world has the qualitative character it does. The beach ball and the sky are constituents of your experience, and their qualitative characters constitute the qualitative character of your experience. That is how experience can be providing you with knowledge of your surroundings. It does so both in providing you with propositional knowledge of how things stand around you, and, more fundamentally, by providing you with some understanding of the concepts of the various objects and properties around you. That's the natural picture. The trouble is that physics seems to undermine that picture, by showing you that the qualitative character of the world is quite unlike anything that shows up in your experience. How then can experience be playing any role in our knowledge of our surroundings?

Yet if we allow physics to push sensory experience back inside the head, then we need some proprietary vocabulary to describe the stuff inside the head. The trouble here, as we shall see, is that we have no coherent conception of sensory experience itself, as something 'internal to the head'. In the end, we have to resist the 'internalization' of sensory experience, the way physics has pushed it into the head.

But how can we resist the way in which physics pushes sensory experience inside the head? Our understanding of sensory experience could be transformed by giving due weight to the idea that reality can be described 'at many levels'. We can acknowledge that there is something fundamental about the physics of our surroundings, at least in that all other facts about our world supervene on the physical facts, while being 'pluralist' about our world, which can be described 'at many levels', and the physical is only one level of description, even if it is a particularly fundamental level of description. There are two developments that make this move particularly appealing. One is the rise of the special sciences, such as psychology, zoology, and economics, which cannot really be regarded as merely branches of physics. The other is recognition of the difficulty of achieving a reduction of conscious phenomena to physical phenomena. These points mean that many philosophers now would acknowledge that the world may be described at many 'different levels'. This opens the possibility that characterizing the qualitative world we encounter in experience, the colours and shapes, the beach ball on the sand, and so on, is simply a matter of saying how things are 'at a different level' than the level of description used by the physicist. This doesn't require that those qualities and objects should be in any way mind-dependent. The dissonance between the qualitative character of our experience and the qualitative character of the world as described by physics may then be merely an artefact of our shifting from one level of description to another. We can keep our natural understanding of the epistemic role of sensory experience, on which the qualitative character of sensory experience is constituted by the qualitative character of the things and properties around us.

In this chapter, I want to set out some of the basic models of the role of sensory experience in grasp of concepts of the objects and properties around us. This is a question about consciousness; but it is not the same as the question whether sensory experience is itself to be reduced to, or explained in terms of, the physical. This is the traditional mind–body problem, and it is arguably secondary to the question I am concerned with, which is the epistemic role of sensory experience. Does sensory experience give us knowledge of our surroundings, or does it play no significant role in cognition? This is a question about both propositional and non-propositional knowledge. Does sensory experience play an essential role in our knowledge that things are thus and so in our surroundings? And, the more basic question, does sensory experience play an essential role in our knowledge of which things and properties there are in our surroundings? That is, does our grasp of concepts of the objects and properties around us essentially depend on sensory experience? Developing models of the relation of sensory experience to our surroundings is, as I said, arguably prior to addressing the mind–body problem. Only when we have a firm understanding of the point of our talking about these phenomena of awareness—do we invoke them to explain our knowledge of our surroundings?—will we be in a position to ask whether they can themselves be explained in terms of physical phenomena.

On one view, still popular today, the epistemic role of sensory experience has to do with the external causes and effects of its phenomenal character. The specific phenomenal characters of your various sensory experiences have no bearing on their epistemic value; all that matters is their characteristic causes and effects. As we shall see, Locke defends this kind of view for the case of our sensory experience of colour.

2.   Locke on Ideas as Signs of Their Regular Causes

Physics drove sensory experience inside the head. Once that happened, there was a question whether sensory experience can really be providing us with knowledge at all. Locke (1690/1975) put it like this: since physics has pushed sensory experience inside the head, it could be that different people are having quite different sensory experiences in response to one and the same external environment. How then can sensory experience be giving any of us knowledge of our surroundings? One way Locke puts it is to say that if our experiences are qualitatively different, then the world out there can't resemble both your experiences and mine. So how could your experiences and my experiences both be giving us knowledge about the world out there? I'll look at his talk about 'resemblance' in the next section. But he has a more basic point.

Locke's point is that, in explaining the epistemic value of sensory awareness, one role of the sensations is to be signs of their regular causes. Here the intrinsic characters of the sensory experiences matter only as a way of differentiating sensations that have different regular causes. So long as your perceptual sensations have the right kind of structure, and have the right pattern of regular causes, they will not be representing the world incorrectly.

Locke illustrates the point by considering the case in which one person's colour sensations have different intrinsic characters to another person's colour sensations:

Neither would it carry any Imputation of *Falsehood* to our simple *Ideas, if* by the different Structure of our Organs, it were so ordered, That *the same Object should produce in several Men's Minds different* Ideas at the same time; *v.g.* if the *Idea,* that a *Violet* produced in one Man's Mind by his Eyes, were the same that a *Marigold* produces in another Man's, and *vice versa.*

(*Essay,* II/xxxii/15)

That's to say: there is no representational error, no 'Imputation of *Falsehood*', for either of the people in this case in which they have different colour sensations. It would not matter for ordinary communication if there were a difference in the intrinsic characters of our sensations. For we don't, ordinarily, know the intrinsic characters of one another's sensations; so communication doesn't rely on them being the same.

For since this could never be known: because one Man's Mind could not pass into another Man's Body, to perceive, what Appearances were produced by those Organs; neither the *Ideas* hereby, nor the Names, would be at all confounded, or any *Falsehood* be in either.

(II/xxxii/15)

Moreover, the palette of colour sensations in one person's mind, despite the intrinsic difference from the colour sensations in the other person's mind, could still be responding to exactly the same pattern of regular causes:

For all Things, that had the Texture of a *Violet,* producing constantly the *Idea,* which he called *Blue,* and those which had the Texture of a *Marigold,* producing constantly the *Idea,* which he as constantly called *Yellow,* whatever those Appearances were in his Mind; he would be able as regularly to distinguish Things for his Use by those Appearances, and understand, and signify those distinctions, marked by the Names *Blue* and *Yellow,* as if the Appearances, or *Ideas* in his Mind, received from those two Flowers, were exactly the same, with the *Ideas* in other Men's Minds.

(II/xxxii/15)

This gives us one basic style of explanation of the epistemic value of sensory awareness. Different types of perceptual sensation have different characteristic causes, and the sensations can therefore function as signs of their regular causes. Sensory awareness—in this analysis, 'sensation'—is coming in only as that which has regular causes in the environment.

As we shall see, this is not all Locke has to say about the epistemic role of sensory awareness. But this is a striking line of thought. It certainly does seem it would be valuable to an organism to have structures that are reliable signs of the presence of their regular causes. However, it now seems obvious that this role does not have to be played by sensations, or as Locke here calls them, 'Ideas'. On the face of it, exactly the same role could be played by patterns of, for example, neural activity. Patterns of neural activity, conscious or not, could represent the world by being systematically responsive to the operation of their regular causes in our environment. So no distinctive epistemic role has been found for consciousness; we could, on this picture, have just the same knowledge of the world without consciousness as we do with consciousness. The fact that we are dealing specifically with *sensations* has been given no significant work to do; all that is being exploited about sensations is the fact that they stand in distinctive causal relations to external phenomena in the environment. But of course, it is not unique to sensations that they stand in such causal relationships to phenomena in the environment.

You might object: sensations are elements in the subjective life of the perceiver, in a way that mere neural assemblies, perhaps remote from consciousness, are not. So maybe the fact that it is sensations we are dealing with is important after all. You might say that sensations bring the external phenomenon into the subjective life of the perceiver in a way that a mere neural assembly could not. Now this is an important objection. If there is a role for sensory experience in our knowledge of the world, it must have something to do with the idea that experience does 'bring the world into' the subjective life of the perceiver.

The difficulty with the objection is this. Sensations themselves are certainly 'in the subjective life' of the thinker. But the mere fact that the sensation stands in a causal relation to external phenomena does not of itself mean that those external phenomena have been 'brought into the subjective life of' the perceiver. The trouble is that though the sensation is, as it were, inertly there in the subjective life of the perceiver, it is doing nothing to explain how the external world is being brought into the subjective life of the perceiver. The sensation stands in causal relations to the external phenomena. So far we do not know why this brings those external phenomena into the subjective life of the perceiver in a way that could not be done by mere neural assemblies. Doubtless the intrinsic characteristics of the sensation are available to the perceiver. But the causal relations of the sensation to aspects of the environment are not themselves intrinsic characteristics of the sensation. There's no presumption that they are available to the subject.

Now you might supplement Locke's account. You might say: it's not just that external objects or properties cause the sensation. The sensation also connects to other thoughts and desires. Maybe you could say, well, the sensation causes the subject to think, 'That's a bank where the wild thyme blows,' for example. You could appeal, more generally, to causal relations between the sensation and other aspects of the subject's mental life: the perceiver's beliefs, for example. Although you could do this, though, you could also do it for a mere neural assembly. You could characterize a neural assembly that is caused by external aspects of the world just as the sensation is, and you could characterize causal relations between that neural assembly and the perceiver's beliefs, for example. Nothing in this would exploit the idea that the neural assembly, or the processes in which it plays a role, are conscious. So the fact that Locke's account appeals to sensations as being the items that stand in the right kinds of causal relations to the external world and to the rest of the subject's mental life is not really explaining what role sensory awareness plays in providing us with knowledge of our surroundings. It leaves it seeming that we could have exactly the same knowledge of our surroundings without having sensory experience.

The root problem in Locke's account so far is that the thing that makes the sensation conscious is doing no work in the account of how the sensation makes it possible for us to think about the world. The sensation is conscious. But that fact about the sensation seems to explain only how we could have knowledge of the sensation itself. What is giving the sensation of colour its epistemic role, on Locke's account, is not 'that which makes it conscious', but its causal relation to the surroundings. It is truly difficult to see how an approach to sensory experience in terms of sensations can do anything to explain how sensory experience makes it possible for us to think about our surroundings. This is one basis of Berkeley's Puzzle. We may indeed feel driven to think of sensory experience in terms of sensations. The trouble is that it is difficult to see how the mere having of sensation as such could provide one with knowledge of anything more than what it is like to have those very sensations. This means that when we try to acknowledge a foundational epistemic role for experience, we will find that all we can ever think about are sensations.

Another example may help to make this point vivid. We already considered Locke's idea that spectrum inversion would make no difference to your ability to think about the colours of objects. However, by Locke's own argument it now looks as though a complete absence of colour sensations would make no difference to your ability to think about the colours of objects. Consider someone born colour-blind. This person has a reliable way to find out about the colours of the objects around them: ask. Why isn't that enough for an ability to think about the colours of objects? You might argue that, well, this person is after all dependent on other people. So perhaps it is only by courtesy of other people that this person can be said to grasp anything to do with colour. So suppose we have someone who has brain circuitry that can determine the colours of objects, but that this happens in a way that is remote from their sensory experience. So, for example, if this person is simply asked to say what colour the object before her is, she naturally replies that she can't do that, she experiences everything in (let us suppose) black and white. However, suppose we ask her to guess, and she does. We may find that she is quite reliable at forced-choice guessing as to the colours of objects in front of her. There is no special puzzle about this; all that is happening is that these verbal reports are being sustained by neural processing that is determining the colours of objects without sustaining sensory experience of the colours of objects. But does this subject know what the colours are? By Locke's argument, there is no confusion in this person's communications with other people. And she has neural states that are reliable signs of the presence of the various colours. Still it seems evident that this subject does not know what the colour words mean, any more than did the person who was born completely colour-blind (that is, without even the circuitry, remote from consciousness, that allowed accurate verbal reports of colour). If that is right, then we have not articulated the role of sensory awareness in our knowledge of the world by saying that it is a matter of sensations being signs of their regular causes. Sensory experience does seem to play an essential role in our knowledge of our surroundings, and if Locke's account were to stop here he would not have acknowledged the force of that idea.

3. Locke on Resemblance

There is, famously, another dimension to Locke's discussion of the epistemic role of experience. He says that some of our sensory experiences are 'Resemblances' of the external physical properties, and some are not:

[T]he *Ideas of primary Qualities* of Bodies, *are Resemblances* of them, and their Patterns do really exist in the Bodies themselves; But the *Ideas, produced* in us *by* these *Secondary Qualities, have no resemblance* of them at all.

(*Essay*, II/viii/15)

By 'primary qualities of Bodies', Locke means shape, size, motion or rest, number, and weight: the properties that he takes to be basic to mechanical explanations of the physical behaviour of objects. By 'Ideas, produced in us by these Secondary Qualities', he means the ideas of colour, smell, taste, and so on produced in us by properties of the external objects.

When Locke says that the ideas of primary qualities resemble those properties, he is making an epistemic point. The ideas of primary qualities give a kind of knowledge of properties of external objects that ideas of secondary qualities do not.

Here it really is specifically experience that is being given epistemic work to do, work that could not have been done without experience. The natural ideas that Locke is working with are something like this:

(a) What is distinctive of sensory consciousness, as opposed to perceptual cognition in general, is the having of sensations, not just perceptual representations (in the sense of: things that are reliable signs of their usual causes), therefore:

(b) If sensory awareness as such can provide you with knowledge of the nature of your surroundings, it must be in virtue of some characteristic of the sensations themselves, not just the representational content (in that causal sense) that perception has.

The upshot of this is that in trying to characterize the epistemic role of sensory experience, Locke is forced to work with the idea that there is something about the intrinsic characteristics of perceptual sensations in virtue of which they yield knowledge of the objects and properties around you.

Of course, you might say that this cannot be right, that it is only the representational characteristics of experience that generate knowledge of our surroundings. But then, since any representational characteristic that an experience has could equally well be there in the absence of consciousness, you will have to abandon the idea that there is any distinctive epistemic role for consciousness. Experiences can be natural signs of external situations, but non-conscious states can also be natural signs of external situations.

However, the view that Locke is driven to, in trying to find the epistemic role of experience, has usually struck commentators as incredible. While I don't, in the end, think the view is correct, it seems to me an important position. I think that feeling the pull of Locke's view is the best way of getting a sense of the radical thinking that is required if we are to find an alternative account of the epistemic value of sensory experience.

The doctrine is that our ideas of primary qualities themselves, considered severally, do each resemble the primary qualities of external objects. Sensory experience has been driven inside the head; but the sensory experiences themselves literally do have characteristics like shape or colour. As he puts it, 'A Circle or Square are the same, whether in *Idea* or Existence' (II/viii/18). An idea can be circular or square; an external object can be circular or square. So from having a circular or square idea, you may derive knowledge of what a circular or square external thing is.

Although your sensory experience can have colour characteristics, just as it can have shape characteristics, however, there is, unlike the case of shape and so on, nothing resembling those characteristics of the experiences in the objects themselves. The blueness of the idea is not to be found in the object itself; all we find in the object itself is 'Bulk, Figure and Motion of the insensible Parts' (II/viii/15). In the case of shape, having the sensory experience can provide you with knowledge of a characteristic of external objects; in the case of colour, having the experience does not provide you with a similar foundation for knowledge of a property of external objects. Blueness is not the same in idea as in existence.

One way to see the appeal of his picture is to consider a simple puzzle about phosphenes. Phosphenes are visual experiences that are not caused by light entering the eye. One familiar case is when you shut your eyes, press a finger gently against your eye and 'see stars'. The visual experience can be caused by pressure rather than light. These experiences are not necessarily projected onto external reality, as in the cases of full-blown hallucinations. More control over the content of the phosphenes is provided by electrical stimulation of the visual cortex, though the results as yet still tend to be somewhat indefinite. Now, suppose that your visual cortex has been stimulated, and you are having what you report as a bright yellow square phosphene, moving from left to right. Is there really something there that is yellow, square, and moving? Here are two answers:

(1) It's just a denial of reality to say there is nothing there that is yellow, square, and moving. That is the only vocabulary we have to describe what the subject is experiencing. And it's not as if this is an extended or metaphorical use of our ordinary talk about colours, shapes, and movement: you are not talking figuratively when you say that the thing is a vibrant yellow.

(2) It's crazy to say there is something there that is literally yellow, square, and moving. We can search all of space and time and there is nowhere to be found anything literally occupying space that has these characteristics, or at any rate, nothing relevant. There is nothing that is yellow, square, and moving.

Both reactions are powerful. In the case of colour terms as applied to ordinary concrete objects, there is a certain complexity in the way we use them. For example, a red pepper painted green isn't a green pepper; it's a red pepper painted green. Nothing parallel seems to apply to phosphenes. But we also speak of film colours, or the colours of flames, where we don't get this complexity, or not in the same way. If 'yellow' applies to both bananas and flames, can't it also apply to phosphenes? Similarly for 'square' and 'moving', which apply, quite literally, to both concrete objects, in which case they have causal significance, and to geometrical patterns, e.g. on a computer screen.

Although the puzzle itself is very simple to state, it is important to realize that contemporary philosophical discussion has no compelling resolution of it. One

school of thought would say that in the case of the phosphene, you are representing the presence of something yellow. But you could represent the presence of
something yellow without there being anything yellow about your experience. For
example, a piece of text can represent the yellowness of a banana without itself
being yellow. What we need to characterize is the difference between merely representing the presence of something yellow, which you could do in a newspaper
report, and the presence of the yellow phosphene itself. I have heard it said that
'in ordinary colour vision, you think about the colours, *in colour*'. This does viv-
idly express the sense that there is something quite special about the way in which
visual experience represents colours; but of course it requires that the visual experience itself should literally be coloured. Somewhat similarly, people sometimes
say that vision does not represent the colours; it *presents* them. But if you ask what
is the intuitive idea that people are trying to express with this formulation, it seems
evident that nothing short of the experience itself being literally coloured will do.
Similar points, of course, apply to the idea that the phosphene is merely representing the presence of something square and moving. We have to acknowledge the
force of the idea that the phosphene itself is, literally, square and moving.

   The only other resource we find in contemporary philosophical discussion is the
idea that there are 'visual sensations' or 'mental paint' that have to be characterized
using some technical vocabulary other than the terms that we use to characterize properties of external objects. The suggestion is that there is a kind of 'mental
paint' that is used in experience to depict one's surroundings, just as regular paint
can be used to depict a forest scene. And just as regular paint has certain intrinsic characteristics, so too mental paint has intrinsic characteristics. Whatever
the intrinsic characteristics of mental paint are, however, proponents of this kind
of idea usually emphasize that they do not include characteristics such as being
yellow, square, or moving. To take a recent example, Ned Block writes: 'To avoid
misunderstanding: I do not claim that there is anything red or round in the head
when one veridically sees a red or round thing in the world as when red pigment
in a painting represents a red barn' (Block 2010, p. 56, footnote 2). For this reason,
mental paint theory simply does not address the puzzle about the phosphene. To
be told that the phosphene has characteristics x13, y44, and z103 (or whatever technical terms one introduces to describe the intrinsic characteristics of mental paint)
does nothing to explain the sense in which it is literally correct to say that the thing
is yellow, square, and moving.

   You might say that the phosphene isn't really yellow; it only *looks* yellow. The
trouble here is to understand why you would use such a cautious formulation.
There the thing is, manifestly, vibrantly, unmistakably yellow. Might it after all be
purple, or plaid? If not, then what is the point of saying that it 'looks yellow'? There

isn't any suggestion that it might really be some other colour. The way we handle this situation in ordinary English is, I think, to use the ordinary vocabulary of colour, shape, and movement, but to say that there isn't anything 'out there' that has those characteristics, there isn't anything 'really' there. The thing is literally yellow, square, and moving, and though it isn't a something, it isn't a nothing either. I do not think that this is a finally satisfactory analysis of the puzzle about phosphenes, but as I said, I do not think that philosophy has, at the moment, anything better to offer.

This puzzle becomes more than a special problem about phosphenes when we reflect on the significance of allowing physics to push experience inside the head. It now appears that in ordinary vision, we have to allow that the visual experiences themselves are literally yellow, shaped, or moving. Nothing less will do justice to the 'special' character of visual 'representation', and talk about an arcane realm of 'mental paint' won't do it either. If we hadn't allowed physics to push visual experience inside the head, of course, we could have acknowledged that in ordinary visual perception, the only yellow, square, moving objects are those outside the head.

For Locke, however, the ideas involved in ordinary vision are 'inside the head', and once you have reached that point, the only way you have of doing justice to the character of visual experience is to acknowledge that the ideas themselves are, for example, literally yellow, square, and moving. Now the question arises, does anything outside the head have the characteristics that those visual experiences do? And as we have seen, Locke's answer is that the external objects don't literally have the very same properties of colour that the experiences do (there is only 'Bulk, Figure and Motion of the insensible Parts') but the external objects do literally have the same properties of shape and motion that the visual experiences do. Consequently, your experiences of shape and movement are giving you a kind of knowledge of the properties of external objects that is not being provided by your experiences of colour.

Notice that this analysis of the epistemic role of experience really does apply specifically to consciousness. It is the phenomenal character of your perceptual experience that is said to resemble the primary qualities around you. Experience provides you first with the character of your phenomenal experience itself, and that provides knowledge of the primary qualities because the ideas of the primary qualities are resemblances of them. There is no suggestion that anything non-experiential in perception could play such a role. So here we do have an attempt to explain the epistemic value specifically of sensory experience. Of course, resemblance could, in principle, hold between structures in the brain, remote from consciousness, and external properties. It could happen that representation of external shapes was achieved by the production of similar shapes in the brain. But merely to have one's brain be in a certain configuration, remote from consciousness, would not of itself mean that one had any grasp of what it is to be in that configuration, even if there is a resemblance between configurations in the brain and configurations in the distal world. In contrast, Locke's picture is that once you have the sensory experience, the resemblance of aspects of the external world to that experience means that from the experience you can find out what those aspects of the world are like.

What causes a lot of difficulty in understanding Locke's text here is that it is often supposed that if the talk of 'resemblance' is to make any sense at all, it must be as a kind of representation. To say that the idea resembles a quality of objects must be a matter of saying that the idea represents that quality, perhaps in some special way. But Locke is not talking about representation here. As we saw, in his discussion of experience of colour, Locke is operating with a perfectly good sense in which experiences of colour can be said to represent the world correctly: sensations of colour are representations of particular microphysical properties in the world around us, those which are the regular causes of those experiences of colour. And those representations are in general correct, even if your and my sensations are intrinsically quite unlike one another. There is no 'Imputation of *Falsehood*' if our colour experiences are intrinsically quite different to, and do not resemble, the textures they stand for. His point here is that further to the talk of 'representation', further to the talk of 'what the Ideas signify', there is another, more fundamental kind of knowledge of the world that sensory experience can give us, in the context of experience of shape but not in the context of experience of colour. In sensory experience of shape, we first have the qualitative character of the sensory experience itself; but our encounter with the sensory experience allows us to go further and find out something about the nature of the quality of shape itself, since that quality resembles the experience.

Notice that the kind of knowledge we are gaining here is not knowledge of the truth of propositions. Really, the story about which representational contents are true can in principle, on Locke's terms, all be told without making reference to any phenomena specifically of consciousness. Ideas are signs of their regular causes; and the story of how the representational system works here does not, as we have already seen, make any indispensable reference to experience. What is doing the work, in the account of representational content, is the fact that something or other is a sign of its regular cause; it does not really matter that it is ideas that, for us, function as signs of their regular causes. What resemblance provides, however, is a kind of knowledge that is not a matter of knowing the truth of propositions, and is a phenomenon specifically of consciousness. When we recognize that the experience of squareness is a resemblance of the property of squareness, we acquire a non-propositional knowledge of what the property of squareness itself is like, knowledge that goes beyond knowledge of the truth of propositions, and is a phenomenon specifically of consciousness; only the *experience* of squareness could resemble squareness in that way. Locke could have got the effect he wants in a quite different way. He could have argued that the qualitative character of our experiences of primary qualities is actually constituted by the primary qualities of the objects themselves that we encounter. This would have saved him from Berkeley's challenge.

4. Berkeley on the Sensory Basis of Concept Formation

Berkeley, like Locke, takes it that the knowledge provided by sensory experience is the foundation of all our knowledge of the world. As we saw, this idea can seem absolutely compelling; ordinary common sense today still finds it compelling that there is a fundamental role for sensory experience in knowledge. As we have seen, moreover, in trying to understand how this can be so, we seem obliged to go beyond thinking of sensory experience in representational terms, for any representational content that sensory experience has could also be had by perception in the absence of sensory experience. So that seems to drive us to try to understand the epistemic role of sensory experience in terms of its non-representational characteristics, which presumably means thinking of sensory experience as a matter of having sensations. But how could sensations provide us with knowledge of our surroundings? At this point, we seem driven to Locke's answer: this happens in virtue of a resemblance between the sensations and characteristics of our surroundings. What else could it be?

Berkeley's first point is that there is no resemblance of the kind Locke needs between our sensations and material objects. 'Resemblance' in this sense is a matter of literally sharing properties. Locke's picture is that the F-ness of your idea is what provides you with your knowledge of what it is for a material object to be F (cf. Jacovides 1999). Berkeley's point is that there are no properties, no replacements for 'F', that are literally shared by ideas and external objects.

> But say you, though the ideas themselves do not exist without the mind, yet there may be things like them whereof they are copies or resemblances, which things exist without the mind, in an unthinking substance. I answer, an idea can be like nothing but another idea; a colour or figure can be like nothing but another colour or figure.

> (Berkeley 1734/975, §8)

It is instructive to think through what happens if this point is resisted, because it then becomes evident that there is a deeper criticism implicit in Berkeley's discussion. I think that the key point here is one that I glossed over in expounding Locke's conception of resemblance in the last section. Suppose that we are trying to explain the epistemic role of experience in terms of a resemblance between our sensations and material objects. And suppose for the moment that the sensations literally do share shapes, for example, with the external objects. Locke has to explain how this resemblance between sensations and external objects can explain our epistemic access to the properties of external objects. So, on the face of it, we must have some epistemic access to the shapes of sensations, and that initial epistemic access to our own sensations is going to be what explains our epistemic access to the properties of material things. So in explaining the epistemic role of experience, we are forced to acknowledge that in the first instance, experience provides knowledge only of experience itself. And knowledge that experience provides of the material world is derivative on this.

This view can seem to have some immediate plausibility; in fact it is sometimes taken for granted in discussions of the epistemic role of experience. Suppose one knows a great deal theoretically about some characteristic of the material world, whether it's colour or shape or something else. And now one encounters the property in experience for the first time. What does one learn? It can seem that the mandatory answer is that what one learns is something about sensory experience itself: what it is like to experience that property.

However, when one reflects on one's visual experience, for example, one typically attends only to properties of the objects one is seeing. It doesn't even seem to be possible to attend to some inner characteristic of 'redness', as opposed to the redness of the external object you're looking at (Harman 1990, Tye 2013). This 'transparency' of visual experience on the face of it means that there is no such thing as first having knowledge of the characteristics of one's visual sensations themselves, and only consequently extending that to knowledge of the material objects one observes. Locke's analysis in terms of resemblance seems to require, though, that our knowledge of our own sensations must come first, and it is our understanding of the resemblance between sensations and material objects that allows us to extend this prior knowledge to the material world.

Locke's view is nonetheless very natural. Suppose you think there's such a thing as 'what it is like' to have a visual experience. And suppose you think that 'what it's like' to have a particular visual experience doesn't at all constitutively depend on what's in your surroundings at the time. That is, your visual experience could have the very same qualitative character as it does now, whatever was in your surroundings. Then you are already working with an idea of 'the qualitative character of experience' that isn't the same thing as the qualitative character of your surroundings (the colours and shapes, the movements and objects around you). This seems to be enough to allow us to ask Locke's question: is there any resemblance between the qualitative character of experience and the qualitative character of the external world? And it's also enough to allow Berkeley to make his deeper point. Berkeley's question is:

Suppose you have an 'internalist' conception of the qualitative character of visual experience. How could our knowledge of the external environment—the things and properties around us—be grounded in the qualitative characters of our visual experiences?

Berkeley's point is that the qualitative character of visual experience, thought of in these 'internalist' terms, could not ground thought about a mind-independent world. It could not ground thought about material things, capable of existing unobserved.

Once it's stated in these terms, Berkeley's point seems absolutely compelling. Our thought about ordinary things and their properties is grounded in our experience of them. But you can't ground thought about mind-independent objects in the qualitative character of perceptual experience if the qualitative character of perceptual experience is thought of in 'internalist' terms; that is, if we assume that the qualitative character of experience could be as it is no matter what's in one's environment.

We are trying to understand the epistemic role of sensory experience in terms of the non-representational aspects of sensory experience. The argument was that any representational characteristic of sensory experience could also be had by perception in the absence of sensory experience. So if we want to understand the distinctive epistemic contribution of sensory experience, we have to look at its non-representational characteristics. But if the non-representational, qualitative character of sensory experience is understood in 'internalist' terms, then it evidently cannot ground thought and knowledge relating to a mind-independent world.

Does Berkeley's point underestimate the resources available to an internalist? You might acknowledge that there is something paradoxical about a remark like 'that (perceptually demonstrated) tree is unperceived'. It's not exactly a contradiction, but it can't be straightforwardly true either. So how do we achieve our grasp of the possibility of that very tree being unperceived? You might argue that the way we do this is by the exercise of sensory imagination. Can't we *imagine* that very tree being unperceived? And isn't that how experience, internalistically conceived, can ground our thought about objects as mind-independent? Here is Berkeley's response:

But, say you, surely there is nothing easier than to imagine trees, for instance, in a park, or books existing in a closet, and nobody by to perceive them. I answer, you may say so, there is no difficulty in it: but what is all this, I beseech you, more than you framing in your mind certain ideas which you call books and trees, and at the same time omitting to frame the idea of anyone that may perceive them? But do you not yourself perceive or think of them all the while? This therefore is nothing to the purpose: it only shows you have the power of imagining or forming ideas in your mind; but it doth not shew that you can conceive it possible, the objects of your thought may exist without the mind: to make out this, it is necessary that you conceive them existing unconceived or unthought of, which is a manifest repugnancy.

(*Principles*, §23)

The usual analysis of this argument is that Berkeley has confused the content of a representation of existence unperceived with the representation itself. When I represent existence unperceived, I do not, of course, represent anyone, including myself, as perceiving the thing. I do, however, have to do the representing. But that does not show that there is anything problematic about a representation of existence unperceived by anyone, including me.

This analysis, however, does not do justice to the challenge Berkeley means to be raising. Berkeley is asking whether the knowledge of the world that we have from sensory experience will ground a conception of objects and properties capable of existing unperceived. It is at this point that his interlocutor objects, and says that sensory imagination can provide a way of grounding the conception of existence unperceived. The role envisaged for imagination here is not merely *exercising* a conception of mind-independent objects, after all, which one could do in free thought just as well as in the use of sensory imagination. The role envisaged for sensory imagination is, rather, to *ground* a conception of mind-independent objects.

In effect, Berkeley's first point is that imagination can't contribute anything relevant to concept formation that was not already available in ordinary perceptual experience itself. We may agree that sensory imagination is not, as it were, a matter of bloodless thought. But whatever sensory imagination brings, over and above bloodless thought, was there already in perceptual experience.

Suppose, for example, you think that sensory imagination involves some qualitative experiential aspects, some qualia, over and above propositional thinking. Those qualitative aspects of sensory imagination were already there anyhow in perceptual experience. So sensory imagination has no distinctive contribution to make to explaining the epistemic role of sensory experience. It adds nothing to an appeal to perceptual experience as grounding propositional thought.

What is so confusing, and leads one to materialism, according to Berkeley, is that it is possible to confront a perceptual sensation without thereby confronting a sensation of oneself. This presumably could happen just as well in ordinary perceptual experience as in sensory imagination. Still, the point is easier to grasp in connection with sensory imagination. One can imagine a sensation of a tree without imagining a sensation of a subject of the experience. This is what is described as 'imagining the tree unobserved'. But the mere fact that one can encounter a sensation without confronting a sensation of oneself does nothing to show that, in encountering the perceptual sensation, one had encountered the sensory basis for a conception of mind-independent existence. Sensations cannot exist unsensed.

We see the force of Berkeley's point when we take seriously the demand to explain the epistemic role of sensory experience. In particular, we see the force of Berkeley's point when we are trying to understand how experience can make it possible for us to think about the mind-independent world we inhabit. There are two basic points about imagination underlying the argument:

(1) The only way experience provides us with knowledge of what is possible is through the way it instructs the (sensory) imagination.

(2) Sensory imagination is a way of understanding what is going on in a mind.

It seems to follow immediately that all that experience can provide one with is the ability to imagine mental states. So there is no way in which experience can provide one with the conception of a mind-independent world. Berkeley's Puzzle is this: to describe the explanatory role of sensory experience without being driven to the conclusion that all we can have knowledge of is experiences.

5. G. E. Moore's Relational View of Experience

As we saw earlier, the key pressure generating Berkeley's Puzzle is physics pushing sensory experience inside the head. Resisting this pressure has become easier since the seventeenth century. We now take it for granted that physical reality has to be characterized 'at many levels'. And those levels may not all be reducible to basic physics. Talk about colours, shapes, and the movements of macroscopic objects may be merely a higher-level description of a mind-independent world, rather than a description of something projected onto physical reality by the mind. Once you grasp this point, you see that sensory experience can be analysed as a *relation* between the subject and an environment described in terms of things, colours, shapes, and so on. The qualitative character of perceptual experience has nothing particularly to do with perception or experience; it is simply the qualitative character of the world observed.

G. E. Moore set out the basic picture here. You might put his point in terms of an analogy between conscious experience and *light*. The concept of light is not all that easy to explain. I remember as a child my cousin trying to explain the concept of 'daylight' to me. We were sitting indoors and she said, 'It's always around. Except it isn't there at night. It's because of the sun.' I was absolutely baffled by this and she said, 'It's outside, really. Suppose we go outside and you'll see what I mean.' So we went outside and she said, 'Look, it's all around you! Daylight!' I stared wildly around me, saying, 'Where? Where?' to her intense frustration. People who have learnt a bit of physics sometimes say that all we ever encounter in vision is light. We don't really see the objects and properties around us: all we encounter is the light that is reflected by them. The right answer to this seems to be that in fact we never encounter light in ordinary vision. All we ever see is the ordinary things and properties themselves. 'Light' is a theoretical construct, that we use in the course of explaining why we sometimes see things and sometimes don't see them. Somewhat similarly, Moore's point is that in fact we do not ordinarily encounter sensory experience at all. All we encounter, in ordinary perception, is the ordinary objects and properties:

[W]hen we refer to introspection and try to discover what the sensation of blue is, it is very easy to suppose that we have before us only a single term. The term 'blue' is easy enough to distinguish, but the other element which I have called 'consciousness'—that which the sensation of blue has in common with the sensation of green—is extremely difficult to fix. That many people fail to distinguish it at all is sufficiently shown by the fact that there are materialists. And, in general, that which makes the sensation of blue a mental fact seems to escape us: it seems, if I may use a metaphor, to be transparent—we look through it and see nothing but the blue; we may be convinced that there *is* something, but what it is no philosopher, I think, has yet clearly recognized.

(Moore 1903, p. 446)

We have a tendency to suppose that blueness itself is something internal to the mind, generated by the external physical surroundings. Moore's point is that the blueness we ordinarily encounter is itself mind-independent. It is an aspect of the mind-independent world. 'That which makes the sensation of blue a mental fact' is not the blueness itself. There is nothing elusive about the blueness. The blueness is the mind-independent property that is right before us in ordinary vision, to which we unproblematically attend directly.

If you think of the blueness encountered in ordinary vision as a 'sensation' or a 'quale', then you will suppose that 'that which makes the sensation of blue a mental fact' is something right before the mind: the colour sensation itself. Moore's point is that the blueness is not itself mind-dependent (as I have been putting it, the blueness itself is merely a higher-level aspect of the physical world). 'That which makes the sensation of blue a mental fact' is not the blueness. It's the *relation* that you stand in to the external phenomenon of colour.

This is perfectly obvious if, say, you are painting a door blue. What you are focusing on, as you attend to the blueness, finding whether it is even or stripy, and so on, is not a characteristic specific to your own current experience. The blueness is a characteristic of the door itself that you're causally modifying. The blueness is one thing, and your seeing of it is a relation between you and it. What makes for the existence of a mental fact is your *seeing* the blueness.

People sometimes put Moore's point by saying that it's impossible to attend to the experience of seeing. You might naturally object that of course you can reflect on what you are seeing, touching, and so on. If you are at a parade and talking to someone by phone, they might ask you what you can see and of course you can answer that: you say, 'I see the trombone player and the bass drum,' and so on, and this reflects your attention to your experience. But Moore's point is that in giving this report, you rely on your sensory attention to the trombone player and the bass drum themselves. Your report of your experience depends on your attention to the external, mind-independent environment.

This transparency of experience is a fundamental problem for anyone who allows physics to push sensory experience back inside the head. The problem has to do with how we are to form concepts that we can use to describe sensory experience, so conceived. The problem here is a kind of inverse of Berkeley's Puzzle. Suppose we acknowledge the transparency of experience: that in sensory experience we encounter only the external, mind-independent objects themselves. How then are we to so much as form the conception of the 'qualitative character of experience', if that is thought of as something internal to the head?

Properly put, the problem here is not whether an internalist conception of the qualitative character of sensory experience is *consistent* with the transparency of experience. You might, after all, say that the qualitative character of experience is constituted by *qualia* (whatever exactly they are), internalistically conceived, and that qualia are somewhat elusive: usually you can't or don't attend to them, but only to the external phenomena. The trouble is rather to understand what you are talking about in the first place when you are talking about qualia, given that they are so transparent.

To give an analogy: consider the concept of spectacles (I mean, the aids to vision). Usually, the wearer looks right through a pair of spectacles, and they are literally transparent. Suppose, however, that you postulate the existence of invisible, intangible spectacles that each person wears, that are located behind the eyes, inside the head. You might postulate that these spectacles are highly transparent, and that you are thereby respecting the transparency of vision. You are not postulating that all we ever experience is the spectacles themselves. The trouble here is not whether your theory is *consistent* with the transparency of vision. In its own terms, the theory has been designed so as to recognize transparency. The trouble is rather that, if the spectacles are as transparent as all that, it is really difficult to know what you are talking about. How are you to explain what you mean by this conception of 'internal spectacles'?

The deeper significance of Moore's point has to do with how we are to make sense of the idea of a 'projection apparatus' constituted by our visual experience, whereby the qualitative world is projected onto an underlying physical reality. Educated people generally today take it that we have 'visual experiences' or 'visual sensations' of colour that are the basis for this projection. The trouble is that there is an ambiguity in how people think about these 'sensations'. On the one hand, they are often treated as though they are theoretical entities, postulated for the explanatory work they can do in characterizing ordinary vision. (Similarly, electrons are theoretical entities postulated to explain the experimental results we observe.) If this way of thinking of sensations were really taken seriously, though, we would expect an attempt to develop a vocabulary to describe the various types of visual sensation, and to state systematically just how they impact visual experience. (Similarly, one could not simply say, of a particular family of experimental results, 'Oh well, that's the work of electrons,' without taking on board the responsibility to say just what kinds of characteristics electrons have and to be explicit and specific about just how those characteristics generate the experimental results.) In fact, however, when people talk about visual sensations, they usually do not accept any such responsibility. The idea seems to be that visual experience itself provides one with all the knowledge one could have or need about the nature and behaviour of these entities. Moore's point is devastating for this idea. All that visual experience even seems to provide one with is knowledge of the colours, for example, of external objects. Visual experience does not provide one with knowledge of the characteristics of some array of internal entities or characteristics. Philosophers do sometimes say, 'When I talk about colour, this is ambiguous as between the colour out there (pointing at the object) and the colour in here (pointing to one's head).' The significance of Moore's point is that the colour 'in here' can at best be a theoretical entity or property; it is not something of which visual experience of itself provides us with any knowledge. But suppose you did manage to give an explicit characterization of these hypothesized entities or properties, analogous to the kind of explicit characterization one has to give of 'electrons' for talk about them to be defensible at all. This would be a characterization of experience that could be understood even by intelligent Martians, who had no sensory systems in common with us. It would be a purely functional characterization of theoretical role. It would, therefore, be something that you could understand without knowing anything about what it is like to have human sensory experience. But the whole point of the talk about visual sensations or visual qualia was to describe what it is like to have ordinary human vision.

At this point you might accept that the talk about visual 'sensations' is irredeemably obscure, but say that we have another way of characterizing visual experience, namely, in terms of what it represents. Perhaps we can say that visual experience represents the external world as having qualitative colours, even if the reality out there does not itself have any such qualitative characteristics, but is entirely as physics describes it. So these representational aspects of experience constitute the 'projection apparatus' of the mind. We represent the world as being qualitatively coloured, though of course there may be no such characteristic out there in the world represented. The trouble with this is that the only accounts we have of what it is for one thing to be representing another are, in one way or another, causal accounts. For a system to be representing qualitative colours is for it to be causally responsive to qualitative colours. But where are these qualitative colours to be found? Not 'in here', because we have dropped the talk of 'sensations' on account of its obscurity. And not 'out there', because all that's out there is the basic physical reality. So we have no way of saying even what it means, that our visual system is 'representing' the colours of things. We still don't have an account of the 'projection apparatus' allegedly constituted by the mind.

If the talk about the colour sensations 'in here' is irredeemably obscure, and the talk about colour representations presupposes that there have to be qualitative colours to which the representational system is causally responsive, then the right reaction is surely to drop the whole idea of the mind as a 'projection apparatus'. We ought rather to accept that the mind merely encounters, in visual experience, the qualitative colours of objects. These qualitative colours are not 'projections of the mind', they are simply high-level characteristics of independently existing objects. Proponents of the idea of 'sensations' have to accept anyhow that human vision can be characterized not just as a basic physical system, but at a 'higher level' as one in which qualia are generated. But once you accept that kind of idea, there is no particular problem about supposing instead that the qualitative colours are fundamentally mind-independent high-level characteristics of the objects we perceive. And then there is nothing standing in the way of Moore's characterization of the qualitative character of experience, in terms of a generic relation of consciousness holding between the subject and the thing observed.

Moore argued that perceptual experience is fundamentally a relation between the observer and the world observed. This relation of sensory consciousness is generic, in something like the sense in which a spatial relation such as '10 feet away from' is generic. You can be 10 feet away from just about anything; the relation is intrinsically the same, whatever it relates. Similarly, there are lots of different things and properties of which you can be sensorily aware; the relation 'x is perceptually conscious of y' is intrinsically the same, whatever it relates. Moore's main point is that the relation 'x is perceptually conscious of y' can hold in an equally basic and fundamental way between the perceiver, on the one hand, and on the other, either:

(a) a material object, such as a blade of grass, or
(b) something like an after-image, or a hallucinatory experience.

The mistake that the idealist makes, on Moore's analysis, is to suppose that the relation between the perceiver and a purely mental object, an inner experience such as an after-image, is the most basic case of the relation 'x is perceptually conscious of y' holding, and that the experiential relation between the perceiver and a material object must somehow be derived from that more basic case.

Moore puts his point by saying that in our ordinary talk of 'consciousness' or 'sensation' we tend to run together the generic relation on the one hand, and the object of which one is conscious on the other. It is the object of consciousness that constitutes its distinctive qualitative character, not the relation of consciousness, which is always intrinsically the same. Moore puts it as follows:

I will call the common element 'consciousness' without yet attempting to say what the thing I call so *is*. We have then in every sensation two distinct terms, (1) 'consciousness' in respect of which all sensations are alike; and (2) something else in respect of which one sensation differs from another. It will be convenient if I may be allowed to call this second term the 'object' of a sensation: this also without yet attempting to say what I mean by the word.

(Moore 1903, p. 444)

Or again:

In every sensation or idea we must distinguish two elements, (1) the 'object', or that in which one differs from another; and (2) 'consciousness', or that which all have in common—that which makes them sensations or mental facts.

(Moore 1903, p. 446)

The mistake is to allow thinking of qualia as internal mental phenomena. There is a fundamental confusion in the very idea of a 'qualitative character of experience', as it is ordinarily used. In ordinary perceptual experience, there are only the qualitative characteristics of the objects in our surroundings. We are related to those objects by the relation of consciousness. To suppose that there is some special set of qualitative characteristics of perceptual experience itself, somehow corresponding to the qualitative characteristics of the objects in our environments, is the fundamental mistake that generates the difficulty of understanding how perceptual experience can have any epistemic role. It is what generates Berkeley's Puzzle. It provides us with a realm of properties of conscious experience itself that somehow have to be playing a role in generating knowledge concerning the external world. Since that can't be done, it looks as though we must in fact be confined to knowledge of sensation itself. Once the relational character of experience is properly acknowledged, however, we can see that there is no reason to give priority to the case in which what one is aware of is an inner mental object, over the case in which what one is aware of is a mind-independent object. And if awareness of an after-image gives me reason to think the after-image exists, in exactly the same way, awareness of a mind-independent object gives me reason to think the object exists. Once we have made the shift from thinking of the qualitative character of experience in terms of monadic properties of sensations, to thinking of experience as a generic relation between oneself and objects and properties one encounters, the case for idealism collapses:

I am as directly aware of the existence of material things in space as of my own sensations, and *what* I am aware of with regard to each is exactly the same—namely that in one case the material thing, and in the other case my sensation really does exist. The question requiring to be asked about material things is thus not: What reason have we for supposing that anything exists corresponding to our sensations? But: What reason have we for supposing that material things do *not* exist, since *their* existence has precisely the same evidence as that of our sensations?

(Moore 1903, p. 453)

2

A Straightforward Solution to Berkeley's Puzzle

John Campbell

1. The Explanatory Role of Experience

Berkeley thought that we cannot but take the existence of a thing to be a matter of its being perceived: 'The table I write on, I say, exists, that is, I see and feel it' (*Principles*, I/3). In general he thought that we couldn't form the conception of an objective, mind-independent reality: 'all the choir of heaven and furniture of the earth, in a word all those bodies that compose the mighty frame of the world, have not any subsistence without a mind... their being is to be perceived or known' (*Principles*, I/6). It is sometimes thought that there must be something wrong with Berkeley's argument. In *The Life of Samuel Johnson*, James Boswell reported:

After we came out of the church, we stood talking for some time together of Bishop Berkeley's ingenious sophistry to prove the nonexistence of matter, and that every thing in the universe is merely ideal. I observed, that though we are satisfied his doctrine is not true, it is impossible to refute it. I never shall forget the alacrity with which Johnson answered, striking his foot with mighty force against a large stone, till he rebounded from it—'I refute it *thus.*'

(Boswell 1791/1992, pp. 295–6)

My aim in this chapter is to formulate the relational, or naively realistic, view of perception that Johnson's argument requires, and to elaborate the argument somewhat. Johnson's point is that the exercise of his own vigorous will is not the only factor affecting the condition of the rock. The other factor is the earlier condition of the rock itself. Often enough, it's true, we do make a difference to the objects around us, and overestimating our own impact may lead us to conclude that the will of the individual is actually the only factor affecting the current condition of an external object. But Johnson's rebound from the rock implies that the principal determinant of the rock's current condition is not the exercise of any will, but the way the rock itself was earlier.

This is central to our conception of objects as mind-independent. We think of physical objects as internally causally connected: the way an object is later depends not only on how other things impinge on it, but on the way the object itself was earlier. And, as we shall see, this internal causal connectedness of the object, which is independent of its relation to a mind, is what constitutes the identity of the object. Johnson's kick brings out the way in which the objects we live among have lives of their own. The obstance of the rock, its resistance to his will, reflects the fact that its identity is established independent of its relation to any mind.

People usually think that Johnson's point is ineffective against Berkeley. The trouble is that Johnson's move comes after we have accepted the conception of sensory experience as 'inner'. As we saw, there are two basic ideas in Berkeley's argument:

(1) Our understanding of concepts of the medium-sized world is grounded in our sensory experience, and

(2) Sensory experience can provide only concepts of sensory experience itself.

More generally, we might say that what is driving Berkeley's argument is the idea that perceptual consciousness has an *epistemic* role to play in our cognitive lives. That is, it is because we are conscious that we have knowledge of particular properties and objects. It is only because we are conscious that we so much as have the conception of the various characteristics and objects that are in our world. And it is only because we are conscious that we have perceptual knowledge of the facts about our world. But, Berkeley is arguing, the only epistemic role that experience can have is to provide us with knowledge of experience itself.

Berkeley's argument is troubling and forceful for us because each of these premises has a lot of plausibility. Certainly, each of these premises would find many supporters among contemporary philosophers. Suppose you simply ask what the point is of perceptual experience, what good it does us that we have sensory experience. The answer that immediately seems compelling is that it's because we have sensory experience that we know about the things around us and their characteristics; it's only because of our experience of ordinary objects and their properties that we so much as have the conception of those objects and properties. At the same time, suppose you ask, 'How exactly can sensory experience provide us with knowledge of the things around us?' People very often think of consciousness as a matter of experience having a certain qualitative character; and how can that qualitative character of experience be a crucial element in our knowledge of anything other than that very type of experience itself? The qualitative experiences, the qualia that we find in our minds, do not provide us with insight into what the external world is like. There are no qualia in any non-mental, physical world. It is hard to see how consciousness as such can provide us with knowledge of anything but itself. So if we accept that it is our experience of ordinary objects that allows us to form the conception of those ordinary objects, we seem driven to the conclusion that we can form the conception only of objects that are themselves merely aspects of our experiences, objects that are themselves creatures of the mind. Berkeley's Puzzle is to understand how it could be that both (a) our grasp of concepts of ordinary objects is grounded in our experience of those objects, and (b) we have the conception of mind-independent objects.

To resolve this puzzle, we have to look again at our conception of sensory experience; we have to think of sensory experience not as a matter of having qualia, for example, but as a matter of our being *related* in the right kind of way to the objects and properties around us. If you don't like that option, there are two radical resolutions of the puzzle:

(1) The conclusion is correct: that we have only the conception of experience itself, and no such idea as that of a mind-independent material object. This is Berkeley's own solution, of course.

(2) Sensory experience plays no role in our understanding of the concepts of the things and properties around. This is the standpoint of contemporary epiphenomenalism about conscious experience.

This second position is quite popular. Its appeal depends, I think, on supposing that sensory experience is an internal product of the functioning of the brain, in an environment that is qualitatively quite different from anything to be found in experience itself. Then it's easy to suppose that sensory experience is simply a fascinating epiphenomenon spun off by the brain. But we don't have to think of brain and consciousness in this way. We can, instead, view the role of the brain as being to sustain the relation of 'experiencing' between the perceiver and the various high-level aspects of the environment that the perceiver encounters.

In opposition to these two radical views, my aim in this chapter is to set out a *straightforward* resolution of Berkeley's Puzzle: that is, one that accepts both that (a) our grasp of concepts of ordinary objects is grounded in experience of those objects, and (b) we have the conception of mind-independent objects. The most important single idea we have to have in play, to give a straightforward resolution of the puzzle, is the conception of sensory experience as a *relation* between the perceiver and scene observed. On a relational view of experience, sensory experience is characterized as a three-place relation holding between:

(i) the observer,

(ii) the point of view from which the scene is observed, and

(iii) the scene observed.

This three-place relation is '*x* is experiencing *y* from point of view *z*', and as we shall discuss, it may itself be adverbially modified (that is, you might use such qualifiers as 'experiencing *watchfully*' or other adverbs). The key point about any such view is that the scene observed cannot be eliminated from a description of the sensory experience. To be having a perceptual experience is, characteristically, to be experiencing a particular scene from a particular point of view; characterizing the qualitative character of the experience involves characterizing the objects and properties in the scene observed. The qualitative character of the sensory experience is constituted by the qualitative characters of the objects and properties in the scene observed. Of course, ordinary visual processing will not sustain experience of absolutely every object and property in your vicinity: you can't see the lot. But the qualitative character of your experience is constituted by the point of view from which you are observing the scene, any relevant adverbial modification of the relation of experience, and the relevant qualitative aspects of the external scene.

With this conception of sensory experience in hand, it is possible to resolve Berkeley's Puzzle straightforwardly: that is, acknowledging both the explanatory role of experience in our conception of the things around us, and our grasp of concepts of mind-independent objects. We first need to say something more about what it means for sensory experience to have a role in explaining our grasp of the conception of objects as mind-independent. Then we need to say something about how sensory experience, conceived as on the relational view, could play this role.

2. Justifying the Use of Objective Thinking

We reason in ways that reflect our conception of objects as mind-independent. Sometimes we have the right to take it, on the basis of observation, without further argument, that we are experiencing one and the same mind-independent object again. And sometimes we do need some auxiliary argument before we can take it that we have one and the same thing again. We engage in reasoning to establish object identity that proceeds by arguing that the later object is the way it is only because the earlier object was the way it was; therefore they are identical. Suppose, for example, that you visit your old schoolroom and find your initials still carved on a desk. You have the right to take it that it's the same desk; the initials wouldn't be there now if it wasn't for your industry all those years ago. More fundamentally, we take ourselves to have a conception of 'the desk itself', on which the concrete object functions as the mechanism by which the influence of your earlier work is transmitted over time to the present. These ways of reasoning reflect a conception of the object as having its identity constituted in a way that is independent of its relation to any mind. Our question is whether we have any justification for reasoning in this way, and in particular, whether perceptual experience could provide us with any justification for reasoning in this way. Berkeley's argument was that perceptual experience provides us with no such justification. Since it is only perceptual experience that can justify our use of particular patterns of reasoning about our surroundings, it follows that these patterns of reasoning are not legitimate and should be abandoned.

An alternative reaction is provided by contemporary epiphenomenalism, according to which perceptual experience plays no role in our knowledge of our surroundings, no role in our grasp of concepts of the objects and properties around us. Someone who holds this view may say that an ordinary individual typically has no access to any justification of those ordinary ways of reasoning. Perhaps there is an evolutionary background that explains and may in some sense validate thinking in terms of mind-independent objects. But that is not something that the ordinary individual has ready access to. This is just the way of our people, to talk and think in terms of mind-independent objects; so far as individual justification goes, here we reach bedrock and the spade is turned.

Neither of these reactions seems particularly compelling. On the one hand, it is hard to believe that perceptual experience licenses us only in thinking and reasoning in terms of objects that are mind-dependent. The view that we can think only in terms of mind-dependent objects is simply impossible to believe, when ordinary perceptual experience seems to provide us at every moment with crowds of mind-independent things. On the other hand, the idea that we actually have no justification for thinking in this way—the idea that perceptual experience cannot underwrite these styles of reasoning—is equally hard to believe. These patterns of reasoning are not simply plucked out of the air, tics that evolution has forced on us, or imposed by us on a malleable reality—perceptual experience confronts us with the very mind-independent things whose being there validates these patterns of inference. That is what makes Berkeley's Puzzle inescapable. We have to explain how it can be that sensory experience is validating our reasoning about mind-independent material things.

How is it that we can conceive of the unity of an object without conceiving of it in terms of its relation to a mind? The example of the school desk suggests that our conception of the unity of an ordinary concrete object is the conception of a causal unity. To have the conception of concrete objects as mind-independent is to have some understanding of their identity conditions; and those identity conditions have to do with the causal dependence of the way the object is later on the way the object was earlier. When we characterize the identity of the object in this way, we do not need to bring in its relation to a mind. That is how we have the conception of the object as mind-independent.

When I put it like this, however, it may look as though we could give a comprehensive characterization of how one has the conception of objects as mind-independent without bringing in one's experience of objects at all. For you could give a theoretical characterization of the causal dependencies here, and how the subject grasps them, without mentioning the subject's experience of objects. So this way of explaining what it is to have the conception of objects as mind-independent may seem to lose any role for the subject's experience of objects. All our understanding of objects as causal unities could be, as it were, theoretical, rather than being grounded in sensory experience.

To see just where experience comes in, notice that in general, we think of causal connections in two ways. First, we think in terms of causation as a matter of there being a counterfactual connection between two variables, Y and X. For Y to be counterfactually dependent on X is for it to be the case that the value of Y would have been different had the value of X been different. Consider, for example, the identity of a handsaw. The kinds of variables that matter for questions of the identity of objects are variables such as 'whether saw Y cut through the wood easily at t2', and 'whether saw X had been oiled at t1', where t2 is later than t1. If saw Y and saw X are different saws, then there will in general be no counterfactual dependence of the first variable on the second. That is, how easily saw Y is cutting through the wood would not have been any different whether or not you had oiled saw X. However, if the value of variables such as that first variable is counterfactually dependent on the value of the second variable, then that is the kind of causal connection that it takes for saw Y at t2 to be identical to saw X at t1. A grasp of this kind of counterfactual connection between variables relating to how the object is later and variables relating to how the object was earlier does not seem to exploit the subject's experience of the object. (Of course, it is a familiar point that the counterfactuals here must not be 'backtracking' counterfactuals. But I will not pursue that issue here.)

There is a second dimension to our ordinary thinking about causation. We do not think merely in terms of counterfactual connections between variables; we think in terms of mechanisms by means of which the counterfactual connections exist. Suppose we consider any finding established by a randomized controlled trial, such as a role for vitamin E in the prevention of heart disease. The trial might establish that interventions on the level of vitamin E in a patient will make a difference to the risk of heart disease. But there is a further, compelling question: What is the mechanism by which vitamin E affects the risk of heart disease? The answer 'There is no mechanism' would seem barely intelligible to most researchers. The truth of the counterfactuals is one thing, and the mechanism implicated in the causation here is something else. The notion of a mechanism here is notoriously difficult to characterize, and I am not going to attempt a general characterization of it, beyond remarking on its importance. For us the key point is that a proto-typical case of a mechanism is provided by our ordinary conception of an ordinary medium-sized object transmitting causal influence from place to place. This is one of the prototypical examples of a mechanism; it provides us with one of the basic pictures of what a mechanism is that we bring to more difficult cases.

Let me give a simple example. Suppose I have two knives, knife A and knife B. And I have a knife sharpener. Knife B is over at the cutting board, with toma-toes ready to be chopped. Knife A is at the other end of the room, beside the knife sharpener. Here are two cases:

Case 1. I sharpen knife A and put it down beside the sharpener. I go to the other side of the room and use knife B to chop tomatoes. The chopping goes faster and better than it would have done if I had not sharpened knife A. Let us suppose that this is established by extensive experiment.

Case 2. I sharpen knife A. I take it over to the chopping board and use it to chop tomatoes. The chopping goes faster and better than it would have done if I hadn't sharpened the knife.

Case 1 is an unusual and puzzling case. How does it happen that the intervention at the sharpener is making a difference to what happens over at the cutting board? The natural question is, 'What's the mechanism?' Surely this must be some kind of conjuring trick. There must be some kind of machinery linking the two places, at the sharpener and at the cutting board, that we haven't yet described. Case 2 seems quite different. What has happened at the sharpener is making a difference to what happens at the cutting board. But there is no puzzle about how this is happening. It's not that there is no mechanism here for transmitting causal influence from place to place. There is a mechanism. It's the movement of knife A. The movement of knife A from one place to another is the mechanism by which causal influence has been transmitted from one place to the other. This point is evidently quite general. The movements of concrete objects from place to place are the mechanisms by which causal influence is transmitted from place to place. This point is so familiar that it is easy to miss. But once you point it out, it is obviously basic to our thinking about cau-sation in the immediate environment. That is what I mean by saying that concrete objects here are prototypical mechanisms by which causal influence is transmitted.

You might say that this is just a matter of what we are familiar with as opposed to what we are not familiar with. We are not familiar with Case 1 interventions whereas we are familiar with Case 2 interventions. But that response understates the contrast. Suppose Case 1 interventions did become commonplace. We would still look for a mechanism explaining why they happened. Similarly we look for mechanisms explaining why light switches turn on lights, no matter how familiar we are with the phenomenon. It is not that there is some a priori guarantee that we will always find what we are looking for. It is just there is some looking to be done. In a Case 2 intervention, however, it is not just that the thing is familiar. The mechanism linking intervention and upshot is palpably there. Ordinary perception confronts us with the mechanism.

One reason it is easy to miss this point is that when we are looking for mechanisms we are often looking for something hidden. For example, it might take a lot of work to find the mechanism linking vitamin E with heart disease. But in this case the mechanism in play is perfectly obvious. You might point out that there is a hidden structure here: the molecular composition of the knife being transported from place to place. But this is not an alternative to thinking of the movement of the knife itself as the mechanism for the transmission of influence. All it provides us with is an equation: the movement of the knife is the movement of a collection of molecules. That identity may be true, but it is still the movement of the knife from place to place that is the mechanism for the transmission of causal influence.

To sum up. A grasp of the identity of knife A over time may consist partly in a grasp of counterfactuals saying that what happened with the thing later wouldn't have happened without what happened with the thing earlier. You know that an intervention on A earlier will make a difference to how it is later. But grasp of the identity of A provides more than this. Your grasp of the identity of A means that you know the mechanism linking what happens at the earlier place to what happens at the later place. In contrast, you could know that an intervention on A is going to make a difference to how B is later. But you might still not know the mechanism involved. Knowledge of the mechanism involved is something over and above knowledge of the counterfactual. This understanding of the physical object as mechanism is not a matter merely of knowing, explicitly or implicitly, various counterfactuals about what would happen under interventions. In the absence of experience of objects, it is difficult to see how we could have such a conception at all. It is our sensory confrontation with the categorical object itself that provides us with our grasp of that which makes the counterfactuals true.

Suppose we do have this conception of physical objects as the prototypical mechanisms for transmitting causal influence from place to place. This is a conception of the concrete object as mind-independent: you think of the mechanism as having a unity that has nothing to do with its relation to any mind. Grasp of this idea cannot be explained as a matter of, for example, understanding in practice that your actions on the object earlier will make a difference to how it is later. You could grasp that there was this fact about the upshot of your actions without having any idea what mechanisms are involved. Our ordinary conception of a concrete physical object does provide us with understanding of mechanism, that must go beyond a mere practical grasp of intervention counterfactuals. So in virtue of what do we have this conception of the object as a mind-independent unity? The great merit of the relational view of experience is that it lets us understand how experience of the object could provide us with this conception.

We think of material objects as the mechanisms by which causal influence is transmitted from place to place and time to time. If we think of perceptual experience as a *relation* between the perceiver and the ordinary, mind-independent objects in the environment, then we can immediately see how perceptual experience could play a role in our having this conception. The key point is this:

On the relational view, the qualitative character of the experience is the qualitative character of the object itself.

As I brought out earlier, and I will return to the point in a moment, there is more to be said than this about the qualitative character of experience, on a relational view. There is the point of view from which the scene is being observed, and there may be adverbial modification of the type of experience in question. But the key point is that once these other parameters are set, on the relational view, the qualitative character of the experience is then constituted by the qualitative character of the object. That is what is distinctive of the relational view of experience.

It is because of this that the relational view of experience can explain how it is that we have the conception of the categorical concrete object as the underlying mechanism by which causal influence is transmitted. The concrete object, such as the knife we discussed earlier, is not a hypothesized cause; it is not known merely as a locus of counterfactual causal connections. Sensory experience brings the thing itself into view, the categorical basis of the counterfactual connections. Consider, in contrast, analyses of perceptual experience on which there is a distinction to be drawn between the qualitative character of the experience and the qualitative character of the object. This means that on these analyses the experience itself does not bring the qualitative character of the object into the subjective life of the perceiver. The qualitative character of the experience is at best an effect of the qualitative character of the object perceived, on these analyses. So these analyses cannot explain how it is that a sensory encounter with the object can be an element in one's grasp of the idea of the object as the categorical basis for the counterfactual connections between the way the thing is at one time and place and the way the thing is at another time and place.

There are characteristic ways in which we think and reason about ordinary physical objects that reflect the mind-independence we usually take physical things to have. We can think of the mind-independence of ordinary concrete objects as showing up in three different types of reasoning:

(1) It's the same object that we encounter over time. The object continues in existence even when it's not being observed. Even when the object is observed continuously over a period of time, there may be changes in the observation of it that don't reflect any change in the object, or any change of the object.

(2) It's the same object we encounter in different sensory modalities. You can see and touch one and the same thing, stick it in your mouth, and so on. There is one and the same thing here, through variation in the way it's being experienced by you.

(3) Different people can encounter one and the same object. The subjective experiences they have of the object are different from one another, but it's one and the same thing. So here there is variation both in who is having the experience and in what kind of experience it is, consistently with it being one concrete thing that is experienced.

There are two dimensions to grasp of a term referring to an ordinary physical object. There is, first, one's grasp of the characteristic patterns of inference to which the term is subject. There is, second, one's grasp of the justification for the use of those patterns of inference in connection with the term. That grasp of the semantic justification for the pattern of use of the term is what provides the most basic role for perceptual experience in our grasp of concepts relating to the medium-sized world.

The relational view of experience can explain how experience justifies these patterns of inference that reflect our conception of objects as mind-independent. Suppose, for instance, that you consider some exercise of reasoning that uses the conception of sameness of object over time. Then, I am suggesting, what validates the correctness of the use of that pattern of reasoning is that the object is identified by your experience of it; and your experience of it is experience of a mind-independent object that is indeed the same over time, despite variation in other aspects of your sensory experience of it, or through gaps in your sensory experience of it. Similarly, in the cross-modal case, what justifies you in using a pattern of reasoning that uses the conception of sameness of object across sensory modality is the fact that your perceptual experiences in different sensory modalities have related you to one and the same object. And in the interpersonal case, what justifies you in reasoning in a way that exploits the sameness of the object that you and the other person have encountered is that you have both been experientially related to one and the same object. Of course, it can happen that you think you have justification for using a particular pattern of inference when you do not. Despite it seeming for all the world as though you have encountered the same object at one time as at another, there may in fact have been a switch. You can take yourself to seeing and feeling the same object when actually the thing you are seeing is not the same as the thing you are feeling. You can take yourself to be encountering the same object as someone else is encountering when in fact you are related to different things. In such cases your perceptual experience is not what you take it to be. Your perceptual experience does not validate the patterns of inference that you suppose it to. Nonetheless, in the good case, your use of these patterns of reasoning is justified by your experience of the object, conceived as a relation to that object.

Even in the cases in which it is in fact the same object that is being encountered, across times or modalities or persons, that mere sameness of object is not enough for perceptual experience to validate the correctness of inferences that exploit the sameness of the object. As we saw already, in setting out the relational view of experience, it would not be right to think of perceptual experience as merely a two-place relation between the perceiver and an object. You experience scenes from a particular point of view, and there may be adverbial modifications of the relation of experience. So we have to say that for one's perceptual experiences to justify the use of patterns of inference that exploit the sameness of the object, it must be not just that those experiences do in fact relate to a single object; they all have to relate one to that object in suitably related *ways*. I will take up this point later.

3. Imagining *de re*

Dr Johnson's kicking of the stone brings out the obstance, the resistance to the will, of the medium-sized world. It suggests that we should think of our project as being to explain the relation of the medium-sized world to microphysics, *then* look for where the mind fits in, rather than to explain the relation of the mind to microphysics, and then explain the medium-sized world as what the mind projects onto the microphysical world. The medium-sized rock is there, independently of us. The question Berkeley's Puzzle raises is: how can experience make it possible for us to think about such a thing? The answer is that if experience is a matter of the generation of sensations, of inner qualia, then experience can play no role in our thinking about such a mind-independent object. If, on the other hand, we think of experience as a relation between the rock and the perceiver, then we can understand how that contact with the object itself could play a role in grounding thought about it as a basis for the transmission of causal influence over time, and from place to place. This role of the object, as possessed of its own internal causal structure, is what makes it resistant to the will of the agent.

The externalist conception of experience that we need here will be quite alien to many readers. I think one big reason for this is the way we picture the role of imagination in an understanding of sensory experience. We think that we can imagine someone's sensory experience without knowing anything about their environment. In principle, you could, in imagination, fully depict someone's sensory experience 'from the inside' in a way that is independent of any assumptions about what's actually there in their surroundings. Moreover, imagination is our canonical way of understanding what sensory experience is like. As Nagel put it:

At present we are completely unequipped to think about the subjective character of experience without relying on imagination—without taking up the point of view of the experiential subject.

(Nagel 2002, p. 224)

This implies that it can't be right to think of sensory experience relationally. If sensory experience is a relation to the qualitative environment, then you can't know about what someone's experience is like without knowing something about their surroundings. But it can easily seem that you could get it right in imagining someone's experience without making any assumptions at all about their surroundings.

The problem here is, I think, not with the idea that imagination is central to our understanding of what sensory experience is like, but with the 'internalist' conception of imagination that is being proposed. I think we need a shift in our picture of imagination that is analogous to a shift that many philosophers have already made in their thinking about belief.

We need to think of 'imagining someone's sensory experience' in externalist terms. I'll call the kind of imaginative exercise that I have in mind 'imagining *de re*' because it involves a relation to a real thing, the '*re*'. Suppose, for example, that your job is to design and make the stage set for a forthcoming performance in a theatre. You have reached the point where you are on the stage surrounded by various pieces and a lot of machinery so you can manipulate your provisional set. However, the auditorium is being repaired so you can't sit in the stalls and view your set directly from there. You have to imagine what your set will be like from there. Will the red and gold you are using be a bit overwhelming, or will the distance have a subduing effect so that it merely seems sumptuously ornate? The set is a bit complicated. Will it seem cluttered, or is its spatial organization lucid enough that it will be evident what is going on? Will the actors be hidden from the spectators by the set, or will it frame them well? More briefly, what will it be like from, say, the rear stalls? That is the imaginative exercise you have to engage in.

There is obviously no difficulty of principle about this, though some people will doubtless be better at it than others. Also, though, notice that this is a *relational*, or real-world, exercise of the imagination. You are imagining what *the set* will be like from various vantage points in the auditorium. This is relational. It involves the physical stage set itself, the perceiver in the audience, and a relation between them.

This relational, or *de re*, exercise of the imagination, seems to me to be the fundamental use of the imagination in understanding of sensory experience. To know what it is like for someone to experience the stage set, you have to know the stage set. Your conception of the qualitative character of someone's experience, as they view the stage, is constitutively dependent on your knowledge of the stage set itself. To engage in this kind of *de re* use of the imagination, you have to know what is there in the environment of the perceiver whose viewpoint you're trying to project yourself into.

For a philosopher who thinks about the conscious life in purely internalist terms, it will seem that this relational exercise misses out the key thing. This is not a matter of imagining what the set will be like from various perspectives. To get onto the conscious life proper, you have to engage in a purely 'internalist' exercise: imagining the mental life of the spectator in isolation from any of the surroundings, regarding the stage set itself as merely a causal prod to the production of inner experiences.

If you think of the project in this way, it is likely to strike you not merely as a skilled exercise that some people might be better at than others. The thing is likely to strike you as altogether impossible. After all, the spectrum of the individual in the stalls might be an inversion of yours, so that the sensations they have when viewing red and gold are more like the sensations you have when viewing green and grey. Or maybe they are nothing like any of your colour sensations at all. Perhaps they are more like the sensations you have when listening to the tones of an organ. Or perhaps they are frankly alien, like nothing in your experience. How could you know? A stage-set designer struck by this thought would really have no way of proceeding. Perhaps God can know what the arbitrary individual in the stalls would experience, but it may be altogether beyond the ken of the humble set designer.

On a relational view of experience, there is no such 'deep' enquiry into the sensory experience of the other to engage in. In the case of ordinary perceptual experience, there is no such thing as the 'inner life' of the other, considered in isolation from its relations to its surroundings. There is *only* the 'surface' enquiry that set designers and other visual artists and technicians routinely engage in. This simply does not require grappling with the unfathomable. This is the exercise of imagining, for example, what the set is like from the rear stalls. This is certainly a question about the conscious life of the perceiver; it is a question about what kind of sensory experience the audience will enjoy, and it is a question that impacts on the kind of aesthetic experience the audience will have. But as I said, it is a relational question. It is a question about the set itself, and the audience's experiential relation to the set.

What I am arguing is that the *de re* or relational use of sensory imagination is as basic as any other use of sensory imagination to understand sensory experience. The basic point here is a simple one. To give an analogy, suppose we consider, instead of 'seeing', a spatial relation like 'being 10 yards away from'. Here are two cases:

(a)   You imagine being 10 yards away from the Brandenburg Gate in Berlin.
(b)   You imagine a fantastical gate, all swooping balustrades and exotic ornamentation, etc., and you imagine being 10 yards away from it.

(By 'fantastical' here, incidentally, I refer not to an architectural style but to the status of the thing as a creature of the mind, rather than concrete.) Cases (a) and (b) seem to be different types of imaginative exercise, and I suppose that in principle someone might be capable of one kind without being capable of the other. For example, it seems possible that someone is well able to imagine being 10 yards away from a real object, but that the cognitive demands of both constructing a fantastical object and imagining being 10 yards away from it reliably overwhelmed them. It's less easy to think of a case in the other direction, but I suppose it could happen that someone found it easy to imagine being 10 yards away from a fantastical object and yet always balked at trying to imagine being 10 yards away from a real thing.

Now there are other uses of sensory imagination than the basic *de re* ones I have described. Suppose, for example, that someone tells you that they're having hallucinations: they see a crowd of children running across a field, even though they know perfectly well there's no such thing there, and in fact the patient is sitting in a hospital bed. What's that visual experience like for the patient? To achieve an imaginative understanding of this sensory experience, you have to do two things:

(1)   *Imagine* a field, with a crowd of children running across it.
(2)   Imagine being the patient, seeing that scene.

If you manage both of those, then you've achieved an imaginative understanding of the patient's visual experience. Notice that in (2) here, you're using the same capacity for *de re* imagining that we talked about earlier. It's just that you are only imagining that there is an object that the subject is seeing. Contrast the earlier, simple case in which you:

(1)   *See* a field, with a crowd of children running across it, and
(2)   Imagine being in the field, seeing that scene.

In both cases, it's the capacity for *de re* imagining that is being used. The only difference is that in the case of the hallucination, imagination comes in twice over. You're only imagining the object that you're imagining the perceiver to see. But the complicated case in which you use imagination twice over is obviously not any more basic than the case in which you imagine the subject's perception of a real object.

You can contrast this account of imagining *de re* with a picture on which there is a kind of imagining *de dicto* that is really the primitive way in which we understand the qualitative character of sensory experience. On this view, 'imagining what someone's sensory experience is like' does not involve the environment, even in the case in which you are imagining their seeing something, and it does not require the double use of imagining that I just described, in the case of hallucination. Rather, what is required is a purely 'internal' exercise in which, as we might put it, the inner qualia of the imaginer somehow reflect or resemble the inner qualia of the imaginee. The trouble with this picture is that, as we have seen, we have no way of making sense of the talk of 'inner qualia' here (I will return to the point in the next section). In our ordinary talk, we characterize the qualitative character of our sensory experience by describing what we are perceiving. We describe the qualitative character of our experience by saying, for example, 'I'm seeing a field with long grass bordered by a row of trees.' And if we want to describe the qualitative character of a hallucination, we do so by using fully factive perceptual vocabulary: we say, for example, 'I'm seeing a field with children running over it,' or 'I'm hearing the voices again.' Only, in the case of something we know to be a hallucination, we qualify the report by saying, for instance, 'Of course, these things aren't really there,' 'They don't exist.' We don't, in practice, have any use or need for the notion of inner qualia in characterizing our imaginative understanding of sensory experience. We can take relational or *de re* imagining as primitive.

The challenge to the relational view of experience was that it's imagination that provides us with our understanding of the qualitative character of sensory experience. And in principle, you could, in imagination, fully depict someone's sensory experience 'from the inside' in a way that is independent of any assumptions about what's actually there in their surroundings. I have proposed that this depends on an obscure conception of 'imagining *de dicto*', as merely reflecting the inner qualia of the perceiver. And I propose that we drop this obscure conception in favour of taking imagination *de re* as our basic format for understanding the qualitative character of sensory experience.

The great insight of much of Nagel's work on consciousness was the indispensable role that imagination has in our understanding of sensory experience, in 'knowing what it's like' to have one sensory experience or another. Nagel made his point in the context of the problem of imagining how the world is from a bat's point of view. He remarked that one could know all there is to know about the physics of the bat and of the surroundings of the bat without knowing the one thing that seems most intriguing and elusive; what it's like to be a bat. Now when you put it like that, 'being a bat' is something that seems to involve only the bat itself. So imagining what it's like to be a bat should involve only aspects of the world that are internal to the bat itself. But this isn't the way we usually understand the phrase 'what it's like'.

In the case of the bat, there is an analogue to the stage-set designer's practical question, but it seems, on a relational view, altogether unanswerable using only the resources of an ordinary human. The designer who wonders what the theatre will be like from the point of view of, let us say, the bats hanging from the rafters, really may find that an understanding of this is beyond his powers. That is not because his question is an intrinsically unanswerable one about the internal mental life of another. It is rather that in this particular case, since it's a bat we're dealing with, many of the things that the bat experiences may not even be visible to the designer, and even if they are visible, the designer may have no idea which things they are. So relationally imagining the bat's sensory experience may be impossible simply because one has no sense of which things the bat is experientially related to. In the case of the bat, it is very difficult for humans to imagine occupying the viewpoint of such a perceiver.

To say all this about our knowledge of another human's sensory experience is not to deny that there is such a thing as depth in one's understanding of another person's mental life. In one of his stories, Borges talks about Droctulft, a warrior of Lombard, 'who no doubt was unique and unfathomable (all individuals are)', and few people would say that they do not recognize that sense of the endlessness of the probing it is possible to do into the inner life of another person (Borges 2007, pp. 127–8). The present point is only that it is quite wrong to suppose that the right location for that sense of depth is in the characterization of sensory experience. If anything is a superficial fact about someone else's mental life, it is the nature of their sensory experience.

4. Learning from Experience

Sensory awareness is what happens when, in Nagel's famous phrase, there is something it is like to perceive (Nagel 2002). Our general question is whether phenomenal consciousness plays any role in our having a conception of the world around us, and if so, what that role might be. Once we have freed ourselves from the internalist conception of sensory experience, we can see how it grounds the ability to think in terms of mind-independent objects. The qualitative character of sensory experience of an object is characterized in terms of the object itself. We think and reason in terms of objects as having their own causal structures; the way the object is later causally depends on the way it was earlier. As we saw, one aspect of this causal dependence is counterfactual: the object wouldn't have been the way it is later but for the way it was earlier. Our ordinary reasoning about what confirms the hypothesis that this is the same object again, and what the implications are of this being the same object again, exploits this idea all the time. If it's my desk, then surely there will be at any rate some trace of my initials still carved there; but if it isn't my old desk, then there won't be. What validates our use of these modes of reasoning is our sensory encounters with the categorical objects themselves, the underlying mechanisms by which causal influence is transmitted. Theoretical reasoning, for example, could only articulate the functional role of the object. A sensory encounter with the object, in contrast, brings that underlying mechanism, the thing itself, into your cognitive life.

The relational account of sensory imagination gives us a way of analysing a popular argument for qualia, namely, Jackson's Mary. Mary lives in an entirely black-and-white environment, and learns all there is to know about colour and colour vision from black-and-white texts and diagrams. Jackson's point was that this person, Mary, may have all the relevant physical information about her world, yet still learn something when she steps from her black-and-white room into the world of colour (Jackson 2002). The suggestion was that what Mary learns when she steps out can only be something about the psychological life: the qualia, the internal sensations, of colour experience. Lewis (2002) suggested that what Mary learns had to be thought of as a matter of her now being able to imagine the psychological lives of colour-sighted people.

These approaches simply assume that what experience teaches us can only be something about experience itself. This assumption is one of the drivers of Berkeley's Puzzle: knowledge of our world is founded on experience of it, but experience can provide knowledge only of experience itself. With that assumption in place, it is hard to resist the conclusion that we can have knowledge only of experience.

You can see that there's something wrong with this assumption by varying the Mary story a bit. Suppose that Mary is born in a black-and-white room and so on, but that she is unlike most humans in that she has no conception of sensory experience. Perhaps she has no concept at all of sensory experience. Or perhaps we should think of it as her having no interest in sensory experience, or the conscious life generally. She is passionately curious about physics and, generally, the inanimate objects around her, let us suppose, but she has no interest in the mind.

Perhaps we could think of this as an innate attentional bias that she has; she simply never directs her curiosity towards the conscious life itself. Now suppose that she finally steps out from her black-and-white room into the world of colour. She certainly will learn nothing about the psychological life from doing so. But when she steps into the blaze of colour, will she then learn nothing at all? It seems perfectly obvious that she will learn something, and it would seem to Mary that she is learning something. She is learning something about characteristics of the objects around her: their colours. These are not psychological; inanimate as well as sentient things have them. Of course, at this point we can drop the assumption of the attentional bias. If, from colour experience, this Mary learns something non-psychological about objects—namely, what their colour properties are—then so too does an ordinary subject learn something non-psychological from colour experience.

Of course, once she has reached this point, and learned about the colours of the objects around us, then, on the relational picture of sensory imagination, our subject is also able to imagine what it is like to experience the colours. But what makes this final step possible is not some leap into the purely internal worlds of other people, but learning something about their surroundings: namely, that they have colours in them. Once you know that, it is not, ordinarily, a difficult further step to imagine what it would be like to encounter those colours in experience.

This is a fully externalist picture of the qualitative character of sensory experience. It is often not realized how weak and unconvincing the alternative, internalist pictures of sensory experience are. A natural thought is that perhaps the qualitative character of sensory experience is constituted by the way it represents the world to be; and it could represent the world as that way however the world actually is. But the obvious problem with this is that perception could represent the world without being conscious at all, and we were trying to describe the 'qualitative character' specifically of conscious experience. So then the natural internalist supplementation is to think that the 'representations' in perception have to be 'charged up' somehow by *visual sensations* in order to achieve consciousness. The trouble with that is that we have no idea what we are talking about when we talk about 'visual sensations'. We have no way of introducing and explaining a vocabulary to talk about them. A quick way to see the basic problem is to ask: is the concept of a visual sensation observational or theoretical? Is the concept of a particular kind of visual sensation to be explained ostensively, by a kind of inner pointing, or is it a theoretical notion, to be explained in terms of its functional role? We can't regard the concepts of particular types of visual sensation as observational, because in ordinary vision we don't encounter inner sensations. All we encounter are the properties of the external objects perceived. It seems then that we must regard visual sensations as postulated entities, there only in a subterranean way in ordinary vision, never directly encountered by us but known by their effects. So we have to give a functional specification of those visual sensations. But at this point we have simply lost track of the project, which was to give a characterization of 'what sensory experience is like', in the most immediate way: to characterize the qualitative character of ordinary experience.

I think a dim recognition of these points is responsible for the fascination that talk of qualia has for many philosophers. On the one hand the talk about qualia sounds rather technical, and one thinks, well, here at last we are making some progress with the problem of consciousness. And one expects that perhaps some technical elucidation will be forthcoming. But at this point one is told that no elucidation is possible or necessary, because qualia are the most immediate characteristics of everyone's sensory experience, and it needs no explaining what they are. This oscillation between two untenable views can easily become the frame through which the internalist thinks about sensory experience.

It is not as if the situation is eased by moving away from talk about sensation to an attempt to describe experience in terms of representation alone. We still face the same dilemma. On the one hand, we can try to give a technical elucidation of the notion of representation that we are using. We know how that will look: it will be some kind of causal-teleological theory. And given an explanation of 'representation' in those terms, it will be perfectly obvious that one could be 'representing' one's environment, in that sense, without being conscious at all. Alternatively, you might say that the notion of 'representation' being used is not to be explained in these terms. The notion of 'representation' that we need here is specific to sensory experience itself. But now we have no way at all of explaining what is meant by this 'specific' notion of 'representation', except by a kind of ostension: everyone has to try to glean what is meant by an inner pointing to their own sensory experience. But when you inspect the qualitative character of your own visual experience, you find that you are simply inspecting your surroundings. Introspection does not provide the materials to enable you to understand the notion of 'representation' that you want here.

This is the general problem with the characterization of sensory experience, and it has been with us since we allowed physics to push sensory experience inside the head. The problem is that we have no way of introducing a vocabulary to characterize the experience inside the head. Various formulations are used: 'ideas', 'impressions', 'sense data', 'qualia', and so on. Each generation announces that the vocabulary used by the previous generation was hopelessly confused, and introduces some new term of its own. But the problem is not the specific vocabulary, but that the general project is hopeless. There is no way of introducing a vocabulary to characterize sensory experience, once that is thought of as something confined to the head.

How should we describe the qualitative character of ordinary sensory experience? We have two kinds of reasonably well understood vocabulary for characterizing the relevant working of vision, for example. These are:

(1) Terms for the characteristics of the objects and properties around us: their colours and shapes, their sorts and behaviours, and so on.
(2) Terms characterizing the information processing taking place in the visual system in the brain—edge detection, symmetry analysis, and so on.

Of course there are other aspects to vision—affective and aesthetic, for example—that have to come into a fuller description. But for a basic description of the role of vision in generating knowledge and action, these will do. Once we think of visual experience in those terms, we have the basis for a solution to Berkeley's Puzzle. Thinking of visual experience as a relation to the external qualitative world allows us to understand how thought of the mind-independent world could be based on sensory experience.

5. Representationalism about the Phenomenal Character of Experience

In a recent discussion, Brian McLaughlin argues that representationalists about the content of sensory experience can do full justice to the epistemic role of experience. McLaughlin explains representationalism as follows:

What it is like for one to have a visual experience is for it to be to one as if one is presented with a scene. This what-it-is-like aspect of a visual experience is its phenomenal character. According to the Representationalist, that phenomenal character is or is constituted by the representational content of the experience. Representational theories can differ markedly in their account of what it is for an experience to have a representational content. But they agree that representational contents are semantic contents, in that they are satisfied or instead fail to be satisfied.

(McLaughlin 2010, p. 240)

Representationalists, according to McLaughlin, think that this representational content is something that could be there whether or not the perception is veridical, illusory, or a hallucination. How can a representationalist acknowledge the epistemic role of perceptual experience? Can the representationalist find the role of perceptual experience in grounding our conception of physical objects as mind-independent? If any representation we might appeal to could, in principle, be there in the absence of sensory experience, how could any explanatory role be ascribed to sensory experience at all? McLaughlin's main point is that characterizing the explanatory role of experience need not, even for a representationalist, be achieved by appeal to the representational content of experience:

The Representationalist will flatly reject the claim that whenever an experience explains something, it does so in virtue of its representational content ... The fact that an experience has a certain representational content will not entail that the experience is an experience of an object. Thus, from the fact that an experience's being an experience of an object explains something, it does not follow that the experience's having a certain representational content explains the something.

(p. 250)

The idea is that as well as its phenomenal content, a perceptual experience may have certain characteristics, such as its causal history, that explain the epistemic role of the experience. One basic problem with this kind of approach is that it threatens to leave experience without any distinctive explanatory role. To be fully explicit about McLaughlin's idea, suppose we take it that it is the causal history of the experience that determines what it is an experience 'of'; and suppose that this is external to the phenomenal content of the experience. And suppose it is the causal history that explains the epistemic role. Since the causal history is not constitutively tied to the phenomenal content, there could be another structure that had a similar causal history, but no phenomenal content. And then that structure would presumably, on this approach, have the same explanatory role as the perceptual experience. Experience as such, on this kind of approach, has no distinctive epistemic role.

McLaughlin nevertheless says that on the representationalist account, there is a role for the representational content of experience in explaining our having the conception of a mind-independent world. One way of being a representationalist is to say that the content of experience is conceptual, of the same kind that we exercise in ordinary thinking and judging. Of course it is possible to hold a view on which this kind of conceptual content is the phenomenal content of experience. As McLaughlin acknowledges, however, this kind of view could not regard our grasp of concepts as being explained by the role of sensory experience. Rather, on this view, sensory experience is simply an exercise of our grasp of concepts, one among many of the ways in which we exercise our grasp of concepts. Still, McLaughlin says, it is open to the representationalist to say that there is a kind of lower-level, 'non-conceptual' content that constitutes the phenomenal content of experience. Having representations with this kind of non-conceptual content would not simply presuppose the subject's grasp of the relevant concepts. And an appeal to this non-conceptual content resolves Berkeley's Puzzle:

The Representationalist can hold that in virtue of their non-conceptual contents, visual experiences, whether perceptual or hallucinatory, 'display the world as objective' …

(p. 254)

There are a number of ways in which the notion of non-conceptual content might be explained (you might want such a notion in talking about the representational states of insects, for example, or various low or high levels of human vision, where you don't necessarily want to suppose that the subject is exercising grasp of concepts). It is, however, difficult to think of a way of explaining non-conceptual content that would have the implication that only conscious states have this kind of content. In general, any kind of non-conceptual content that could be ascribed to sensory experience could also, in principle, be ascribed to perceptual states in the absence of sensory experience. This means that the fact that sensory experiences are conscious is ultimately being given no work to do in our understanding of the world as mind-independent. We do not have here a way in which the representationalist can acknowledge the explanatory role of experience. From the point of view of understanding our grasp of concepts of mind-independent objects, on this analysis we would be just as well off with perceptual states that had this capacity to 'display the world as objective', even if those perceptual states were not themselves conscious states.

The problem raised by Berkeley's Puzzle is to understand how experience can play a role in our grasp of concepts of mind-independent objects. Now an appeal to non-conceptual content, however 'objective' the content, cannot anyhow be a direct solution of this problem. All that we have so far is a different kind of content, non-conceptual content, and the thing has to be completed by explaining how the non-conceptual content in perception might be related to our concepts of mind-independent objects. McLaughlin seems to think that the thing is somehow obvious; once we have objective non-conceptual content we will naturally have objective conceptual content. But really it is not obvious how this connection is to be made.

I proposed that we think of grasp of concepts of mind-independent objects as relating to grasp of patterns of reasoning that exploit the identities of concrete objects over time, across sensory modality, and across persons. The role of sensory experience comes in, I suggested, when we think of the way in which the subject grasps the semantic foundation for our use of those patterns of inference. Ordinary sensory experience relates us to the mind-independent objects that validate our use of those patterns of inference. If we are interested in the validation of the patterns of reasoning that reflect our grasp of objects as mind-independent, how could an appeal to non-conceptual content help? There will presumably be some patterns of use governing non-conceptual contents too. Perhaps what it comes to that non-conceptual contents 'display the world as objective' is that they are governed by patterns of use quite like those that we have for conceptual contents relating to mind-independent objects. Perhaps the suggestion is that the patterns of inference governing conceptual contents actually are justified by their relations to the similar patterns of use governing non-conceptual contents. But then we have simply pushed the problem back to the validation of the patterns of use governing non-conceptual contents. We have no idea how such a validation might be given and still less do we have any idea what role sensory experience might play in such a validation. Perhaps McLaughlin's thought is that we do not need to bother with this validation of patterns of reasoning. We should take it as a given that non-conceptual content relates to mind-independent objects, and regard conceptual content as a kind of direct translation of that non-conceptual content into another style of representation, conceptual representation. The trouble is that we have no idea how to go about translating non-conceptual content into conceptual content. In fact, the whole point of drawing the distinction in the first place seems to have been lost if direct translation from one to the other really is possible.

My aim has been to give a straightforward resolution of Berkeley's Puzzle: that is, one that acknowledges the role of sensory experience in our grasp of concepts of objects, but shows how sensory experience can play a role in grounding our grasp of concepts of mind-independent objects. The key point in the straightforward solution is the appeal to a relational conception of sensory experience. The literature on sensory experience has, however, tended to suppose that sensory experience must be characterized not in relational terms, but as a matter of having perceptual *representations* of one's surroundings, or as a matter of having perceptual *sensations*. I think that an appeal to the idea that sensory experience has representational content offers little prospect of explaining how sensory experience can ground our concepts of mind-independent objects. You might, however, still wonder whether an appeal to the idea of perceptual sensations might provide an account of the explanatory role of experience.

As I said, it seems compelling to common sense that sensory experience has a fundamental epistemic role to play; sensory experience is our window on the world. On the other hand, it's not quite easy to see how that can be so. If we think of sensory experience as a matter of having sensations, then it's hard to see how sensory experience can be providing knowledge, in the first instance, of anything but those sensations themselves. If you think of sensory experience as a matter of representing how things are, then it's not obvious how awareness can have a fundamental epistemic role to play, since you can have representations without awareness; why wouldn't representations without awareness provide just as good epistemic access to objects and properties? Moreover, the use of representations seems to presuppose, rather than to explain, the very knowledge of things and properties that we are trying to explain. The natural thought is that we should combine the representationalist and sensationalist approaches. Perhaps we can say that our representations of the mind-independent world are grounded in sensational aspects of perception. But now we face Berkeley's argument. Put in terms of representation and sensation, his argument is this:

(1)   There is a distinction between representational and sensational aspects of perceptual experience.
(2)   All the representations we can form have the contents they do in virtue of their connections to the sensational aspects of experience.
(3)   Representations that derive their meanings from their connections to sensation can only relate to how things are with sensations.

It seems to follow from this that we cannot form representations of a mind-independent reality.

Summing up, here we have looked at two different ideas: that we can characterize the epistemic role of sensory experience in terms of representational content, and that we can characterize the epistemic role of experience in terms of sensations. These ideas face different problems. The appeal to representations ultimately forces you to abandon the idea that there is an epistemic role for sensory experience, because one could have the representations without the experience. The appeal to sensation keeps hold of the connection to experience, but cannot explain how it is that experience has an epistemic role. Trying to combine the appeal to representations with the appeal to sensations leads, as we have just seen, directly to Berkeley's conclusion.

It seems to me that what is problematic is the idea that the non-representational aspects of experience are to be thought of as sensations. As I have said, it seems to me arguable that the non-representational aspects of experience are not constituted by sensations. They are, rather, constituted by the experiential relations that the subject, occupying a particular point of view, stands in to the objects and properties in the environment. When we restate Berkeley's assumptions in these terms, we have:

(i)   There is a distinction between representational and relational aspects of perceptual experience.

(ii) All the representations we can form have the contents they do in virtue of their connections to the non-representational, relational aspects of experience.

(iii) Representations that derive their meanings form their connections to non-representational, relational aspects of experience may relate to how things are in an objective, mind-independent world.

The premise that would now be regarded as most obviously problematic in Berkeley's argument is his (2). The argument for (2), though, is that only an approach that connects representational content to perceptual sensation can do justice to the sense in which representational content enters into the subjective life of the perceiver. Recasting the premise as (ii) aims to recognize this point. Accepting premise (ii), you can still find a place for causal considerations in a theory of content. For causal considerations will matter for the existence of the relation 'perceives' between subject and object, or subject and property; it is not to be supposed that what one is experiencing is a matter independent of some underlying level of physical and causal facts. Causal considerations matter because they have a constitutive role in determining what one is experiencing, and in consequence of that they have an impact on what one can represent or think about. This gives us a way of recognizing what is correct in Berkeley's argument, while also acknowledging that our conscious experiences can ground thought about an objective, mind-independent world.

3

Experiencing Objects as Mind-Independent

John Campbell

1. What Can Vision Science Tell Us about the Ways We Experience Things?

We've seen that our understanding of mind-independence has to do with the kinds of reasoning we engage in about physical objects, reasoning that reflects our picture of them as internally causally connected over time. As we saw, there are a number of types of inference that reflect our understanding of objects as internally causally connected. They include some that exploit our grasp of it being the same object that we encounter over time, or in different sensory modalities, or that different people encounter the same object. With what right do we use these patterns of reasoning? I have suggested that justifying our use of these patterns of inference is the role of perceptual experience. I have been arguing against internalist conceptions of perceptual experience on the grounds that:

(a) experience, internalistically conceived, cannot ground our use of these patterns of inference, and

(b) the transparency of experience means that it is difficult to see how we can so much as formulate a coherent conception of internal 'qualia', whether in terms of representations or sensations. (One way to put the problem is to say that we face a dilemma over whether our conception of 'internal qualia' is observational or theoretical. It can't be observational, because all we observe in ordinary sensory experience is the external environment. It can't be theoretical, because a purely theoretical concept can't give a characterization of something distinctive specifically of conscious experience.)

Instead, I've been arguing, we should characterize sensory experience in externalist or relational terms. On a relational view of experience, we describe sensory experience first by saying what we are (for example) seeing: that it's a red chair, a yellow balloon, and so on. As I said earlier, however, a relational view of experience can think of sensory experience as a three-place relation: there is not only the perceiver and the chair, for example, but the point of view from which the observer is seeing the chair. And it is also possible to modify the perceptual relation adverbially, as when you say that you are looking steadily at the chair. Summing up, we could put these points by saying there is not only the scene you are observing; there is the *way* in which you are observing it.

Our problem is to explain how sensory experience, thought of like this, can be grounding use of patterns of inference that reflect the conception of objects as mind-independent. And to give the explanation, it's not enough merely that we specify which objects and properties the subject perceives. We also have to specify the *way* in which the scene is being perceived. We cannot say simply that the perceptual experience consists in one's being related to various objects and properties around one, without saying *how* the experience relates one to those objects and properties. We will see, however, that we can explain the experiential relation in terms of its attentional structure; and we can characterize attentional structure in terms of the way in which the objects and properties in the scene contribute to the causal structure of the perceiver's experience.

In specifying the way in which the scene is being perceived, we have to resist appealing to qualia, or anything else that smacks of an attempt to describe sensory experience in purely 'internal' terms. That is, we have to resist trying to give a description of an 'inner' aspect of experience that it could have whatever was in one's surroundings. For it does not seem possible to form a coherent vocabulary to describe that 'inner' aspect of experience. So will it be possible to characterize a *way* of experiencing objects as mind-independent?

The gist of the account I will propose is this (though it will take most of the present chapter to get it properly articulated). In visually attending to a scene, one dimension of your experience has to do with the characteristics of objects that you would report them to have, act with respect to, or report yourself as experiencing. But another, more fundamental dimension of visual experience has to do with how you grab the object visually in the first place; how, in vision, you snatch it out from the rest of the visual array as something on which you are going to focus. This is not a matter of you representing the object in experience; it is not a matter of experiential representation at all. It has to do with the relation between you and the object. It makes a constitutive difference to your visual experience. And it reflects the mind-independence of the thing.

Consider the way in which vision scientists characteristically approach questions about visual attention. In a classical vision science experiment, the subject is set some task. This is defined in terms of how the subject has to respond to some external scene, such as a display on a computer. This is a relation between the subject and the environment: here is the subject, there is the computer screen. In performing the task, the subject has to select some aspect of the display and make a response. It is assumed that the potentialities and limitations of the subject in performing this task reflect, in part, the potentialities and limitations of underlying neural processing. This is a second level, at which we think of attention as having to do with what's going on in the brain. The discussion characteristically moves seamlessly back and forth between two levels: thinking of attention as:

(1) a relation between the person and the environment, and:
(2) a characteristic of information processing in the brain.

Do we find sensory experience at the level of the relation between the subject and the environment, or is sensory experience rather at the level of internal brain processing? If we have to choose, it seems quite evident that sensory experience is found at the level of the subject looking at the computer screen, for example, rather than at the level of information processing in the brain. Still, the possibilities and limitations of visual experience are taken to be explained by the possibilities and limitations of the underlying neural processing.

Attention, whether at the level of subject's experiential relation to the computer display, or at the level of brain processing, has usually been taken to require some kind of *selection*. Psychologists have thought of this selection as reflecting some kind of resource limitation in the visual system in the brain, some kind of ceiling on the visual system's processing capacity.

You might argue that this gets things round the wrong way. It is possible to argue that selection is demanded at level (1), at the level of the subject's attention to the external scene, and that this is what explains the limitations on brain processing. It's possible, for example, to argue that the generation of knowledge, or intentional action, in themselves require selection. The arm can only move in one direction at a time, for example, so in order for current visual perception to control what direction the arm moves in, there will have to be selection of one visual parameter rather than another to direct the movement of the arm. You might argue that this kind of consideration, rather than any processing limitation of the visual system, is what explains the role of selective attention in knowledge and action (see Allport (1989, p. 648) and Wu (2011) for exploration of the line of thought). The trouble with this line of thought is that (a) as Allport remarks, it is not obvious that intentional action as such really imposes much limitation on parameter selection for the control of action (for example, in moving your arm to reach the diamond protected by the beams of an alarm system, you may have to be monitoring your arm location with respect simultaneously to many spatial parameters), and (b) there seem to be quite definite limitations on selective attention that aren't predicted merely by its role in the generation of knowledge and action. For example, consider the basic finding by Liqiang Huang and Harold Pashler (2007) that assessment of the symmetry of a variously coloured display has to proceed by selecting and assessing for symmetry, one at a time, the regions of each particular colour. This isn't predicted merely by the demand that vision should generate knowledge and intentional action. It seems rather to reflect some deeper processing limitation on the brain. So the mainstream view is that the possibilities and limitations of selection at the level of sensory experience of the external scene are consequences of the possibilities and limitations on selection at the level of neural processing.

Can we press further the work that vision science can do in explaining visual experience? I suggest that there are contexts in which:

(a) We can argue that experience of object O is causally made possible by experience of property F, and

(b) At the level of information processing in the brain, visual representation of O is causally made possible by representation of F.

In this kind of case, property F will constitute the visual 'mode of presentation' of the object O. There are two strategic issues we face in making out this kind of argument. You might argue that all the causality is found at level (a), the level of information processing in the brain, so that there is no prospect of finding a causal relation at the level of specifically experiential phenomena. If, though, we are to find an epistemic role for sensory experience at all, we shall have to resist this kind of cognitive epiphenomenalism about experience. Finding an epistemic role for sensory experience requires that we find it a causal role. The second strategic issue is that you might say that the natural interpretation of the situation at level (a), in terms of experience, is that 'experiential representation' of O is being made causally possible by an 'experiential representation' of F. But this really would leave 'consciousness' seeming like a kind of optional glow with which visual representation is sometimes enlivened. It makes it baffling what kind of causal contribution that 'glow' could be making, that wasn't there in the mere visual representation itself. We need to explain why we have to appeal to the idea it could be your experiential relation to the external property F that was making it causally possible for you to consciously attend to the object, and thus constituted your 'mode of presentation' of the thing. So in making the case that experience of O is causally made possible by experience of F, we will have to resist both cognitive epiphenomenalism and the idea that if colour figures in experience, it does so as the content of a representation. Let's look at how this could go.

2. Selection vs Access

Huang and Pashler (2007) draw a fundamental distinction between selection and access in visual attention. This is a distinction between two ways a perceived property can function in relation to an object or region. Grabbing the thing out from its background (selection) is one thing, and characterizing it (access) is another. So a property may be used to *select* the object or region. Or the property may be *accessed* as a property of that object or region. Selection is what makes the object or region visible in the first place; selection is what makes it possible for the subject to focus on that object or region in order to ascertain its various properties. Access is a matter of the subject making it explicit, in one way or another, just which manifold properties the object or region has.

The key point is that whether a property is being used to select an object in experience is one thing, and whether the subject is accessing that property of the object is another. You can use a property of the object to snatch it out. It is a further step to make it explicit that the object has that property.

You can draw this distinction between selection and access at two different levels:

(1)   The level of the relation between the perceiver, trying to perform some task, and the external environment.
(2)   The level of information processing in the brain.

Level (1) is, I suggest, the level of such phenomena as ordinary *seeing*; it is the level at which we find conscious experience.

Here's how the distinction between selection and access looks at level (1), the level of the conscious relation between the subject and the environment. Here you can explain the distinction in terms of two different dimensions along which the difficulty of a task can be varied. For example, suppose you are presented with a display of variously coloured letters of the alphabet. Suppose you have to report which letters are coloured red. Here your task could be made more difficult in two ways. (a) Your task can be made more difficult by including letters that have colours similar to red, such as pink or orange, rather than only letters that are either red or green. That makes it harder to select a target as opposed to a non-target letter (red vs pink, for example). Alternatively, (b) your task can be made more difficult by including many different letters all coloured red, all of which have to be reported. In this case, your task has been made more difficult not by making it harder to select a target, but by giving you more reporting to do. You have to access the shapes of more targets (cf. Huang 2010). For another simple example of the distinction between selection and access, again as drawn at level (1), consider

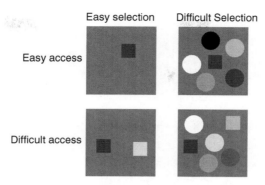

Figure 3.1 This diagram illustrates the distinction between selection and access, at the level of the subject's relations to external displays for which a task has to be performed. The task is to report the colour of any squares in the display (colours not shown). In the left column, selection is easy, because there are no distractors, only targets (squares). In the right column, selection is difficult, because there are distractors (circular disks). In the top row, access is easy, because there is only one target whose colour has to be reported. In the bottom row, access is difficult, in that there are two targets whose colour has to be reported (from Huang and Pashler 2007).

Figure 3.1. Here your task is to report the colour(s) of any squares in the display. The difficulty of selection in this case has to do with how many distractors (how many non-squares) there are in the display. More distractors may make it harder to identify the target. The difficulty of access, on the other hand, has to do with how much reporting of colour you have to do; hence, with how many squares there are in the display. As I said, we can interpret the idea of a *way* of being conscious of an object in terms of the properties that are being used to *select* that object. Access is a further step. That, I think, is how the distinction between selection and access looks at level (1).

How does the distinction between selection and access look at level (2), the level of the underlying neural processing in the brain? Huang and Pashler presuppose an underlying architecture of Treismanian feature maps, in which the locations of various features of different sorts are plotted: the locations of various colours, shapes, orientations, movements, and so on. In *selection*, a particular property—say, a particular colour—is used to identify a particular region or object. So, for example, an area might be selected as the locus of all the redness in the observed scene. Huang and Pashler say that what is being selected is: 'a collection of locations. It should be emphasized that those locations are regions exactly covered by relevant stimuli (i.e., one should imagine the map as being, as it were, shrink-wrapped to conform tightly to the object)' (p. 601 footnote 2). I do not think, though, that we should see them as taking an undefended stand on the idea that attention is always to location rather than to objects. Rather, we could understand them as saying merely that when an object is selected, it is selected by selecting the region it currently occupies. In *access*, the various maps are interrogated again, now to make explicit the various properties of this selected region or object (cf. Campbell 2002b, ch. 2, 'The Double Use of Feature Maps'). Huang and Pashler diagram the situation as shown in Figure 3.2.

Now I have suggested that we should think of sensory experience as occurring at level (1), the level of the relation between the subject and the external display. Sensory experience has to do with what the subject sees. And at level (1), we can characterize the way in which you are conscious of the object in terms of the properties of the object that are being used to select it. But we can ground our understanding of the causal structure here by looking at its relation to this level (2), the causal mechanism that underpins the use of a property to select an object.

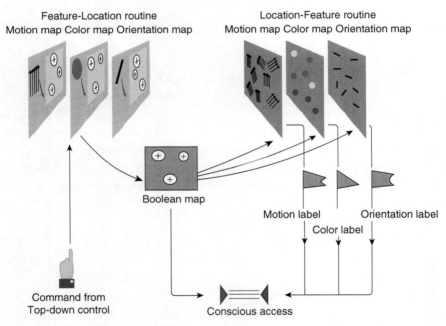

Figure 3.2 Boolean map theory depends on an underlying architecture of Treismanian feature maps. In the example shown, a feature, redness, is used to select all and only the red areas. A first consultation of the feature maps is made, to find which regions have red at them. This yields a Boolean map, which at this stage is not thought of as labelled. The underlying feature maps are then consulted again to determine what features are found at the region selected, and the labelling then makes those features explicit (from Huang and Pashler 2007).

Let's look at how it could happen that you use a property to select an object even though you may be quite incapable of visually accessing the object's possession of that property. Let's take a relatively simple kind of example: the use of tests for colour vision in which all that separates a particular figure from its background is the hue. So, for example, you may be presented with an array of variously coloured blobs of varying luminance in which all that there is to systematically separate a figure 5 from its background are the colours of the various blobs (Ishihara colour test plates).

In such a case, it is hard to imagine how you could see the 5 without having conscious experience of the various colours involved. If you did not have conscious experience of the various colours, you might perhaps have a hunch that there is a 5 there in the scene. You might, if forced to guess which figure is present, actually guess that the number in the scene is a 5. But if the 5 is visibly there, as a 5 can be present in ordinary vision, then we cannot imagine how that could be unless you had phenomenal awareness of colour. It is not exactly that there is a contradiction in the idea of seeing the 5, in this kind of case, without experiencing its colour. The problem is rather that the experience seems entirely unimaginable; we can make nothing of the idea of such an experience.

You might argue that wavelength discrimination is possible even in the absence of colour perception. In particular, consider patients with cerebral achromatopsia (for a classic introduction, see Sacks 1995). Patients with this rare condition have a deep loss of colour experience, because of damage to brain areas that determine the colours of things. So such a patient's retina may be perfectly all right, and the processing of wavelength information at early stages in the brain—in particular, in the primary visual cortex—may be fine. So a patient like this may be able to use their intact capacity for rudimentary wavelength discrimination to use wavelength differences to extract the shapes of things (Barbur, Harlow and Plant 1994; Heywood, Cowey and Newcombe 1991), or to perceive motion in moving gratings (Cavanagh et al. 1998). Couldn't a patient like this discriminate the 5 in our Ishihara plate, even though they have a deep loss of colour experience?

Even for such a patient, though, the basic point I am making applies. The basic point is this: when the visual system is using a particular property of an object as the basis on which the object is selected from its background, experience of the object depends on experience of that property. The visual experience of someone with cerebral achromatopsia is, of course, quite different from the visual experience of an ordinary subject. The preserved wavelength discrimination is making a difference to their visual experience, even though it does not constitute perception of colour. You might argue that the wavelength discrimination makes a difference to visual experience in that it allows experience of shape or movement that the patient wouldn't otherwise have had. In that case, my general point is: if the object is being selected on the basis of shape or movement, then experience of the object depends on experience of shape or movement. Or you might argue that the preserved wavelength discrimination itself allows the object to be discriminated from its background. In that case, my point is that experience of the object depends on experience of the differences in wavelength. You might think of the differences in wavelength as showing up in visual experience as, for example, an extra dimension along which the various greys, whites, and blacks in the scene are ordered. Experience of the object still depends on experience of the property being used to select the object.

The Ishihara plates were, of course, not designed to test for whether someone has cerebral achromatopsia. In fact, though, many people with this kind of colour-blindness cannot see the figure 5 (for example) at all. About 29 per cent can, though the significance of the number is hard to determine because there is a lot of variety in the severity of cerebral achromatopsia (Bouvier and Engel 2006). For present purposes, I'll assume that the Ishihara plates fulfil their intended purpose, in that full colour vision is required to see the objects, such as the 5, as figures against their backgrounds.

Ordinarily, then, when someone can see the 5, the colour and location of the object are the properties of it that are causally responsible for the object being singled out at all. That colour has to be used to single out the object in visual experience is the whole point of the test; there is ordinarily nothing other than hue that could causally differentiate the thing from its background. Of course location too is being used, as becomes evident if you consider a variant on the Ishihara plate that has two figure 5s, of the same hue as one another, at different places on the same dappled or brindled background. All that differentiates the two 5s is their location; but you have absolutely no difficulty in focusing on one rather than another of the two 5s. So there is a contrast here between hue and location on the one hand, and shape on the other. Hue and location are causally involved in allowing you to see the object against its background. But the shape of the thing—whether it is a 5 or a 3 or something else—is, we are supposing, playing no such causal role. You would still be singling out the object on the basis of its hue and location whatever shape it had.

Still, although you may have used your conscious experience of the colour to select the 5, and can then go on to access various properties of the 5, such as its size, shape, and orientation, it seems entirely possible that you could select the 5 on the basis of colour without yet having any capacity to access colour properties. This is evident if you consider the mechanism underlying visual experience, described in Figure 3.2. Here it is an entirely logical point about the mechanics of selection and access. Merely having the capacity to select objects of regions on the basis of colour does not of itself automatically imply that one must have a capacity to access colour properties.

It is not difficult to find illustrations at level 1, the level of the subject and the environment, of the possibility of selection on the basis of a property without access to that property. Human children have colour vision in place long before they have anything in the way of a colour vocabulary; it is entirely possible that a child a few months old could see the 5 in the kind of display I am describing, without having any ability to give a verbal report of its colour. You might object that verbal report is only one way in which access to a seen property could manifest itself. That is correct; there are other ways in which access to colour could show up. For example, it could be that one is capable of colour induction: having been exposed to red berries that were not good to eat, one is in the future reluctant to eat red berries. But the same point applies here. A mere ability to see the 5 against its background does not yet imply that one has a capacity for colour induction. Nor, to take some further obvious examples, does it imply that one has a capacity for colour matching, or a capacity for ordering objects by their colours. If one sees the 5, then, I have said, one must have experience of its colour; but that experience of colour may be quite deeply recessive, and not show up in any way other than in a capacity to use it to distinguish objects from their backgrounds.

Incidentally, as you can see from Figure 3.2, Huang and Pashler have their own interpretation of where consciousness fits into their picture: they suggest that it is a consequence of the kind of processing they describe at level 2 that the accessed properties of a selected region will be the contents of consciousness, the various aspects of the phenomenal experience of the subject. Now it seems to me that the empirical basis for Huang and Pashler's distinction between selection and access, and their way of locating the distinction against a broadly Treismanian background, is forcefully and persuasively made out. But their way of locating sensory awareness in the picture seems to me questionable. The key point is that as we have just seen, properties that are used in selection, but not accessed by the subject, may themselves figure in experience. So it's a mistake to suppose that the properties that figure in awareness are those that we access. The way to connect awareness to attention is, rather, to connect awareness of a property to the possibility of that property being used as a basis for selection of an object or region.

So we should:

(a) Locate consciousness at level (1) the level of the relation between the subject and the environment, the level of *seeing*, rather than at level (2), the level of neural processing, and

(b) Regard a property's figuring in awareness as a matter of that property being available for use as a basis for selection of an object or region (rather than as a matter of that property being accessed in vision).

I've been arguing that visual experience of the 5 can be made possible by experience of the colour of the 5, even though the subject cannot access the colour of the 5. This means that we can regard colour as specifying the *way* in which the 5 is experienced. Now in this simple example, we do not yet find anything that seems to be distinctive of a way of experiencing the 5 as mind-independent. So we will look at more realistic examples in a moment.

3. Selection without Representation in Visual Experience

Before going on to mind-independence, though, I want to pause over this causal structure that we have uncovered in visual experience. Let us go back over what we should say about the visual experience of a subject who sees the 5 in our display. Suppose the subject is not able to access the colour of the object, though able to see the thing. Does the colour of the object enter into the subject's visual experience? For anyone who ties visual experience to what the subject can access, colour can play no role in characterization of the subject's experience. For the subject cannot access colour. So suppose colour plays no role in the subject's visual experience. How would the subject be able to see the 5? There is now nothing in the subject's visual experience to differentiate the thing from its background. You might argue that this is consistent with the subject nonetheless being capable of some forced-choice guessing as to the presence of a 5 in the display. You are surely right about this. The trouble is that if this is what is going on, then the usual tests for colour vision are useless; passing the test (identifying the 5) is consistent with the subject having no experience of colour at all. Moreover, forced-choice guessing about the presence of the object does not seem to be what is happening when a tiger, for example, which may be incapable of accessing colours, makes a strike against an insufficiently camouflaged victim. The tiger does not merely have some hunch that there may be food in the long grass: the tiger can see its target perfectly well. You might wonder whether we couldn't have the following situation:

(a) the subject can't access the colour of the thing,

(b) the subject has no experience of the colour of the thing, yet

(c) the subject has perfectly ordinary experience of the thing itself, sees the thing perfectly well, even though it is only colour that differentiates the thing from its background.

It is difficult to understand the situation envisaged here. The problem is not that there is a contradiction in the description, or that it is somehow linguistically incoherent. The trouble rather lies in envisaging the situation being described. The situation is one in which one has no experience of the colour of the thing. So there is nothing in one's experience itself that differentiates the 5 from its background. The point about these colour vision test images is that there is nothing but colour to differentiate the number from the background. So one's experience might as well be in black and white. Nonetheless, you can see the 5 perfectly well, because of some sub-personal information processing remote from consciousness that is providing spectral information. I don't find any internal contradiction in this description. The trouble is that the situation described is completely unimaginable. We have no idea what such an experience would be like. If, as in the case of the 5, colour really is all that differentiates the object from its background, it is not something we can visualize that there might be visual experience not involving colour that nonetheless does involve seeing the thing. This argument is a direct appeal to what is imaginable in visual experience. We can make nothing of the idea that there might be visual experience not involving colour that is nonetheless experience of the 5. If that is right, then it is a mistake to tie visual experience of a property to the ability to access that property. We should rather think of visual experience in terms of its role in selection. We should think of visual experience of a property as being what makes it possible to use that property as the basis for selecting a region or object. We should tie visual experience to selection, rather than to access.

As we saw, it seems quite coherent to suppose that our subject may be using the colours of things *only* for object perception. We saw that a natural model of the brain mechanisms of selection and access seems to allow for the possibility of selection without access. And it is not hard to find real examples. Passing this kind of test for colour vision, being able to see the 5, is consistent with your being unable to give a verbal report of the colour of the object. This is obvious from the case of animal colour vision. A tiger padding through the veldt may be able to distinguish its prey from the foliage because of the colour of its target; but that does not mean that the tiger has any interest in the colour of things; it may not even be able to attend to the colour of the object. All it cares about is the object itself. The tiger may be incapable of attending to the colour of the object, even though it uses the colour of the thing to select the object from its background. A parallel point applies to humans: the use of colour to discern the object against its background is one thing, and the ability to form beliefs about the colour of the object is another. There are various ways in which we can illustrate this point. Human children have a lot of difficulty in learning colour words. Even after more than 1,000 trials, a child who already has hundreds of words in their vocabulary may still be quite unable to go on to apply the words 'red' and 'green' (Rice 1980, Franklin 2006). Darwin thought that his children were colour-blind, because of the great difficulty they had in learning colour words. There is even a word for the phenomenon, '*Farbendummheit*' (Davidoff 1991, p. 149). Yet ordinary colour vision is in place in children from a very young age. As early as four months' old, categorical colour perception seems to be in place in children (Franklin and Davies 2004). Of course, you might point out that the capacity to give verbal reports of the colours one sees is one thing, and the ability to conceptualize the colours one sees is another. Merely establishing that young children can see colours without having the ability to give verbal reports of them does not of itself show that these children do not have a capacity to conceptualize the colours they see. There does not seem to be decisive evidence in support of this idea (cf. Kowalski and Zimiles 2006 for discussion and further references). But even if it is true, the basic point is still in place, that the ability to use colours to define the objects one sees is one thing, and the ability to conceptualize those colours is another. One could be using colours to define the objects to which one attends without having any ability to attend to the colours themselves, and, consequently, without having any ability to conceptualize those colours.

Of course, a personal-level representation of the colour in experience might be functioning to allow the subject to perform a number of other operations than verbal report. But the same basic point still applies: the use of the property to define the object as figure from ground is one thing, and the use of the property in these further computational tasks is another. Ordinarily we are, for example, able to engage in a variety of sorting tasks with regard to colour. Given a stack of variously coloured chips, you might, for instance, be able to sort them into piles of like-coloured chips, or to sort all the green ones into a sequence from light green to dark green. Performing this kind of task is one use to which you might put a personal-level representation, supplied by vision, of the colours of the chips. But the mere use of the colour of a chip to differentiate the chip from its background does not of itself imply that one will be capable of these kinds of matching and sorting tasks.

It is usually assumed that if colour figures in your visual experience, that must mean that there is a *representation* of colour somehow figuring in your visual experience, which in turn means that you must be able to form beliefs about the colours of things, use their colours as a guide to action, or form beliefs about what colours you are experiencing (cf. Siegel 2010). Yet what we have just seen is that none of this is right. If you can see the 5, then colour does figure in your visual experience. Yet, consistently with that, you may be incapable of forming beliefs about the colours, using colour itself as a guide to action, or forming introspective beliefs about what colours you are experiencing. The idea that colour figuring in visual experience must be a matter of colour being represented to the subject seems to be a consequence of thinking that visual experience must be confined to properties that are being visually accessed.

To say that we should tie visual experience to selection, rather than to access, is to say we should prefer one family of theories over another; we still have to explain in detail just how experience is tied to selection. In particular, one question is whether experience of a property should be tied to the actual use of that property to select some region or object; or if the tie is rather between experience of a property and the possibility of using that property as a basis for selection. If we take the second route, we have to say something about what it is for a property to be capable of being used as a basis for visual selection. Here is one approach; I assume that others are possible too. We could:

(a) Define a notion of the 'visual field' of the subject. In the first instance you might think of this as a continuous external spatial region, a region defined by angles to the subject. Only objects in this area affect the subject's visual experience; objects behind the subject, or too far to the left, don't make any difference to the subject's visual experience. Of course, this is only a first approximation. We have to reckon in factors such as blind spots, or the fact that vision is not altogether ephemeral and that even as the subject moves around visual experience at one moment leaves an impact on visual experience moments later. But suppose that we can manage this, that we can define some suitable notion of visual field.

(b) Define a notion of 'visible property'. Not all properties of objects affect the visual experiences of those who see them; factors such as the age of the object, or exactly what happened to it ten years ago, may not make any immediate difference to the visual experience of someone looking at it. On the other hand, properties such as size, shape, and motion do seem to make an immediate difference to the visual experience of someone looking at the thing. That is not a complete account of the idea of a visual property: there is a lot to do to determine whether, for example, the species of an animal should be regarded as a visible property of the thing, or if it's rather inferred from visible properties. Suppose, though, that we can in the end give a suitable explicit characterization here.

If we can complete (a) and (b), then we can say that for a property to be visually experienced is for it to be a visible property of an object in the perceiver's visual field. And the reason this matters causally is that visible properties in the perceiver's visual field are the bases on which regions or objects are selected, so that the properties of those regions or objects can be accessed.

I am proposing, then, that we should not think of visual experience of a property as a kind of epiphenomenon that is spun off when one accesses an object's possession of the property. Given (a) and (b) above, we can say that the properties that are visually experienced are those that are available as bases for visual selection; and 'basing' here is a causal relation. Visual experience of the property is something that plays a causal role in allowing one to use that property in selection of an experienced object or region.

I think we can use this kind of point to begin articulating what we might call the 'attentional structure' of someone's experience of a scene. Experience of the object—the 5—is made possible by, causally facilitated by, experience of the colour of the object. If you can report on the shape of the object—if you can say that it is a 5, for example—then your experience of the object (caused by your experience of the colour) and your experience of the shape of the object are jointly playing a role in causing your verbal report. But there is a distinction between the causal roles of your experience of the colour and your experience of the shape of the object, in this case. Your experience of the colour is not (we may suppose, in your case) capable of causing a verbal report of the colour of the object, even though you are experiencing the 5. In contrast, your experience of the shape of the object is capable of causing a verbal report of the shape of the object, in the context of your experience of the 5. But your experience of the shape of the object is not what is causally facilitating your experience of the object itself; it is the colour that is doing that work.

Similarly, there is an asymmetric causal dependence between your experience of the object and your experience of the shape of the object, in the roles they play in verbal report. It is only because you are experiencing the object that you can experience its shape in such a way as to cause verbal report of its shape. You could, however, experience the object without experiencing its shape, in such a way as to cause you to have the capacity to make verbal reports of other aspects of the object.

The sense in which colours are 'given' to us in sensory experience, on this approach, needs careful glossing. It is natural to equate being 'given' the colours of things in experience as a matter of accessing those colours for potential further use; but that is not what I am suggesting. I am proposing that we are given 'colours' in experience in the sense that the various colours we encounter are available for use in the selection of objects as figure from ground; having selected those objects, we may then go on to access their various properties.

On this approach, the correct way to formulate a relational account of perceptual experience is to think of the relation as holding between a thinker and an array of visible properties at various locations, available for use in the selection of objects as figure from ground. Objects figure in sensory experience only when selected as figure from ground, ready to have their further characteristics accessed. It is possible to attend to an object without accessing any of its characteristics, though it may not be what usually happens. Consider, for example, a child watching a beetle. The child may keep the most careful track of the thing, singling it out from its background, over quite a long period of time, without having accessed any particular properties of it, such as its colour, shape, or movement. There may have been no further cognitive tasks the child was poised to perform with regard to those properties; all the child was doing was watching the beetle.

I have emphasized the distinction between selection and access, and in particular the possibility of selecting an object on the basis of a characteristic of it, such as colour, that one does not access. I have emphasized the relation between a property's figuring in experience and the possibility of using it as a basis for selection. But an understanding of the concept of a property also seems to depend on being able to access that property, when it figures in visual experience.

You might propose that not only is it true that:

(1)   There is a range of *basic* properties we encounter in perceptual experience, such as colour, orientation, shape, and size, that we can use as the basis for selection of objects as figure from ground.

But also that:

(2)   Grasp of the concept of any one of those properties has as an element the ability to *access* that property when that property figures in one's visual experience.

Consider the case of shape concepts. The point that is always made about the ideas of shape that we have for ordinary physical objects is that some causal understanding is involved in grasping them. Given that something is conical, that has implications for how it will behave when liquids are poured into it, for example, given other factors about, for example, the rigidity and liquid resistance of the stuff it is made from. You might make a long list of the causal expectations that a subject ordinarily has of an object, given the facts about its shape, conditional on the other properties of the object. You might argue that grasp of these causal conditions is part of what it is to have the concept of shape. Indeed, following Shoemaker (1984), you might argue that this is *all* there is to grasp of a shape concept. What I am suggesting is that this is not all there is to grasp of a shape concept; one must also have the capacity to access the shape of the object when one encounters the object in experience.

The question here is about the causal structure of the relation between the capacity to access the shape of the object in experience, and the capacity to use the shape of the object as a basis for selection of the object in conscious experience. I have just suggested that grasp of colour and shape concepts depends on the ability to access colour and shape in perception; but it seems to matter, in these cases, that we are accessing colours and shapes that figure in experience. What I have argued in the case of colour, and seems equally to be the case here, is that selection of an object as figure from ground in conscious experience has to be done on the basis of conscious experience of the properties of the object. We can make nothing of the idea that the figure 5 might be experienced on the basis of perceptual representation of its colour, even though that representation had no reflection in conscious experience. You can have experience of the 5 only on the basis of conscious experience of its colour. But now, suppose that you are experiencing the 5, and you access its colour. Should we think of your access to colour here as caused by perceptual processing that has nothing particularly to do with consciousness, and could well be performed in the absence of any experience of colour? In that case we might think in terms of there being a common cause for the experience of colour used in selecting the 5, and your ability to access the colour of the 5. But your conscious experience of colour would play no role in causing your access to the colour of the 5. Alternatively, you might think that in ordinary cases in which you are accessing the colour of the 5, your judgement as to colour causally depends on your experience of the colour of the thing. Similar points apply, of course, to the case of shape. The suggestion is that when grasp of colour concepts exploits your ability to access the colours of objects you can see, it matters that you are accessing colours that are there in your visual experience. This is a different role for experience of the property than its role in making it possible for you to see the object in the first place.

4. Experience of Mind-Independence

Suppose you can see the figure 5 against its background, and you form the judgement 'That figure is a 5.' The simplest form of the relational analysis describes the situation by saying that you are related by the two-place relation of consciousness to the figure 5, and to the properties of colour, location, and shape. But what I have just been arguing is that we can give a more informative analysis of the situation by distinguishing between the kinds of causal roles played by the properties of colour and location on the one hand, and shape on the other.

Our discussion so far allows us to give a relationalist explanation of the notion of a *way* of experiencing an object, without appealing to anything in the way of internal 'qualia'. Consider a demonstrative mode of presentation, such as expressed by 'that 5' said by someone pointing at the 5 in our display. If you say that the mode of presentation here is descriptive, for example 'the red region', then you suggest that the description has to be grasped by the subject in order to understand the demonstrative. This implies that the subject has accessed the redness of the region, and indeed had to do so in order to refer to the object. But our previous discussion suggests that this is not necessary. To have selected the 5, the subject had to use the colour of the figure, but the subject need not have accessed the colour of the figure, and indeed the subject might be quite incapable of grasping any such description.

This suggests that the mode of presentation of a perceptually demonstrated object has to be characterized not in terms of any internal 'qualia' or any description that the subject accesses, but rather in terms of an external property of an external thing that the subject uses to select that object perceptually. Sameness of mode of presentation is the same thing as sameness of the external property on the basis of which the object is selected; difference of mode of presentation is the same thing as difference of the property on the basis of which the object is selected. This gives us an externalist mode of presentation for the perceptual case.

Though the mode of presentation is non-descriptive and may not be accessed by the subject, it is not remote from consciousness. On the contrary, on this approach the mode of presentation is an aspect of the subject's conscious experience, and will affect the causal role of the subject's demonstrative thoughts. For the property on the basis of which selection of the object is made enters into the characterization of the subject's conscious state, and the subject's conscious experience makes a difference to which beliefs the subject actually forms.

Let's look now at what it could be to experience the objects around you as mind-independent. We have been talking about visual attention as a matter of selecting an object whose properties you will go on to access visually. So far I have been considering a particularly simple example, selecting the number 5 in a display on the basis of its colour. Now in this simple case, it's hard to see that there is a decisive case to be made that you are selecting the object on the basis of anything related to its mind-independent status. Let's now take a look at a rather more realistic case. You and I are watching someone who's digging a hole in the road. We are talking together about the scene. Let's suppose that this is a case of joint attention. That is, it's not that we just happen, by accident, to be focusing on the same person. Let's suppose that what's causing you to focus on that man is, in part, my focusing on him, and that what's causing me to focus on him is, in part, your focusing on him. You are selecting that man as an object whose characteristics you are accessing visually. I am selecting that man as an object whose characteristics I am accessing visually. What is the relation between the properties that you are using to select that man, as figure from ground, and the properties that I am using to select that man, as figure from ground? And what is the relation between the properties of that man that you are accessing, and the properties of that man that I am accessing? Finally, what is guiding your and my individual visual systems' selections of an object here?

This example makes apparent one of the ways in which our case of the 5 is particularly simple. In the case of the 5, there is only one property that can be used to select it visually, namely its colour. So if you and I are to jointly attend to the 5 on the colour test plate, we both have to select it on the basis of its colour. But in the case of the workman, there is a much richer and more complex set of properties that can be used to distinguish him as figure from ground. You may be seeing him from a different angle than I am. Quite different aspects may be visible to you than to me. Your objective is to select the same object visually as I am attending to. My objective is to select the same object visually as you are attending to. There may be nothing more substantial than that to be said about the relation that has to hold between the properties that you are using to select that man as the object of attention, and the properties that I am using to select that man as the object of attention. The case of the 5, in which we both have to be using the same properties as the basis for selection if we are to attend to the same object, thus seems to be quite unusual.

I have been arguing that visual experience has to be characterized in terms of the principles governing selection of the object attended. If what I have just said is correct, then in joint attention, the only way we have to specify the principle governing selection is in terms of the object itself that you and I are both attending to. There are no particular properties that you and I both have to be using to select the thing, and as you and I and the workman move and change over time we each may be using different properties as the basis for visual selection, in order to sustain our joint attention on the thing. The only principle governing which properties you and I have to be using to select the thing is that they be properties of that very thing. For each of us, the visual experience in this case of joint attention thus has to be characterized in terms of the object itself that both you and I are experiencing. It's implicit here that the object in question is mind-independent. It can't be internal to your mind, because it's what I am attending to. And it can't be internal to my mind, because it's what you are attending to.

Does this give us a satisfactory response to Berkeley's Puzzle? Remember that the puzzle was:

(1) Our knowledge of our environment has to be grounded in sensory experience.

(2) Sensory experience can provide knowledge only of sensory experience itself.

Here I have characterized a sense in which a mind-independent object has to be recognized as a constituent of a visual experience in joint attention, being visually selected in a way that requires its mind-independence. The subject may not be visually representing the mind-independence of the object; what the subject is visually representing has to do with the level of visual access, not the level of selection. There is, nonetheless, a sense in which we can say not just that the object is there as what the experience relates you to, in joint attention, but that the object is there *as* a mind-independent constituent of experience. This is not a matter of the subject *representing* the object as mind-independent, but doesn't it give us enough objectivity in experience to be able to say that experience of this type can be grounding thought about a mind-independent world?

There is, however, at least one dimension of our ordinary conception of a concrete object that this picture does not do justice to. As we saw in Chapter 2, we can think of the mind-independence of physical objects as a matter of their having a particular type of causal structure. The object itself has a particular counterfactual structure: the way the object is later counterfactually depends on the way the object was earlier. The object later would have been different had the object earlier been different. Interventions on the object earlier would have made a difference to how the object was later.

Now it seems possible that you and I could jointly attend to an object that did not have this kind of causal structure: a 3D projection of a human figure, for example. Here the way the object is later does not causally depend on the way that very object was earlier. Making a difference to the way the hologram is earlier, for example by shining a light on it, will make no difference to the way the hologram is later. The way the hologram is earlier and the way it is later are both effects of the projection apparatus, rather than one depending directly on the other. (Berkeley's own picture seems to have been a bit like this: you and I can jointly attend to an idea that is an artefact of the mind of God.) I argued, however, that we want to understand the sense in which our experience relates us to objects that have their own immanent causal structures, where the way the thing is earlier really does causally affect the way the thing is later.

We could try to address this by considering someone visually keeping track of an object over time. An object can change colour and location. It might change its shape as it moves around. And yet it can still be visibly the same thing. Vision does, though, make a sharp distinction between the case in which it is the same object, merely changing its properties, and the case in which one object has been substituted for another. Here again there may be nothing systematic to be said in terms of properties about how the subject is keeping track of the thing over time; it may be changing as it moves, and perhaps the only concise systematic thing to say about the principles governing the subject's selection of the thing over time is that the selection is sustained by it being the same object over time. We might think of this in terms of the counterfactual dependence of the way the thing is later on the way the thing was earlier. However, I think that reflection on this approach suggests that there is a deeper consideration at work.

I think it is a familiar point to most students of causation that it is natural to explain causation in terms of some kind of counterfactual connection. For A to be a cause of B is for it to be that were there a difference in A, there would be a difference in B. This kind of idea needs a lot of development; for example, you might argue that the key idea is that were there to be an intervention on A, there would be a difference in B. But I think it is also a familiar point to most students of causation that there is invariably a sense here that this is not all there is to causation; we have some intuitive picture of the 'mechanism' that underpins this kind of counterfactual connection, and we tend to think of this underlying 'mechanism' as the true locus of causation. But a third familiar point is that this notion of 'mechanism' has proven extremely difficult to explain. And in fact, generally what happens is that the notion of 'mechanism' is itself explained by the theorist in counterfactual terms: it's a mechanism if making a difference to one of the input elements would make a difference to one of the output values. I think the reason we find ourselves in this situation is that our intuitive picture of what a 'mechanism' is, is provided by our understanding of simple contact phenomena among medium-sized objects; what Locke called the transmission of motion by impulse. This is the prototype that governs all our other thinking about mechanisms; we're looking for something *like that*. Now central to our understanding of the prototypical mechanisms is our conception of a continuing physical object as the mechanism by which causal influence is transmitted from place to place over time. But if you ask 'What is this conception of the categorical physical object that sustains counterfactual dependencies across time and place?' there is no obvious analysis to be given. I think the reason for this is that our understanding of physical objects as categorical mechanisms here is something that is provided *ostensively*: it is our experience of objects that provides us with this conception of the categorical thing itself.

It is *because* it is one and the same categorical object that the way the thing is later counterfactually depends on the way the thing was earlier. The later thing would have been different if the earlier thing had been different. And that is because it is one and the same thing. The continuing categorical object functions as the mechanism that explains the transmission of causal influence over time.

Your sensory experience of the object provides you with insight into *why* the object's later condition depends on its earlier condition. We do not ordinarily experience concrete objects merely as collections of causal powers. We select a concrete object from the visual scene as the mechanism by which causal influence is transmitted from place to place over time.

This bears on what we say about the joint attention case too. In seeing an object, we do not ordinary observe it as a mere potentiality to affect the other person's beliefs as well as one's own beliefs. Rather, you experience the categorical object itself. You experience the ground of the potentiality to affect the other person's beliefs and your own beliefs. You see why the other person and you are reacting as you do. Similarly, if a hot object moves from one place to another, you do not experience merely a potentiality for the way things were at the earlier place to affect how things are at the later place. You see the thing itself, the mechanism by which causal influence is being transmitted from one place to another. Finally, the present point also bears on Dr Johnson's kicking the rock. It is important that Johnson's kicking the rock is a multimodal affair. It would not have had the same visceral impact if Johnson had rebounded off the thing while kicking it in the pitch dark. That would merely have established the presence of some force or other. The reason Johnson's reaction is powerful is that in vision he is experiencing the categorical object itself: the underlying thing that is responsible for the rebound. It is the presence of the mind-independent thing itself, categorically there in visual experience, that allows us to respond to Berkeley's Puzzle.

5. Is the Visual World a Grand Illusion?

Here is one version of the form that the mind–body problem takes in the recent literature on visual attention. The difficulty is that as we study the visual system in the brain—in particular, when we look at what properties of the scene seem to be accessed by the systems of visual attention in the brain—we find only incomplete, transient representations of aspects of our surroundings. We find no assembly of detailed, stable representations that could ground our apparent visual experience.

One, perhaps the most common, reaction to this point is to suppose that we are under a kind of persistent and pervasive illusion about the nature of our visual experience. It seems to be richly detailed and stable, but it is not (see, e.g., Cohen et al. 2012). To bring out the idea here, consider a thought experiment. Suppose you are fitted with an eye tracker, and you are looking at a large, blank white wall. Suppose that a projector is linked to the eye tracker, and it projects onto the wall a small circle of letters. So what an observer sees when they walk into the room is you seated on a chair moving your head around while a small circle of letters moves around on the wall. To you, though, as the subject of this experiment, it seems as though you are facing a vast, stable array of letters on the wall, reaching from floor to ceiling and the full length of the wall, though of course you can only select and access—focus on—the characteristics of some small group of stimuli at a time. In this kind of case, it really seems that you are being subjected to some kind of illusion about the character of your visual experience. The suggestion is now that this is not a special or unusual case. In ordinary life we are continually subject to just that illusion about the character of our ordinary visual experience. There seems to be simultaneously present in our experience a rich, stable array of properties and objects when in fact there is not.

This is a perplexing conclusion. Isn't there any way we could rescue the idea that our ordinary experience is usually detailed and stable in the way it seems to be? The trouble is that this is impossible so long as we think that the nature of our visual experience must be entirely grounded in the characteristics of the brain. If we think of the relevant brain characteristics as representational, the trouble is that there aren't the detailed, stable representations to be found. If we think in terms of a kind of 'mental paint' that presents characteristics of the brain to us in a 'phenomenal' way, the trouble is that there isn't enough mental paint to go around, there isn't enough mental paint to constitute that detailed, stable picture.

The only way in which we can sustain our common-sense conception of visual experience is to be externalist about experience: to acknowledge that the physical grounding of experience is found not just in the brain, but in the relation of the brain to the external environment itself. After all, the external array of objects and colours and so on is there, detailed and stable. If we think of the external objects and colours and so on as literally constituting the phenomenal content of visual experience, then we can take our ordinary visual experience at face value.

These points bear on the interpretation of inattentional blindness and change blindness (see, e.g., Simons and Chabris 1999). In these cases, aspects of what we might take to be the detailed, stable world of visual experience are simply not noticed by subjects, and change in them is simply not noticed by subjects. This is really startling if you do not distinguish between:

(a) the detailed, stable world of phenomenal visual experience, and
(b) the subject's access to properties of various regions and objects in the perceived scene.

The basic point here is that stability and detail are characteristics of the rich visual scene, out there in the external world, that we actually experience. I have suggested that we should be thinking of the visible characteristics of the scene as being there in experience, in the sense that they are available for use as the basis on which we select objects or regions whose characteristics we can go on to access visually.

Stability and detail, on the other hand, are not characteristics of our visual access to the properties of objects and regions around us. Visual access really does seem to be transitory and incomplete. But the sense of paradox vanishes once we let go of the idea that visual experience has to be described entirely in terms of what we access visually, rather than in terms of the external scene to which visual experience relates us.

One way to bring out the point is to reflect on Huang and Pashler's demonstrations that access to the colours in a scene is serial: you can in fact access the colours in a scene only one at a time. At first this seems counter-intuitive: surely in ordinary visual experience the entire multicoloured blaze is all there in front of you simultaneously? What I am suggesting is that there is no tension here, once we let go of the idea that it is only what we have access to that is there in visual experience.

To illustrate Huang and Pashler's point about the serial nature of access to colours, consider the following study. You are shown two arrays of variously coloured discs, and asked whether for each disc in the array on the left there is a disc in the corresponding location on the right. This task can be accomplished at a glance. You can tell in a moment whether the total configurations of the two sets of discs are the same. The implication of this is that the locations of all the discs on the left, and the locations of all the discs on the right, can each be accessed simultaneously. In contrast, suppose you are shown two arrays of variously coloured discs and asked whether for each disc of a particular colour on the left, there is a disc of that colour in the array on the right. You cannot perform this task in a moment. You have to work through the discs, colour by colour. You verify that there are two red discs on the left and two red discs on the right, for example, and then move on to consider how it goes for the green discs. Suppose, however, that you could access all the colours of the various discs simultaneously. Then you ought to be able to determine whether the total 'configuration in colour space' on the left is the same as the total 'configuration in colour space' on the right. You should be able to do this in a moment, if all the colours are given to you simultaneously. Since you cannot do this in a moment, but must work through colour by colour, it follows that you are managing to access the various colours in the scene only one at a time.

Huang and Pashler (2007) argue that this serial access to colour, and other observable properties of your surroundings, is at the root of inattentional blindness and change blindness. Since spotting visible features of your environment, or identifying specific changes in them, can be done only on the basis of a serial scan, there is always the possibility of unnoticed features or changes inside your visual field that are not accessed. If you think of visual experience as the upshot of such a serial scan, then you have to explain what is going on when these features that seem so visible are present yet unnoticed right in front of your nose. These cases seem to write large the idea that our impressions about the detail and stability of our current visual experience are somehow entirely illusory. We can, however, give a straightforward resolution if we think of the detailed, stable content of visual experience in externalist terms, as simultaneously present, and available as the basis for selection and access.

As we saw, Huang and Pashler do try to hold on to the equation of visual experience with visual access, though they distance themselves somewhat from other writers who take this line: 'Some writings inspired by change blindness would seem to imply that human visual experience is akin to the experience of looking at the world through a long cardboard tube' (Huang and Pashler 2007, pp. 623–4). Their point is that the spatial structure of visual attention is significantly more complex and flexible than this picture allows. Still, it is difficult to achieve a recognizable picture of visual experience until we let go altogether of the idea that it is only what we visually access that we visually experience.

We do have to let go of that idea anyhow. That was already implicit in our discussion of the figure 5. Recall the case of someone who has colour vision but uses colour vision only for object identification, not in order to visually access the colours of things. As we saw, someone like this who sees the 5 in a colour test plate has visual experience of the colour. But that is not because they are accessing the colour. They are accessing only the object and various of its properties, other than colour. The situation seems to be that if you are to have conscious experience of an object whose characteristics you can access, you must be able to select that object on the basis of properties that are making a difference to your visual experience. Experience of those characteristics is presupposed by your ability to attend to the object: to select that thing and access its characteristics. The detailed, stable world of visual experience is not a product of attentional selection and access: it is a background precondition of selection and access, if selection and access are to constitute attention to experienced objects.

This is not to say that visual access makes no difference to visual experience. Visual attention to one aspect or another of an object is a specifically visual matter, and it surely does make a difference to your visual experience just what things or regions you attend to, and what aspects of them you make visually explicit. But we have to distinguish between the rich phenomenology of visual experience in which we find, for example, arrays of various colours all simultaneously present, and the relatively bloodless sense in which, for example, it makes a difference to your visual experience of a display when you notice that it is symmetrical.

4

The Role of Sensory Experience in Propositional Knowledge

John Campbell

1. Does Sensory Experience Matter for Propositional Knowledge?

Epiphenomenalism in general is the view that mental properties don't have any causal role. There may be causal explanations for an organism coming to have those mental properties, but the properties themselves don't have any further effects, physical or mental. This view has seemed less compelling for mental properties in general than it does for properties relating to consciousness in particular. So, for example, you might argue that the information-bearing characteristics of an organism—which, you might say, it can have independently of whether it is conscious—are causally significant, and do make a difference to what the organism does. You could still hold that properties of the organism that relate to consciousness in general, and sensory awareness in particular, have no causal outcomes. Or at any rate, even if they have some causal outcome or other, they make no difference to our knowledge of our surroundings.

From one perspective, it can seem very appealing to hold that sensory awareness makes no causal difference to human cognition. Consider the honeybee. Quite a lot is known about honeybee cognition. For example, there are two navigational problems that honeybees have regularly to solve: to get from where they are to home, to the hive; and to get from where they are to their food sources. It has long been known that bees can keep track of the directions and distances they travel when outbound from the hive, even if their outbound path is zigzag, and then use path integration to find their way home. They use the sun and time of day as a compass, in recording directions, and landmarks in recording distance travelled (Wehner 1992, Wehner, Michel, and Antonsen 1996, Graham and Collett 2002).

However, recent studies suggest that although bees can use these simple strategies, they are also capable of navigation by means of a cognitive map of their targets. That is, when displaced from their flight paths, and simply set down at a new location, they will not merely try to retrace their steps. They will fly around and 'get their bearings' before flying direct to their target of choice, hive or feeder (Gould 1986, Menzel et al. 2005). The informational significance of the 'dance' bees engage in on returning to the hive after finding new food sources has also been extensively discussed (von Frisch 1967, Dyer 2002). So too has the bee's representation of the times at which various events characteristically happen (Kolterman 1974).

Are honeybees conscious? My point is that the study of honeybee cognition does not depend on our having any way of answering that question. Perhaps they are not conscious at all. The results on mapping and so on would still stand; they still have and use cognitive maps of their surroundings. Perhaps honeybees do have some rudimentary consciousness. Even if they do, it may play no role in their cognition. Perhaps honeybees do occasionally experience pangs of hunger or the joy of arriving home. But that may make no difference whatever to their cognitive engagement with their surroundings. We could put the point by saying that our working hypothesis, in studying bees, is that bee consciousness, if it exists, is 'cognitively epiphenomenal'. It makes no difference to bee cognition, even if bee cognition is one of its causes. Bee consciousness is regarded as 'cognitively epiphenomenal'. Even if there is such a thing, the serious study of bee cognition in no way depends upon it, for 'bee consciousness' is simply not a working part of bee cognition. At best it may be thrown off by bee cognition, as an epiphenomenon.

Now you might argue that the scientific study of human cognition similarly has no such dependence on phenomena of consciousness. That is not to deny that there is such a thing as sensory awareness, for example. It is just that sensory awareness is not itself a component of the mechanisms of human cognition. In the end, all that we have are various cell assemblies responding differentially to various external stimuli, and the description of their various impacts on one another in information-processing terms. It may be possible to view sensory awareness as an epiphenomenon thrown off by this cognitive processing. And of course there may be fascinating puzzles as to how this can happen. But sensory awareness is not itself an element in the explanation of how it is that we have knowledge of our surroundings. In general, there can be perception in the absence of sensory awareness, and there can be perception that is accompanied by sensory awareness. Representation is one thing, and awareness is another. But whether there is sensory awareness may not of itself make any difference in the generation of knowledge. Again, we might think of this view as 'cognitive epiphenomenalism'. It need not say that human consciousness has no causal outcomes at all, only that there are none that matter for our knowledge of our surroundings.

Although I have tried to set out the basic case for cognitive epiphenomenalism, it is not the perspective of traditional epistemology, or, for that matter, ordinary common sense. Ordinarily, we would take it that sensory experience has some epistemic role to play, that it does *something* for our knowledge of our surroundings, but more than that, it is the *fundamental* way in which we acquire knowledge of our surroundings. Sensory experience certainly *seems* to play a role in our knowledge of the world around us. It has often been observed that when you try to focus on the nature of your visual experience, for example, your attention typically falls onto the world itself. When you try to introspect the nature of the experience of green, for example, you find yourself simply focusing on the colour of the tree before you. Sensory experience seems simply to be displaying the world itself to you, and its value seems to be in the knowledge it provides of your surroundings.

There are two types of knowledge that might be in question here. There is your knowledge of how things are around you: knowing that the book is on the table, that the tree is full of birds' nests, and so on. Secondly, and more basically, there is knowledge of which things and properties are to be found in your surroundings. For example, consider knowledge of the colours. I don't just mean knowledge that there is such a phenomenon as colour, but knowledge of which property scarlet is, for example. We usually find it compelling that this knowledge can be provided only by experience of the colours. A capacity for correct, blindsight-style guessing as to the colours of things would not be enough for knowledge of what the colours are; you wouldn't know what scarlet is, in the absence of experience of it. Or again, we take it that to know which particular thing someone is trying to draw your attention to, you have to experience the thing; a mere capacity for blindsight-style guessing, a mere hunch that someone is there, isn't enough. This kind of knowledge is, on the face of it, not a matter of knowing that things are thus and so. It seems to be a precondition of knowing that things are thus and so. To know that the apple is red, for example, you have to know what an apple is, and you have to know what redness is. So our question has two parts: (a) Does sensory awareness play any role in our knowing that things are thus and so?, and (b) Does sensory awareness play any role in our understanding concepts of the world around us, does it play any role in our knowledge of what the various objects and properties around us are?

For ordinary common sense, it seems obvious that we know about the world around us only because we have sensory experience of it. Sensory experience is, as it were, your window on the world. Consider again cases in which there is perception without sensory awareness, such as cases of subliminal perception or blindsight-style cases. In classical cases of subliminal perception, a stimulus was flashed briefly, 'below the threshold of awareness', yet made some difference to your behaviour. The whole point about cases of subliminal perception was that you were supposed to be affected by the stimulus without knowing that it was there. In blindsight, patients with no explicit awareness of things in one half of their visual field were systematically responsive to the characteristics of objects in the blind field. No matter how fast, reliable, and confident the patient becomes, the patient is still said to be 'guessing' what is in the blind field. Because of the absence of awareness of the blind field, we do not describe the patient as 'knowing' about what is there. Or again, the motion-blind patient who catches the ball tossed to her, for example, does so without knowing that it's moving.

Classical cognitive psychology has no place for the distinction we ordinarily make between probabilistic belief and knowledge. It describes the brain processing entirely in terms of the various levels of probability assigned to different conclusions. Classical cognitive psychology has no more of a place for the distinction between knowledge and probable belief than it does for the distinction between perceptions that are conscious and perceptions that are not conscious.

So it looks as though for common sense, sensory experience is what explains our knowledge that things are thus and so. And cognitive psychology has no objection to make to this, because cognitive psychology does not address the phenomena of sensory experience or knowledge (as opposed to probable belief). Similar points apply to our understanding of concepts; to our knowledge of the objects and properties around us. Mere subliminal exposure to any quantity of apples, for example, would not provide you with any insight into what apples are. Similarly, knowledge of what colour and shape properties are seems to depend on experiencing them. It isn't enough that you have a perceptual system that allows you to respond differentially to this shape or to that. Mere perception of colour without sensory experience of colour, for example, wouldn't provide you with any knowledge of what the colours are. And classical cognitive psychology does not address the common-sense distinction between the subject 'grasping a concept' and merely having an information-processing representation in the brain.

So far in this study we have been looking at how our concepts of mind-independent objects can be grounded in sensory experience. Once we shift away from thinking of sensory experience in terms of inner qualia, whether representational or sensational, we can see how sensory experience could have a distinctive role to play in grounding our concepts of mind-independent objects, such as rocks or mountains. It is a further question whether sensory experience has any distinctive role to play in grounding propositional knowledge of our surroundings. That is, it's one thing to say that sensory experience has a role to play in grounding concepts in mind-independent objects. It's a different thing to say that sensory experience has a distinctive role to play in grounding knowledge *that* things are thus and so in your surroundings. It's one thing to say that sensory experience has a distinctive role to play in grounding your grasp of the concept of a *rock*. It's another thing to say that sensory experience has a distinctive role to play in grounding your knowledge *that*, e.g., the rock is blue-black and massive. In this chapter, let's look further at the role of sensory experience in propositional knowledge.

2. Perceptual Experience as an Intervention on Belief

One way to get at what seems special about sensory experience is to consider the kind of causal impact it has on our formation of belief. Suppose, to take an example of Austin's, that I am wondering whether it's true that there is a pig roaming these woods (Austin 1962, pp. 114–15). I've heard that there is one, but it seems quite unlikely. Then I come upon one in a clearing. I see it in good light. I walk all round it. I prod it with a stick. I sniff it a few times. The pig here has a causal impact on my beliefs. But it's not just that the pig is *influencing* my beliefs. In the ordinary case, the pig here has a *decisive* impact on my beliefs, in quite a strong sense. It's not just that it is one factor among many causally determining my belief. In this case, where I see it in good light, walk all around it, and so on, the pig itself suspends all other factors from having an impact on whether I believe there's a pig there. I did have a certain prior scepticism about whether it was at all likely that there was a pig in the woods. But my sensory encounter suspends the influence of those prior biases. The experiential encounter with the pig is not just one consideration among many affecting whether I think there's a pig there. Once it comes into play, it is the *only* factor specifically affecting what I believe on this point.

I am suggesting a reading of Austin's remark on which the point is that per-ception of the pig is an *intervention* on my belief as to whether a pig is present. That is, once the thing is in full view, my prior expectations as to whether a pig will be present are no longer causally influencing what I believe. The notion of 'intervention' is central in the recent literature on causation, and is usually illus-trated by an experimenter's action on some system. The experimenter reaches in from outside, and seizes control of the value of some variable X, suspending the influence of all other variables on X, to find what happens to the value of some other variable Y. (Cf., e.g., Woodward 2003 for a fully explicit definition. Notice that the idea of 'intervention' is illustrated by action. It is not *explained* in terms of action. We can make sense of a 'natural experiment', in which there is intervention without agency.) Now when you think of intervention in terms of agency, it is hard to see how there could be interventions on the human mind. For an external agent to intervene on someone's beliefs would seem to involve violating the rational autonomy of the subject. And free agency with respect to one's own beliefs seems impossible; one can't, e.g., voluntarily decide what to believe. But in perception, the external state of affairs itself intervenes on the subject's beliefs, without any violation of rational autonomy.

It seems compelling that this causal organization is normatively correct. This is how we ought to be organized in forming our perceptual beliefs. I will put the causal point by saying that perceptual experiences are *decisive* in the formation of beliefs about one's surroundings. I will put the normative point by saying that perceptual experiences are *authoritative* in the formation of beliefs about one's surroundings.

Sensory awareness has a kind of authority in our formation of beliefs that is not had by perception in the absence of consciousness. It is quite different with, for example, blindsight, or subliminal perception. If I am wondering whether there is a pig about, and one is in my blind field, at best my inclination to guess that there is one there has to be weighed against my prior views as to whether this is likely. My hunch that there is one there has to be weighed against, and may actually be outweighed by, my other beliefs and expectations. I am simply engaged in balancing various causal forces impacting specifically on my belief. Perception without awareness does not have the kind of decisive impact on belief possessed by perception with awareness. It is not an intervention on belief.

The point I am making about the decisive role of sensory experience in our formation of beliefs does not extend to every case in which a belief is formed on the basis of sensory experience. Consider, for example, threshold judgements about whether two things are exactly the same colour, or whether one pattern has higher contrast than another. These we ordinarily regard as decision-making under uncertainty; in these cases we don't usually regard perception as providing anything more than probable opinion. These kinds of case are quite unlike the case of the pig. I will not here try to make explicit the principled distinction between these kinds of cases; I remark only that there is obviously such a distinction to be drawn. You can have as much as you like in the way of prior reasonable beliefs about whether there is likely to be a pig in the woods. When you prod it with your stick, your experience is decisive in resolving the issue.

The point I am making here is so obvious and elementary that it is easy to take it for granted, so let me labour it a little. Suppose that you are going out and setting a timer to switch on a lamp, the lamp being plugged into a power supply. We can suppose that you're familiar with all the mechanisms here and know them all to be reliable. You set the lamp to go on at 6.00 pm. Quite rationally, you have a very high level of subjective confidence that the lamp will be on at 6.00 pm. Suppose you live in a bad neighbourhood and your house will be raided if there isn't a light on at 6.00 pm. You may, literally, be betting the farm that the lamp will be on at 6.00 pm. And this may be quite reasonable. But if you get back early and get a good look at the situation at 6.00 pm, that is decisive in determining whether you now believe that the light is on. Once you can see whether the light is on, your earlier beliefs are no longer causally relevant to whether you now believe the light is on. Your perception of the light is an intervention on whether you believe that the light is on at 6.00 pm, in that it cuts out the influence of your former beliefs on your current belief. If you have a forecast as to whether p is true, the beliefs that you form in setting up the forecast have no effect on whether you believe that p is true, once you are in a position to observe whether p. And that is, of course, normatively correct. (Cf. Glymour and Danks 2007, for an interesting discussion of this example. I depart somewhat from their analysis.) Notice this is a point specifically about sensory experience. Merely being told that the light was off at 6.00 pm, or having a blindsight-style non-conscious perceptual representation that the light was off, at 6.00 pm, would not have the same decisive force.

I am proposing that one element in the epistemic role of consciousness is this distinctive causal role played by sensory awareness. Subliminal perception or blindsight-style guessing doesn't have this causal role. The question is, how can it be right for sensory experience to have this decisive role? On a relational view, experience is a relation between the subject and the scene viewed. If you see Sally running, then the probability of the hypothesis that Sally is running, given your experience, is 1. Of course, you may have some room for doubt as to whether you have the kind of evidence you think you do. You may question whether you really are seeing Sally run. So perhaps your subjective confidence in the proposition will be a bit short of absolute certainty. But if you are trying to conform your level of subjective confidence in the proposition to the objective probability of your hypothesis, given your evidence, then in the good case, your experience of Sally running ought to make a big difference to your level of subjective confidence; it will typically make enough of a difference for it to be decisive in making your mind up. For it to be right for a perceptual experience to be decisive in the formation of belief, it must be that the probability that things are so, given the evidence of perceptual experience, is 1.

On a representationalist view of experience, in contrast, it is hard to see how it could be right for experience to have this decisive role. In the absence of experience, one could have a blindsight-style representation of Sally running, and assign that a particular level of subjective confidence. Suppose now that the representation of Sally running becomes conscious. Why should that make any difference at all to one's level of subjective confidence in the proposition that Sally is running? The probability that Sally is running, given that one has a blindsight-style representation of Sally running, may be exactly the same as the probability that Sally is running, given that one has a conscious representation of Sally running.

The point I am making here is in sharp contrast to Quine's picture of the relation between belief and experience. Quine wrote: 'Total science is like a field of force whose boundary conditions are experience. A conflict with experience at the periphery occasions readjustments in the interior of the field ... The total field is so underdetermined by its boundary conditions, experience, that there is much latitude of choice as to what statements to reevaluate in the light of any single contrary experience ... Any statement can be held true come what may, if we make drastic enough adjustments elsewhere in the system' (Quine 1953, pp. 42–3). On this picture, perceptual experience is *never* decisive in generating any particular piece of belief or knowledge. All that happens is that the experience, if 'recalcitrant', may occasion probabilistic reasoning, in the light of 'total theory', as a result of which one set of beliefs rather than another may seem like the most reasonable to form. So experience is not a decisive intervention on belief; at best it may occasionally outweigh other causal factors determining one's belief.

Although Quine's empiricism notionally aims to give due weight to sensory experience as the final arbiter of what we ought to believe, it actually seems impossible for his picture to recognize the decisive role that it plays. As a matter of fact, we do allow sensory experience to definitively resolve the correctness of a hypothesis about the perceptible facts. If you see it's so, well, that's that. Quine's account, like that of the representationalist about experience, cannot explain why sensory experience should ever have that role.

Why should we have this phenomenon of experience as decisive in the fixation of belief? Recall for a moment the position of the epiphenomenalist about sensory experience. For the epiphenomenalist, it cannot be any part of the *point* of our perceptual systems to generate conscious experience. The epiphenomenalist agrees that perceptual processing does generate conscious experience, but says that this conscious experience has no further impact on the working of the system; so it can hardly be the point of perceptual processing to generate conscious experience. But if we say, surely there must be some value for the organism in the production of sensory experience by perceptual processing, what kind of value could it have? Let us go back for a moment to the honeybee. As I remarked earlier, the waggle dance that honeybees do to indicate the location of food has been intensively studied. Gallistel reports:

[A]n experiment in which Dyer and his colleagues (the fullest account is in Gould and Gould 1988) manipulated the dance of returning honey bee foragers so that it indicated a food source in the middle of a small lake. Other bees could not be recruited by this dance.

If, on the other hand, the dance of returning foragers indicated a site on the far shore of the lake, other bees were recruited by the dance.

(Gallistel 1990, p. 139)

Here the bee's large-scale map of the terrain is used in evaluating the information provided by returning foragers; the input information is implicitly being weighed against the prior information provided by the map. For a Quinean animal, this kind of thing could happen with perceptual input: that is, an animal presented with perceptual evidence that there is, say, a food source at a location that it knows to be the middle of a small lake could have this perceptual evidence outweighed by prior information that there is no food source there. Actually this kind of thing can happen when an animal is hardwired so as to discount some particular possibility, like, for example, a local reversal of gravity: the animal may simply not be able to factor that perceptual input into its web of belief. But in many other cases, the animal will merely update its cognitive map or other informational structure in the light of perception.

The big difference between other animals and human beings here is that human beings have extensive capacities for the generation of endlessly elaborated theories about their environment and their own place in it. We tend not to grasp just how developed our own theories are, since they are largely implicit, until we observe the kind of variation that happens across cultures in deeply developed theorizing about the nature of the world, or in patients with more or less complex delusions about the nature of their surroundings, or in the development of philosophical positions, such as those on which there are only one's own sensations. If we really operated with Quine's holistic web, the input from experience would constantly be vulnerable to being completely overwhelmed by prior information from our vast network of prior theorizing, which is on a quite different scale from anything the honeybee might achieve. That really does happen in the case of certain delusional patients, whose prior beliefs overwhelm the input from perception. But it does not happen in ordinary humans, just because of the decisive role played by perceptual experience. As I emphasized earlier, it is because perceptual experience has the qualitative character it does that it has that decisive role. Blindsight, or subliminal perception, is merely put into the scales and weighed against one's prior expectations. In the case of an animal like the honeybee, with relatively simple, revisable informational structures, that does not matter. But what keeps humans, with their endlessly complex theorizing, anchored in reality is the role played by sensory awareness as an intervention on belief.

What makes this point so difficult to recognize is the tendency of philosophers to regard the evidence provided by sensory experience of the world as if it were just the same kind of evidence as is provided by hallucinations. The idea is that the qualitative character of experience is just the same whether one is having an experience of the objects and properties around one or whether one is dealing with but a creature of the heat-oppressèd brain. This makes it seem that the probability of the belief that the thing is there, given the experience, is just the same whether the experience is an ordinary perceptual experience or a hallucination. That in turn would make it quite wrong for experience to have the decisive role that I have been describing. The probability that a dagger is there is hardly affected by the evidence provided by a hallucination of a dagger (cf. Kennedy 2010). But then sensory experience always ought to be put in the scales with the other evidence that one has. It could not be right for sensory experience, as such, to be an intervention on belief.

If we think of cognition as something that does not particularly involve sensory awareness, we have no way of getting beyond this point. The perceptual input states that we are dealing with, in blindsight or in subliminal perception, or in honeybee cognition for that matter, assuming honeybees not to be conscious, are all informational states that could be there whether or not the distal stimulus existed. As such, it could not be normatively correct for them to have the kind of decisive role I have been saying sensory awareness has in the fixation of belief.

Our problem earlier was to understand how the qualitative character of experience could be responsible for its epistemic role. If you think of the qualitative character of experience as a matter of epiphenomenal qualia being spun off by the underlying brain machinery that is truly the level at which the mechanisms of knowledge are found, then you cannot find an epistemic role for the qualitative character of experience. It is different if you think of the qualitative character of experience as being constituted by the qualitative character of the objects and properties around you.

A similar point was made by G. E. Moore in his classic, 'Proof of an External World' (Moore 1939). Moore's point was this. Suppose, for example, that you are confronted by a complex, brilliant, persuasive sceptical argument; the sceptic argues that you never encounter anything but your own sensations, and that you cannot even make sense of the idea of material objects, such as hands, existing. Suppose moreover that you have not had the benefit of the philosophical training that will, presumably, enable you to meet the sceptic's points on their own terms. Nonetheless, confronted, in ordinary experience, by your hands, or indeed by any other similarly manifest material objects, the sceptical argument will not in fact exert any influence on your formation of beliefs. Your experience of the objects will exert a decisive influence on the formation of belief. Other factors, such as the sceptical argument, simply exert no influence whatever on your formation of belief at this point. The other aspect of Moore's point was that it is not just that this is how people are causally organized, with perceptual experience playing this role in shutting off other factors from having any impact on the formation of belief. Moore's point was that this causal organization is normatively correct. This is how we ought to be organized in forming our perceptual beliefs.

3. Illusions

It is often suggested that the existence of perceptual illusions is a decisive objection to relational views of experience. On the face of it, thinking that this objection is decisive merely reflects not having sufficiently got oneself free of representational-ist ways of thinking about perceptual experience. On the face of it, the objection relies on the idea that for the relationalist, perceptual experience must after all be a representation, only always a veridical representation. To that view, the point that perceptual representation is not always veridical, that there are illusions, is indeed a decisive rejoinder. But, of course, it is not an objection to the relational view of experience. It is only an objection to the view that perceptual experience is always a matter of having veridical representations of one's surroundings.

Still, illusions are important here, for two reasons. In an illusion, there is nothing out there that is as you experience it, so how can experience be merely a relation to the external scene? Secondly, suppose the relational view can resolve this problem; how are we then going to be able to hold on to the epistemic value that we thought we had found for sensory experience? Suppose we interpret experience as a relation that can hold between the subject and the external scene even though the perceiver is subject to an illusion. How can it then be right for sensory experience to have the decisive role that it does in the formation of belief?

As we saw earlier, there are two levels at which vision is studied. One level has to do with the relation between the subject and the external scene: the level at which we say, for example, that the subject sees the computer screen and is performing some task defined in terms of the external display. The other is the level at which we talk about the information processing that is going on in the brain. In identify-ing and analysing visual illusions, vision science of course has to operate at both levels. On the one hand, you don't even know what the visual illusion is until you have characterized the kind of external scene that is in question, and the kind of task that the subject has to perform on it. On the other hand, detailed understand-ing of how the illusion is being generated often seems to require some knowledge of how the stimulus is being processed by the brain. As we saw, the first level, the level at which we talk about the subject seeing the display and noticing various aspects of it, is the level at which we have sensory experience.

A moment's web search will show the bewildering diversity of visual illu-sions and the extent of the debate that each one generates over its explanation in information-processing terms. For concreteness, and to have an example that is easily reproduced in print, consider the Ebbinghaus illusion. Here we have two central discs, one surrounded by smaller discs, the other surrounded by larger discs. Though the central discs are in fact both the same size, one seems larger than the other. Though the explanation is by no means definitively sorted out, one possibility is that the relative sizes of the discs surrounding the central disc lead to overestimation of the size of one disc and underestimation of the size of the other.

This is an explanation of the illusion at the information-processing level (or rather, it would be if properly filled out to specify exactly what computations are being performed on the initial visual representations of the stimulus). How exactly is the illusion to be characterized at the level of sensory experience? Here it is worth bearing in mind a remark of Nagel's that I quoted earlier: 'At present we are completely unequipped to think about the subjective character of experi-ence without relying on imagination—without taking up the point of view of the experiential subject.' This is Nagel's central insight on consciousness, and I think it is fair to say that it has not been effectively challenged in the subsequent extensive discussion. To have an understanding of vision at the level of sensory experience requires the exercise of imagination. Now suppose you're told that Sally has been visually presented with two discs of identical size and made the mistaken judge-ment that one is larger than the other. How strange! Sally is quite sane and has good vision. How could that have happened? What you want here need not be some information-processing account. In fact, you might regard it as beside the point to be told 'Something went on in Sally's brain that made her say one was larger than the other.' Well, sure: but what you want is some empathetic or imaginative under-standing of how it could have happened that Sally came to this conclusion, given that she could see the two discs perfectly well.

What would really help, at this point, is to get a look at Figure 4.1, or something like it. What would help is to see the kind of display that Sally saw. That's what will provide you with an empathetic or imaginative understanding as to how Sally came to her mistaken conclusion. When you see Figure 4.1, the puzzlement van-ishes. Of course, this requires that you actually see Figure 4.1 (or something like it), and that it really is the same kind of thing as Sally was looking at. This is the kind of *de re* exercise of the imagination that we discussed in Chapter 2. It requires that you have the external display to look at, and it requires that it is the same kind of thing as the external display that Sally was looking at. In Chapter 2, I discussed this kind of relational exercise of the imagination in connection with a stage-set

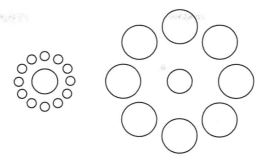

Figure 4.1 The Ebbinghaus illusion (Wundt 1898, Figure 49). The centre circles in both diagrams are the same size. However, the one on the left seems larger than the one on the right.

designer thinking about how *the set* will look from various positions in the auditorium: will it seem too gaudy or too cluttered, for example; will the actors be plainly visible from here and there? This, I suggested, is an exercise of the visual imagination, but it has *the set itself* as a component; it's not properly thought of as a matter of the generation of internal qualia that might or might not match those of a potential audience. If we could make sense of the idea of such qualia, the project would strike one as altogether impossible in a way in which the set designer's imaginative project is not. But anyhow, I said, we have no coherent conception of these internal qualia.

As I remarked, it is often said that to understand visual illusion we must move away from thinking of experience as a relation, and instead postulate the existence of a 'visual representation'. The idea is that whenever there is a visual illusion leading the subject to form a mistaken judgement that p, one can explain the phenomenon by postulating a visual experience with the representational content that p. So, for example, in the case of the Ebbinghaus illusion, the idea is that anyone looking at the display is going to form a 'visual representation' to the effect that one disc is larger than the other.

The difficulty with this idea is to know at what level it is supposed to be pitched. Is it intended to somehow amplify or deepen our imaginative understanding of visual experience? In the case of Sally, who looks at the Ebbinghaus display and judges one disc to be smaller than the other, what kind of understanding do we get from being told that she has a visual representation of one disc as smaller than the other? If you don't already have some empathetic grasp of her situation, this talk about 'visual representations' is not going to give it to you. On the other hand, if you have already seen the Ebbinghaus display, and thereby do have an imaginative understanding of why Sally came to her judgement, the talk about 'visual representations' seems to add absolutely nothing. Alternatively, you might say that the talk about 'visual representations' is meant as a contribution to information-processing psychology. Of course, this simply leaves behind the idea that you are characterizing sensory experience here; but anyhow this is manifestly not much of a contribution.

This difficulty points towards the fundamental problem we have seen before: that we have no way of explaining the notion of 'visual representation' that is intended here. What is a 'visual representation'? One answer is that everyone knows what a visual representation is from their own experience: merely by seeing the Ebbinghaus display, you know what it is to have a 'representation' of one thing being smaller than another. But of course, that is just wrong: in seeing the Ebbingahus display, you see only an array of discs: the 'representation' is not itself an object of your experience. The other answer is that the 'representation' is a theoretical entity, hypothesized to explain why you have some inclination to make the judgement that one disc is smaller than the other. If it's a theoretical entity we need some explanation of it in terms of its causal role. That can be done, and we arrive at something like the familiar causal-teleological notion of representational content. This is certainly of value in giving an account of the information processing that goes on in the brain. But it seems of no direct value in giving an account of what sensory experience is, in itself.

This is not to say that vision science can't illuminate the nature of visual experience in general and visual illusion in particular. Indeed, vision science already implicitly has a powerful methodology for explaining why, at the level of experience, we have the visual illusions we do. Suppose, for the sake of argument, that we accept an explanation of the Ebbinghaus illusion in terms of the sizes of the central discs relative to their surrounding discs. (As I said, the explanation is still debated, and likely more complex, but, for the sake of the example, suppose this is the key point.) Now it is a matter for experimental study whether this explanation, in terms of perception of the absolute sizes of the discs being affected by their sizes relative to the surrounding discs, is correct. And it's not just a matter of what happens under the manipulations of various variables in an Ebbinghaus display (the sizes of the discs, their locations relative to one another, and so on). The account here has to be part of a convincing general analysis of how visual processing of size works. But let's suppose that it turns out that the sizes of the central discs relative to their surrounding discs is indeed the key factor. Then at the level of experience, we could say that the subject's assessment of the sizes of the two central discs is being causally affected not just by their experience of the discs themselves, but by their experiences of their sizes relative to the surroundings discs.

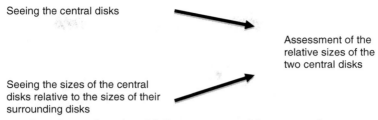

Figure 4.2 Causal contributions of different perceptual factors to subjective assessment of size.

Notice, incidentally, that this is not a view on which sensory experience of the absolute sizes of the central discs in the Ebbinghaus display is *correct* or *veridical*. These terms only make sense in connection with representations. And the point I have been making is that we have no coherent conception of 'representation' to use here. Rather, what the Ebbinghaus illusion, like many other illusions, really brings out is that in general, our perception of a particular magnitude or dimension of an object is not the only factor causally affecting the perceiver's subjective assessment of that magnitude or dimension. Other, related factors can come into play.

The role of vision science in characterizing our visual experience of illusions is, I am suggesting, to find causal structure in our experience that would not have been discernible on the basis of introspection alone. We have, in fact, come upon this kind of point before. I remarked that the relation of consciousness is modulated by the mechanisms of selection and access that we discussed in Chapter 3. Recall the example we considered earlier (in Chapter 3), of the properties used to select an object as figure from ground in conscious perception, as opposed to the properties of the object that one goes on to access. Remember the 5 in a test for colour-blindness, made of blobs of various sizes and luminances, on a field of blobs similarly varying in size and luminance, so that the only systemic way in which the 5 is differentiated from its background is by colour. If you can see the 5, then you do have visual experience of colour; that's the assumption on which the colour test is used (the Ishihara plates). Of course, this is a simple example, but the point here is quite general. Whenever an object is differentiated from its background, there will have to be some account of the characteristics of the object that, together with its location, are causing the object to be experienced as figure on ground. This is the realm of classical Gestalt psychology, or more recently, work on perceptual organization. The point was this. Suppose you can see the figure 5 against its background, and you judge, 'That figure is a 5.' The simplest form of the Moorean analysis describes the situation by saying that you are related by the two-place relation of consciousness to the figure 5, and to the properties of colour, location, and shape. But what we saw was that we can give a more informative analysis by distinguishing the causal roles played by the properties of colour and location on the one hand, and shape on the other. We could state this distinction by talking about the 'point of view' from which the scene is being observed, or we could put it in terms of adverbial modification of the kind of experience of the scene one is having. And this kind of causal structure in one's observation of the scene is what underpins one's selection of a figure as the target of one's attention, and a particular dimension—shape or orientation or whatever—of the object as the aspect of it about which the experience can generate knowledge.

Of course, none of this is to question the point that our understanding of sensory experience is always an imaginative understanding. At the moment we really do not have any alternative way of understanding sensory awareness. But our imaginative understanding of visual awareness can be enriched by vision science, which finds causal structures that could not have been established simply by reflection. And of course, there are mechanisms by which visual experience exhibits the kinds of causal structure I have been describing, in how an object is lifted out as figure from ground, or in visual illusion. These mechanisms are described by brain science.

This way of thinking of visual illusion does not, of course, pose any threat to the epistemic value of sensory experience. On the contrary, our *de re* imaginative understanding of visual illusion simply requires that there be an external scene out there that you are seeing. Being subject to the illusion requires that there are objects and properties that you are seeing. As has often been remarked, visual illusion requires a background of visual knowledge.

4. Hallucinations

Hallucinations are sometimes treated as a central topic in philosophy: one distinguished philosopher once said to me that hallucination is the central problem facing the philosophy of perception. It seems to me that hallucination and perception are quite different problems. People do in fact suffer hallucinations. This is an arresting and interesting phenomenon, though it has drawn relatively little scientific study, and very little in the way of philosophical analysis. In *Sim's Symptoms in the Mind*, the classical text on descriptive psychopathology, the author writes, 'the possible range of bizarre schizophrenic false perceptions and interpretations is limitless' (Oyebode 2008, p. 112). To give some sense of the possibilities here, consider a couple of cases of hallucination:

(1) One man believed that he could feel semen traveling up his vertebral column into his brain, where it became laid out in sheets.

(Oyebode 2008, p. 112)

(2) As a doctor was writing in his case notes during his interview of a female patient, she said, 'I can feel you writing in my stomach.'

(Oyebode 2008, p. 116).

This seems to me a quite different thing from ordinary perception. It is also a quite different phenomenon from imagining or dreaming. A helpful perspective is stated by Oliver Sacks in his review of neurologically based hallucinations:

Hallucinations often seem to have the creativity of imagination, dreams, or fantasy—or the vivid detail and externality of perception. But hallucination is none of these, though it may share some neurophysiological mechanisms with each. Hallucination is a unique and special category of consciousness and mental life.

(Sacks 2012, p. xiii)

Philosophers have sometimes pointed out that the causal role of a hallucination may result from its being indiscriminable from a perception. In an influential discussion, M. G. F. Martin writes: 'Why did James shriek like that? He was in a situation indiscriminable from the veridical perception of a spider. Given James's fear of spiders, when confronted with one he is liable so to react; and with no detectable difference between this situation and such a perception, it must seem to him as if the spider is there and so he reacts in the same way' (2004, p. 68). Whatever we say about the specific case of spiders, it does not seem likely that this could give us a general approach to the causal role of hallucination (it does not seem to have been intended to). In particular, it does not seem that this kind of analysis can apply to the cases above. It is perhaps not even nomologically possible for humans to perceive semen travelling up their spinal columns to be deposited in sheets in their brains, or to feel doctors writing in their stomachs. So I do not see how we could speculate about the possible causes or effects of such perceptions. Rather, we have to regard these hallucinations as *sui generis* phenomena, to be studied, if at all, as phenomena in their own right, with their own distinctive causes and effects.

In an instructive discussion, William Fish gives the following 'formal definition' of 'the hallucinatory state':

For all mental events, e, in doxastic setting D with cognitive effects C (in its subject), e is a pure hallucination *of an F*, if and only if e lacks phenomenal character, and there is some possible veridical visual experience *of an F*, V, that has a rational subject who is in D and produces C, and C is nonempty.

(Fish 2009, p. 94)

Again, it does not seem as though our cases above will meet this criterion, since there are no relevant 'possible veridical visual experiences' whose cognitive effects we might consider.

The philosopher's idea of a hallucination (as opposed to the empirical phenomenon of hallucination) is the idea of a mental state that is intrinsically just like seeing something, but without the external world being there. Recall Moore's point about the transparency of visual experience: 'that which makes the sensation of blue a mental fact seems to escape us: it seems, if I may use a metaphor, to be transparent—we look through it and see nothing but the blue'. The implication of transparency, and the relational view of experience that we have been developing, is that we do not have the conceptual materials even to formulate the idea of such a 'hallucinatory' state. To describe the experience I have when I am seeing something, what I have to do is describe what I am seeing. The point about hallucination is this: you are asked to imagine a visual experience that is, for example, just like seeing an airport, only without the airport being there. But what is left of seeing the airport if the airport is not there? The philosopher's answer has been: 'the visual experience'. But the point about transparency is that your ordinary introspective knowledge of the experience of seeing an airport gives you no knowledge of any such internal state. Introspection of the experience of seeing an airport amounts merely to inspection of the airport itself. Subtract the airport, and there is nothing left to inspect.

The natural idea is: well, I can imagine having an experience that is just like seeing an airport, only without the airport being there. But what exactly do you do in this imaginative exercise, when you imagine what it is like to see an airport? All there is for you to do is to imagine an airport. Within the context of your imagining the airport, you can suppose further that you are seeing this thing. But that exercise does not amount to an understanding of what it is to have the experience of seeing an airport, only without an airport being there. That makes no sense. It is like saying: imagine a state that is just like being a mile away from a hotel, only there is no hotel. Subtract the hotel, and there is not enough left of the original state for you to have a coherent imaginative exercise to perform.

The natural contrast here is between visual experience and a sensation such as pain. You can attend to the features of your own headache—is it sharp or dull, pulsating or steady?—without attending to any aspect of the non-mental world. Now it is often thought that the nature of pain must be immediately given to one in introspection. (There is, therefore, a problem about how it can be that pain is a physical state (cf. Kripke 1980).) Philosophers have usually thought of knowledge of your own visual experience on the model of knowledge of your own pain. That is, they assume that the nature of visual experience is immediately given to you in introspection, without the need to attend to anything non-mental. (And that there is, therefore, a similar problem about how visual experiences can be physical states.)

Now in the case of pain, it seems evidently imaginable that there could be a state just like one's current headache but which has a different distal cause. For example, suppose stress at work caused my current headache. It seems possible that there could be a state that is intrinsically just like my current headache but which had a different cause, being brought about by, say, dehydration. Just so, people suppose, I could have a state that is intrinsically just like my current visual experience of an apple, but brought about by quite different causes than my current visual experience. But the implication of transparency is that there is no such introspective knowledge of the nature of my current seeing of the apple, independent of my knowledge of the apple. Somehow it has seemed compelling to many philosophers to suppose that the nature of visual experience is immediately given to the subject in introspection. You think: '*That* visual experience, (pointing at the head), *that* I could have whatever was going on in the external world.' The nature of this visual experience is then thought to be evidently distinct from the nature of the environment, for after all the nature of the environment is not given immediately to the subject in introspection. But Moore's point implies that there is no such thing as being given the intrinsic nature of one's current visual experience of seeing, independently of one's knowledge of one's surroundings.

Recall our two levels for thinking about visual attention: as a personal-level, task-involving relation to an external scene, and as a neural process making it possible for one to execute the task. Someone might argue: 'If you see something yellow, then your experience has a particular qualitative character, and your brain is in some particular neural state. Therefore, if you're in that very neural state even though there's nothing there, you will have a hallucination of something yellow.' This doesn't follow. If you think of seeing as a relation to something external that's yellow, and hallucinating as involving, e.g., a yellow sensation (whatever that is), it's not a priori that the neural state that facilitates seeing the yellow thing will, if left to itself, generate a yellow sensation. To think that, you'd have to be supposing that seeing a yellow thing required one to be not just seeing the yellow thing, but also in a neural state that generated a yellow sensation. That's not a credible position: we don't usually have this situation of a 'double awareness' of yellowness, external and internal, and some problem of keeping them in register. If you are an internalist about perceptual experience, you will say that there is no 'double yellowness' because the qualitative character is constituted entirely by your inner qualia. But the whole thrust of our discussion has been to query the coherence of this position.

In what sense are hallucinations experienced as 'real'? Hallucinations are often experienced as relating to an independent reality: relevant to one's own emotions, needs, or actions; expected to be perceptible through another sense modality; existing even if not experienced; the experience is involuntary (Aggernaes 1972, quoted at Oyebode 2008, p. 104). However, consistently with this:

> One further quality of normal object perception was found to be absent more often than not with hallucination. This is the quality of *publicness*, in which the experiencer would be aware that anybody else with normal sensory faculties would be able to perceive this something. Often, the hallucinator does not believe that others could share his experience (delusional explanation may be given for this).
>
> (Oyebode 2008, p. 105)

Sometimes, in fact, there seems to be a heightened sense of reality, as if what is being experienced is a deeper or higher reality than ordinary perception reveals:

> I had long wanted to see 'true' indigo, and thought that drugs might be the way to do this. So one sunny Saturday in 1964, I developed a pharmacologic launch-pad consisting of a base of amphetamine (for general arousal), LSD (for hallucinogenic intensity), and a touch of cannabis (for a little added delirium). About twenty minutes after taking this, I faced a white wall and exclaimed 'I want to see indigo now—*now!*'
>
> And then as if thrown by a giant paintbrush, there appeared a huge, trembling pear-shaped blob of the purest indigo. Luminous, numinous, it filled me with rapture: It was the color of heaven, the color, I thought, which Giotto had spent a lifetime trying to get but never achieved—never achieved, perhaps, because the color of heaven is not to be seen on earth. But it had existed once, I thought—it was the color of the Palezoic sea, the color the ocean used to be. I leaned towards it in a sort of ecstacy.
>
> (Sacks 2012, p. 110)

The analysis of these phenomena of course has its own intrinsic interest. As I said, they have attracted relatively little in the way of serious scientific or philosophical study, and they may well repay investigation. They seem, however, at best tangentially related to the study of perception. Philosophers talking about hallucination have generally been trying to discuss some much more limited class of cases. Internalism about perceptual experience seems to be the only motivation for the idea that there is such a limited class of cases to discuss, however. The usual philosophical discussions of hallucination, from Descartes on, merely show the internalist trying to work with internalist ideas about experience; they cannot establish the correctness or even the coherence of these ideas.

5. Transparency

We began, in Chapter 1, with the sense in which physics seems to alienate us from our surroundings: it seems to imply that sensory experience does not provide us with knowledge of our environment. Now certainly sensory experience does not in any immediate way provide us with knowledge of the world as described by particle physics. I suggested, though, that we can think of ordinary talk of people and trees, colours and shapes, as relating to the external, mind-independent environment at a 'higher level' of description than the level addressed by basic physics. And we can then think of sensory experience as providing us with knowledge of our mind-independent surroundings, as described at this high level.

The main obstacle to this picture is internalism about sensory experience: the idea that sensory experience has to be described in terms of *qualia*, 'internal to the head', whether this is in terms of representations or sensations, that are independent of what is going on in the immediate environment of the perceiver. It is not obvious how sensory experience, conceived as the internalist conceives it, could play any foundational role in our knowledge of the things and properties around us. If we conceive of sensory experience in terms of representations, we face the problem that the same epistemic work could be done by representations that are not conscious. If we conceive of sensory experience in terms of sensations, then it is hard to find any epistemic work it can do, beyond yielding knowledge of itself. Yet we have also seen that there seems to be no coherent way of formulating a conception of 'qualia' so conceived, whether in representational or sensational terms. We do not ordinarily observe *qualia* in this sense, in ordinary perception. But nor can the *qualia* be thought of as purely theoretical postulates, since they are supposed to be the first and most immediate aspects of perception. If we did think of them as purely theoretical postulates, they would lose the status they are supposed to have, as directly constitutive of the most immediate elements of sensory experience. We have no coherent way of saying what we are talking about when we talk about *qualia*.

Even the most ardent supporter of *qualia* has to acknowledge that there is a question about how qualia can be aspects of the physical world. And here the enthusiast has not much choice but to endorse the idea that talking about 'qualia' is talking about the world at a different level than that of basic physics. But once we have the idea of there being 'different levels' at which the world can be described, we see that we could have made that move earlier. We did not have to allow physics to push sensory experience inside the head. We could have argued that the qualitative world, the buzzing blooming world we encounter every day, is itself merely the mind-independent physical world, described 'at a higher level'.

Russell gave sharp expression to the basic problem here: 'Naive realism leads to physics, and physics, if true, shows that naive realism is false. Therefore naive realism, if true, is false; therefore it is false' (Russell 1950/1995, p. 15). The problem with this, I have been arguing, is that if naïve realism—the view of sensory experience as a relation between the perceiver and the surroundings—is false, then sensory experience could not be the foundation of our knowledge of physics, for sensory experience could provide knowledge of nothing but sensory experience itself. We would have a problem about how sensory experience could have generated knowledge of a mind-independent physical world.

That was the source of Berkeley's Puzzle: since sensory experience is the foundation of all our knowledge of our world, and sensory experience can provide knowledge of nothing but sensory experience itself, we can have knowledge of nothing but sensory experience. The resolution, I have been arguing, is to quarrel with Russell's claim that 'physics, if true, shows that naïve realism is false'. Once we move to the idea that the mind-independent world can be described at many levels, we can hold on to the idea that perceptual experience is simply a matter of standing in the relation of consciousness to the characteristics of the mind-independent world found at a level of description much higher than that of basic physics. And that allows us to recognize the epistemic significance of sensory experience.

There is, of course, a significant problem about how the higher levels of description—talk about, for example, the colours of physical objects—relate to the level of basic physics. There is a basic question about whether, and if so how, we can explain the colours of objects in terms of basic physics. Once you grasp the difficulty of this problem, it is natural to try to shuffle it back to being a question about how colour qualia can be generated by physical objects. But this shuffle generates nothing but confusion, because we have no coherent vocabulary in terms of which to discuss these 'qualia'. There is a great advantage to posing the question about the relations between descriptions of the world in terms of the relations between talk about, for example, the colours of objects, and talk about basic physics. The advantage is that these vocabularies make plain sense. The question is plainly well posed. In contrast, regarding talk about the relations between higher and lower levels of description as fundamentally a question about the relation between *qualia* and basic physics means that we do not have a well posed question to begin with, given the questionable coherence of talk about qualia.

In everyday life, we certainly suppose that the colours of objects are mind-independent characteristics. Consider what is going on when we manipulate the colours of objects. Ordinarily, we use paints or inks or dyes without supposing that there is any great mystery about what is happening. When you are painting a chair, you ordinarily suppose that you know exactly which property of the chair you are affecting. It is not as though you are fumbling in the dark with your paints, doing something that, in some as yet unknown way, seems to make some difference or other to perceptions of observers. There is such a thing as acting on a variable to produce a given outcome, without having much idea which variable you are acting on. For example, suppose you have an ancient and temperamental TV set. Occasionally the volume suddenly booms out much more loudly than it should. You can fix this by banging the side of the set; but it's an inconstant business, you have to vary just how you bang the side of the set from time to time, and sometimes it actually works better to strike the set from behind, just below the top corner. When you correct the volume in this way, you take it that there is some hidden variable on which you are acting, to make a difference to the volume. But you have no idea what that hidden variable is. The case of colour seems quite different. When you manipulate the colour of part of a painting, in order to affect the perceptions of people who look at it, you do not seem to be acting in a hit-or-miss way on some hidden variable or other—a presumed underlying molecular structure, for example. But if you really took seriously the way in which physics seems to push experience back inside the head, that would the right picture to have of what is happening here. You ordinarily take it that you are acting on a manifest property of the thing, its colour, and you can see exactly what you are doing to it. But once physics has pushed experience back inside the head, it turns out that you are merely fumbling in the dark with an unknown molecular structure, observing the impacts of your fumbling on your own qualia, and wondering what the upshot will be for other people's qualia. We do not, ordinarily, take this picture seriously. Someone trying to get right colour composition, the colour balance in a painting, for example, takes it that they are affecting the colour balance of *the painting*, not merely juggling with unknown physical magnitudes to produce some unknown impact on the qualia of other people. Unless we move to thinking of sensory experience as a relation to high-level characteristics of a mind-independent world, though, we are threatened with this kind of alienation from our own agency.

Our original problem was to understand how sensory experience can ground the conception of objects as mind-independent. The response I have given is, in spite of some occasional superficial complexity, Dr Johnson's. I explicitly characterized the mind-independence of an object in terms of its identity being constituted by an immanent causal structure—the causality that works within an object over time. If an object is mind-dependent, if for example the object is constitutively dependent on your mind, or the mind of God, then the way things are later with that object depends on how things are then with your mind, or God's, rather than being directly dependent on how the thing itself was earlier. But with a mind-independent object, the way it is later causally depends on the way it was earlier. Characterizing the causal dependence here is not straightforward. As we saw, it is not merely a matter of law-like or counterfactual dependence between the way the thing is later and the way the thing is earlier. There could be a law-like or counterfactual dependence between the way a thing is at one place later, and the way a thing is at another place earlier. This could be a case in which there is a so-far-unexplained 'action at a distance' between two different objects. But if we are dealing with a case in which the object has simply moved from one place to another, then the identity of the object constitutes the *mechanism* by which causal influence is transmitted from place to place. This conception, of the identity of the object as a causal mechanism by which influence is transmitted from place to place, is more fundamental than a conception of immanent causation as law-like or mere counterfactual dependence. We appeal to it in explaining the transmission of causal influence over time. This is the root conception of objects as mind-independent, and it is ostensively explained. What makes this conception available to us is our experience of concrete objects as mind-independent. And to understand what is going on here, we need the conception of sensory experience as a relation to the mind-independent object itself. So Berkeley's Puzzle is resolved not by challenging the role of experience in our knowledge of the mind-independent world, but by arguing that it is only by way of sensory experience that we have the conception of objects as mind-independent.

5

Berkeley's Puzzle

Quassim Cassam

In his *Principles of Human Knowledge* Berkeley writes:

Some truths are so near and so obvious to the mind, that a man need only open his eyes to see them. Such I take this important one to be, to wit, that all the choir of heaven and furniture of the earth, in a word, all those bodies which compose the mighty frame of the world, have not any subsistence without a mind, that their being is to be perceived or known; that consequently so long as they are not perceived by me, or do not exist in my mind or that of any other created spirit, they must either have no existence at all, or else subsist in the mind of some eternal spirit; it being perfectly unintelligible and involving all the absurdity of a contradiction, to attribute any single part of them an existence independent of spirit.

(PHK 6)[1]

I take it that what Berkeley says in this famous passage can't be right. Even if he has good philosophical arguments for the view that things like tables and apples depend for their existence on being perceived or known, it certainly isn't *obvious* that bodies are, in this sense, mind-dependent. Berkeleyan idealism is not the standpoint of common sense and it takes considerable ingenuity to make it look like a serious option.

There are passages in which Berkeley shows that he is well aware of this. He admits that:

It is indeed an opinion strangely prevailing amongst men, that houses, mountains, rivers, and in a word all sensible objects, have an existence natural or real, distinct from their being perceived by the understanding.

(PHK 4)

---

[1] All references in this form are to numbered sections of Berkeley's *Principles of Human Knowledge* in Berkeley 1975. This is the 1975 Everyman edition of Berkeley's *Philosophical Works*, edited by Michael Ayers.

His basic objection to this prevailing opinion is not, or not just, that it is false or inadequately supported but that it is incoherent, by which he means that it involves a 'manifest contradiction' (PHK 4). For Berkeley, idealism is the only serious option because realism, the view that things like houses and rivers are mind-independent, ultimately makes no sense.

For the most part, Berkeley's objections to the idea of a mind-independent object are objections to the idea of matter or corporeal substance. He takes it that realists conceive of mind-independent objects as material, and argues that 'the very notion of what is called *matter* or *corporeal substance*, involves a contradiction in it' (PHK 9). Matter, as the realist conceives of it, is both non-mental and the bearer of sensible qualities like shape, smell, and colour. Berkeley thinks that sensible qualities are ideas, which he equates with sensations. Since sensations are mental entities they cannot inhere in something non-mental, and this is what ultimately gets realism into trouble. The notion of material substance is self-contradictory and absurd if matter is supposed to be the *non-mental* bearer of *sensations*. Indeed, once we think of ordinary objects like apples and tables as collections of sensible qualities, and therefore as collections of sensations, it follows immediately that they cannot exist unperceived. The table in my study can exist unperceived by me but this only means that someone else is perceiving it or that I would perceive it if I were in my study. When it is not actually being perceived by anyone the table only exists hypothetically.[2]

If this argument seems less than compelling it is because it is hard to believe that sensible qualities *are* ideas or sensations. On Berkeley's view, the shape of the table in my study is not the cause of corresponding shape sensations. His view is that the shape of the table *is* a sensation, and that is why it is not possible to regard its shape as something that can exist unperceived. Berkeley does have arguments in support of the identification of sensible qualities and ideas but, for reasons we don't need to go into here, these arguments are not convincing.[3] Neither, by the same token, is the claim that the notion of material substance is unintelligible or self-contradictory. We can think of matter as a non-mental substance in which *sensible qualities* inhere without thinking of it as a non-mental substance in which *sensations* inhere.

It might be tempting to conclude at this point that Berkeley's arguments for idealism have no force because they rely on premises which we have no reason to accept. According to Campbell, however, this would be a mistake. His discussion

---

[2] Here, as elsewhere in this chapter, what I say Berkeley says is heavily influenced by the interpretive work of Michael Ayers. There is a particularly helpful discussion of Berkeley on existence unperceived in Ayers 1975.

[3] See Ayers 1970 for further discussion.

implies that the discussion so far fails to get to the heart of Berkeley's thinking, or to uncover his deepest philosophical motivations. Campbell's proposal is that what is actually doing the work for Berkeley is not the suggestion that the idea of objects existing unperceived is self-contradictory but rather the plausible assumption that:

1. Our understanding of concepts of ordinary objects and their properties is grounded in our sensory experience of those objects and properties.

Call this *experientialism*. One sense in which concepts of ordinary objects and their properties are grounded in sensory experience is that sensory experience has a role to play in explaining our grasp of such concepts. Campbell refers to this as the explanatory role of experience, and elsewhere he gives the example of the relation between colour experience and colour concepts: 'someone who is blind or entirely colour-blind from birth, or someone who is normally sighted but simply never encounters colours, cannot understand colour predicates as we ordinarily understand them' (Campbell 2006, pp. 31–2).

What is sensory experience? Berkeley takes over from Locke a *sensationist* model of sensory experience. Sensationism is, among other things, the view that:

2. Sensory experience consists of sensations.

A further defining commitment of sensationism is that:

3. Sensations are non-representational.[4]

One way of bringing out the significance of this view of sensory experience is to bear in mind the traditional distinction between sensations and perceptual experiences. As Christopher Peacocke writes:

Historically, the distinction between putative perceptual experiences and sensations has been the distinction between those experiences which do in themselves represent the environment of the perceiver as being a certain way, and those experiences which have no such representational content.

(1983, p. 5)

The representational content of a perceptual experience is given by a proposition, or set of propositions, which specifies the way the experience represents the world to be. On the view that Peacocke describes, sensations have no such content, and this is how sensationism sees things. If sensory experience consists of

---

[4] This aspect of sensationism is emphasized by Rolf George, who reads Kant as a sensationist. See George 1981.

sensations, and sensations lack representational content, then sensationism is denying that to have sensory experience is to have perceptual experiences in Peacocke's sense. Alternatively, it is inviting us to think of such experiences on the model of sensations. Either way, sensationism views sensory experience per se as non-representational.

This account of sensationism needs to be qualified in one respect. Even if sensations lack representational or 'intentional' content the sensationist needn't deny that different types of perceptual sensation can have different characteristic causes or that they can function as signs of their regular causes. The sensationist insists, however, that their causal relations to the environment are not intrinsic characteristics of sensations. *In themselves*, sensations do not represent objects and properties in the environment as being a certain way. As far as their intrinsic character is concerned the sensationist regards sensations as mere 'blank effects', as conscious states with no representational content of any sort.

We now have the premises which form the basis of Berkeley's Puzzle: if our concepts of objects and their properties are grounded in sensory experience, and sensory experience is understood in the way that sensationism understands it, then it looks as though our concepts cannot be concepts of mind-independent objects. Given that the sensations which constitute sensory experience do not represent mind-independent objects (or, for that matter, anything else) there is nothing in sensory experience per se which could possibly explain our grasp of concepts of such objects. That is why, as Campbell puts it:

It is truly difficult to see how an approach to sensory experience in terms of sensations can do anything to explain how sensory experience makes it possible for us to think about our surroundings. (p. 7)[5]

On a sensationist account, the most that sensory experience can do is to make it possible for us to think about sensations, but sensations are mind-dependent entities.[6] What is missing is any account of how, from a sensationist perspective, we can have the conception of mind-independent objects. So experientialism and sensationism drive us to the conclusion that our concepts of objects can only be concepts of mind-dependent objects. For those who find this conclusion intolerable, the puzzle—Berkeley's Puzzle—is to 'understand how it could be that both (a) our grasp of concepts of ordinary objects is grounded in our experience of those objects, and (b) we have the conception of mind-independent objects' (p. 27).

---

[5] All references in this form are to Campbell's chapters in this volume.
[6] Actually it's not even clear that if sensory experience just consisted of sensations one would still be able to think about sensations. Barry Stroud made this point in an APA talk on Berkeley's Puzzle.

So far I have represented Berkeley's Puzzle as focusing on what is required for grasp of concepts of mind-independent objects and properties but it would be just as accurate to regard it as focusing on what is required for *knowledge* of mind-independent objects and properties. So instead of 1, which gives expression to what might be called *experientialism about understanding*, we can see the puzzle as turning on a commitment to *experientialism about knowledge*. This says that:

1* Our knowledge of our surroundings and of what is going on around us is grounded in sensory experience.

When experientialism about knowledge is combined with sensationism 'it's hard to see how sensory experience can be providing knowledge, in the first instance, of anything but…sensations' (p. 47). Accordingly:

Berkeley's Puzzle is this: to describe the explanatory role of sensory experience without being driven to the conclusion that all we can have knowledge of is experiences. (p. 18)

Assuming that sensory experience *does* provide us with knowledge of mind-independent objects and properties the Kantian-sounding question to which an answer is now needed is: how is this so much as possible?[7]

How should we respond to Berkeley's Puzzle? Suppose we define *realism* as the view that our concepts of ordinary objects and their properties are concepts of mind-independent objects and properties. Then what Berkeley is saying is that experientialism and sensationism are jointly incompatible with realism. Since he thinks that experientialism and sensationism are non-negotiable, he draws the obvious conclusion: it is realism that has got to go. So one response to the puzzle would be to ask whether it is true that experientialism and sensationism cannot be combined with realism. If experientialism and sensationism are compatible with realism then there is no puzzle. There is also no puzzle if there are independent objections to experientialism or sensationism which make it better to reject one or other of these doctrines than to reject realism. Why worry about the fact that experientialism and sensationism are at odds with realism if there are major problems with experientialism or sensationism? The obvious weak link is sensationism since it is not clear why we should think of experience as consisting of sensations, conceived of as the sensationist conceives of them. Experientialism is less obviously

---

[7] What I'm suggesting here is that Berkeley's Puzzle can be expressed in the form of a 'how-possible' question. Questions of this form ask how something that is assumed to be actual is even possible, given the factors that make it look impossible. I give an account of 'how-possible' questions in Cassam 2007. There is more in my Epilogue at the end of this volume about the significance of reading Berkeley as asking a how-possible question.

problematic but it is still worth considering whether this doctrine is as secure as Campbell's discussion implies.

A philosopher who tried to combine realism with experientialism and elements of sensationism was Locke. As M. R. Ayers points out, the whole tenor of Locke's approach is to 'portray ideas as blank effects in us' (1991, p. 62), that is, as non-representational. The 'ideas' which Locke portrays as blank effects are sensations. Confusingly, he also describes ideas as 'the materials of Reason and Knowledge' (1975, p. 104). In this context ideas are not sensations but concepts. Our ideas in this sense include ideas of the primary qualities of bodies, such as shape, solidity, and extension. These qualities 'are in the things themselves, whether they are perceived or no' (1975, p. 141), and our ideas—concepts—of primary qualities are ideas of mind-independent properties of mind-independent objects. How, in that case, can concepts of such properties be grounded in sensory experience? Locke argues that some of our sensations *resemble* primary qualities of objects, and that in virtue of this resemblance they can ground our concepts of primary qualities despite being intrinsically non-representational. By resembling primary qualities sensations not only ground the corresponding concepts; they also give us some insight into the nature of primary qualities.

This attempt to reconcile experientialism, sensationism, and realism is derided by Berkeley, who objects that 'an idea can be like nothing but an idea; a colour or figure can be like nothing but another colour or figure' (PHK 8). For a sensation of, say, squareness to resemble the squareness of ordinary things it would have to be the case that the sensation is itself literally square, but that makes no sense. Resemblance is a matter of sharing properties and the relevant properties cannot be shared by ideas and external objects. So it seems that Locke has no viable solution to Berkeley's Puzzle. If experience is to ground our concepts of mind-independent objects and their properties it cannot be because it consists of sensations which resemble such properties. Given the resources available to Locke, there is, as Berkeley sees, no way for him to establish the requisite link between experience and the conception of objects as capable of existing unperceived.

One reaction to this line of thinking would be to agree that Locke fails to reconcile experientialism, sensationism, and realism but to insist that these doctrines are not, as a matter of principle, irreconcilable. Perhaps there are ways of fitting them together which do not rely on the notion of resemblance. For example, one might think of Kant as someone who tried to combine sensationism with a form of realism and a form of experientialism. He does not rely on Lockean resemblance and so cannot be refuted by the observation that an idea can be like nothing but another idea. Maybe Kant's account fails for other reasons but pending further discussion it seems premature to conclude that experientialism, sensationism, and realism form a strictly inconsistent triad.[8]

I think that the appropriate reaction to this suggestion is just to concede the point. It is true that Berkeley hasn't proved that experientialism, sensationism, and realism are strictly irreconcilable, and that the most that can be said on the basis of the discussion so far is that Locke fails to reconcile these doctrines. However, even if there is a way of reconciling them there remains the question whether one should be a sensationist or, for that matter, an experientialist in the first place. Suppose, for example, that sensationism is rejected in favour of a form of representationalism according to which sensory experience includes representations of mind-independent objects. In that case it no longer seems puzzling how sensory experience can ground concepts of such objects. It can ground concepts of mind-independent objects because such objects figure in its representational content. To put it another way, it might be held that experience displays objects as mind-independent and thereby makes it possible for us to conceive of them as mind-independent. This *representationalist response* to Berkeley's Puzzle seems particularly forceful because, apart from the fact that it deals with the puzzle, representationalism is regarded by many philosophers as giving an independently attractive account of the content of experience.[9]

Campbell thinks that the representationalist response to Berkeley's Puzzle fails. He argues that 'an appeal to the idea that sensory experience has representational content offers little prospect of explaining how sensory experience can ground our concepts of mind-independent objects' (p. 47). In that case, Berkeley's Puzzle does not have an obvious solution; the problem with Locke's view which Berkeley identifies cannot be dealt with by substituting a representationalist view of experience for a sensationist view. And once it is agreed that neither sensationism nor representationalism can explain how sensory experience can ground concepts of mind-independent objects it starts to look like a genuine question how our concepts of objects can be concepts of mind-independent objects. Campbell thinks he can avoid drawing Berkeley's unwelcome conclusion because he believes that sensationism and representationalism are not the only options. He has a different

---

[8] There is much more to be said about Kant in this connection. See Cassam 2011.

[9] There are many different ways of defining 'representationalism' in philosophy. I understand it as the view that sensory experience has representational content. This characterization leaves it open whether (a) sensory experiences also have non-representational properties, (b) the representational content of sensory experience is conceptual or non-conceptual, and (c) sensory experiences have their representational content in virtue of their conscious character or just in virtue of their causal role. The representationalist solution to Berkeley's Puzzle which I will ultimately be defending turns on the idea that the representational content of sensory experience is partly non-conceptual and determined by its conscious character.

view of experience, which he calls the 'relational view', and which he thinks really can explain how sensory experience grounds our concepts of mind-independent objects. His point is that unless we accept the relational view, or what I will call 'relationalism', there is no viable solution to Berkeley's Puzzle.

Why does Campbell think that representationalism fails to solve the puzzle? Some representationalists think that representational content of experience is a form of conceptual content.[10] This implies that sensory experience can represent mind-independent objects only if one already has concepts of mind-independent objects. But if one already has to have concepts of mind-independent objects in order to have sensory experiences which represent mind-independent objects then 'this kind of view could not regard our concepts as being explained by the role of sensory experience' (p. 45). One would instead have to think of sensory experience simply as one among the various ways in which we *exercise* our grasp of concepts rather than as *grounding* our concepts.

The alternative is to view the representational content of sensory experience as a form of non-conceptual content, that is, as a type of representational content which does not presuppose the experiencer's grasp of the relevant concepts.[11] So now the proposal is that sensory experience can explain our grasp of concepts because it represents mind-independent objects in a way that does not presuppose our grasp of concepts of mind-independent objects. Campbell extracts a proposal along these lines from a paper by Brian McLaughlin and then argues against it on two main grounds. The first is this:

In general, any kind of non-conceptual content that could be ascribed to sensory experience could also, in principle, be ascribed to perceptual states in the absence of sensory experience. This means that the fact that sensory experiences are conscious is being given no work to do in our understanding of the world as mind-independent. We do not have here a way in which the representationalist can acknowledge the explanatory role of experience. From the point of view of understanding our grasp of concepts of mind-independent objects, on this analysis we would be just as well off with perceptual states that had this capacity to 'display the world as objective', even if those perceptual states were not themselves conscious states. (p. 46)

This argument turns on a distinction between sensory experience and mere perceptual states. Sensory *experience* is, by definition, conscious but mere perceptual states are not. The usual example given to illustrate this distinction is that of blindsight.[12] In a recent discussion of this phenomenon, Burge argues that even though

---

[10] The classic statement and defence of this view are in McDowell 1996.

[11] Peacocke 2001a gives a useful account of the idea that the representational content of perception is non-conceptual.

[12] Weiskrantz 2007 quotes the dictionary definition of blindsight as 'a condition caused by brain damage in which a person is able to respond to visual stimuli without consciously perceiving them'.

blindsight patients perceive environmental conditions 'there is strong reason to believe that some of these patients lack phenomenal consciousness in the relevant perceptions' (2010, p. 374). He concludes that 'perception can, and apparently does, occur without any sort of consciousness' (2010, p. 368). Campbell agrees: 'in general, there can be perception in the absence of sensory awareness, and there can be perception that is accompanied by sensory awareness' (p. 76). Yet perceptual states which occur without consciousness are still representational, and this is what causes difficulties for representationalists who want to be experientialists. The problem is that if we view sensory experience as consisting of perceptual states that are accompanied by sensory awareness, and we also regard perceptual states as representational, as bearing the representational content of experience, then we are no longer thinking of sensory *experience* as explaining our grasp of concepts of objects. The subtraction of the conscious, strictly experiential element of sensory experience would leave something—a mere perceptual state—which, in virtue of the fact that it represents objects as mind-independent, would still be quite capable of grounding our grasp of the conception of objects as mind-independent. We can call this the *redundancy problem* for representationalism, since it implies that the fact that sensory experience is conscious is redundant relative to the project of explaining our grasp of concepts of objects.

A different problem for representationalism is the *justification problem*. The key to this problem is *experientialism about justification*. This kind of experientialism agrees with experientialism about understanding that our grasp of concepts of ordinary objects and their properties is grounded in our sensory experience of those objects and properties. However, it sees the grounding relation as a justificatory as well as an explanatory relation, the suggestion being that sensory experience plays some role in justifying our concepts of ordinary objects and their properties. To the extent that these are concepts of mind-independent objects they go with the conception of objects as mind-independent, and to have this conception is to 'think and reason about ordinary physical objects [in ways] that reflect the mind-independence we usually take physical things to have' (pp. 33–4). Experience matters because it plays a role in justifying these ways of thinking. More generally, justificatory experientialism says that the sense in which experience plays a role in justifying our concepts is that it plays a role in validating the associated patterns of reasoning. Representationalism has to explain how this can be so.

Suppose that representational content is a form of conceptual content. In that case, sensory experience 'is simply an exercise of our grasp of concepts' (p. 45) and cannot do anything to justify our concepts. The alternative is to think of representational content as non-conceptual, and this is where the justification problem kicks in:

If we are interested in the validation of patterns reasoning that reflect our grasp of objects as mind-independent, how could an appeal to non-conceptual content help? There will presumably be some patterns of use governing non-conceptual contents…Perhaps what it comes to that non-conceptual contents 'display the world as objective' is that they are governed by patterns of use quite like those that we have for conceptual contents relating to mind-independent objects. Perhaps the suggestion is that the patterns of inference governing conceptual contents actually are justified by their relations to the similar patterns of use governing non-conceptual contents. But then we have simply pushed the problem back to the validation of the patterns of use governing non-conceptual contents. (pp. 46–7)

The problem with pushing the problem back to the validation of patterns of use governing non-conceptual contents is that 'we have no idea how such a validation might be given and still less do we have any idea what role sensory experience might play in such a validation' (p. 47). If this is right then neither form of representationalism can meet the demands of experientialism about justification. Whether we view representational content as conceptual or as non-conceptual, representationalism cannot explain how sensory experience can play a role in validating ways of thinking that reflect the mind-independence of ordinary objects.

How convincing are these objections to the representationalist solution to Berkeley's Puzzle? I will return to this question below. For the moment, let us suppose that they show that representationalism, like sensationism but for rather different reasons, has no solution to Berkeley's Puzzle. It is at this point that relationism is supposed to come into its own. So we now have three questions to consider:

(a)   What is the relational view of experience?
(b)   How is the relational view supposed to solve Berkeley's Puzzle?
(c)   Does the relational view actually solve the puzzle?

On the relational view, sensory experience is a three-place relation between the observer, the point of view from which the scene is observed, and the scene observed. One consequence of this is that 'the scene observed cannot be eliminated from a description of the sensory experience' (p. 28). A related consequence is the following *constitutive thesis* (CT):

The qualitative character of the sensory experience is constituted by the qualitative characters of the objects and properties in the scene observed. (p. 28)

It is this thesis which Campbell regards as 'distinctive of the relational view of experience' (p. 33). So, for example, CT implies that when you see a beach ball against a blue sky, 'the beach ball and the sky are constituents of your experience, and their qualitative characters constitute the qualitative character of your experience' (p. 2).

How does any of this help with Berkeley's Puzzle? The discussion so far points to a number of different ways of understanding the puzzle, corresponding to the various different versions of experientialism I have distinguished. Campbell's account of the relevance of the relational view for experientialism about understanding turns on three ideas:

(i) One grasps concepts of mind-independent objects only if one has the conception of objects as mind-independent.

(ii) The conception of objects as mind-independent is the conception of them as mechanisms for transferring causal influence from place to place.

(iii) Only the relational view can explain how experience can ground the conception of objects as mechanisms for transferring causal influence from place to place.

The second and third of these ideas need some explaining. Starting with (ii), Campbell's thinking is that to have the conception of objects as mind-independent one must grasp the identity conditions of concrete objects. Specifically, one must understand that in specifying these conditions we do not need to bring in the relation of objects to a mind. Instead, identity conditions of objects 'have to do with the causal dependence of the way the object is later on the way the object was earlier' (p. 29). Causal dependence is partly a matter of counterfactual dependence but 'we do not think merely in terms of counterfactual connections between variables; we think in terms of mechanisms by means of which the counterfactual connections exist' (p. 30). A prototypical case of a mechanism is provided by our ordinary conception of 'an ordinary medium-sized object transmitting causal influence from place to place' (p. 31). Only with this conception in place can one think of objects as mind-independent.

With regard to (iii), Campbell's proposal is that we can understand how sensory experience is able to play a role in grounding the conception of objects as mechanisms for transferring causal influence only if we take it that the qualitative character of sensory experience is the qualitative character of the objects and properties experienced. This is the constitutive thesis, which is one of the defining commitments of the relational view. Non-relationalist analyses of experience, on which there is a distinction between the qualitative character of the experience and the qualitative character of the object, cannot account for the explanatory role of experience. To put it another way, the key issue is whether sensory experience brings objects into view. Sensory experience can play an explanatory role in relation to the conception of objects as mechanisms only if it brings objects into view, and only the relational view regards sensory experience as bringing objects into view in the sense that matters.

These considerations also have a bearing on experientialism about justification and knowledge. On a relational view, sensory experience can justify patterns of inference that reflect our conception of objects as mind-independent because mind-independent objects, with their qualitative characters, are constituents of sensory experience. The particular way in which, on a relational view, sensory experience brings mind-independent objects and their qualitative characters into the subjective life of the perceiver also makes it intelligible that sensory experience can be providing one with knowledge of one's surroundings, whether the knowledge in question is knowledge that things are thus and so or 'knowledge of what the various objects and properties around us are' (p. 77). For example, knowledge of what colour and shape properties are seems to depend on experiencing them but Campbell argues that only relationism can do justice to this dependence because only relationism can do justice to the sense in which sensory experience brings such properties into view.

To sum up, Campbell's view is that:

(A) Representationalism cannot solve Berkeley's Puzzle.
(B) Relationism can solve Berkeley's Puzzle.

I believe that this is exactly the wrong way round and my main aim in this essay is to show that this is the case. I claim that it is actually the representational rather than the relational view which has a viable solution to the puzzle, to the extent that this puzzle is genuine. I say 'to the extent that this puzzle is genuine' because I believe there are also questions about the various forms of experientialism which form the basis of the puzzle. My immediate task, however, is to give a preliminary indication of my reasons for rejecting the relational solution and recommending a representational solution.

There are problems with the relational view which do not specifically relate to the puzzle and there are problems which do relate to the puzzle. Starting with the former, one question is whether the constitutive thesis can be reconciled with physics. Doesn't physics show that the 'qualitative character of the world is quite unlike anything that shows up in your experience' (p. 3)? Isn't this a problem for the constitutive thesis? Even if the relational view has an answer to this question one might wonder how the constitutive thesis can deal with everyday phenomena such as the following: two people have their eyes tested by visiting the same optician and looking at the same eye chart from exactly the same position. To one of them, the fourth row in the chart is crystal clear. To the other, the letters looks blurry. There is no difference in the qualitative character of the observed scene—it is the very same chart after all—and also no difference in the point of view from which the chart is observed by the two individuals. Yet there is a significant difference between the qualitative character of the first person's experience and the qualitative character of the second person's experience. How, then, can the qualitative character of sensory experience be constituted by the qualitative characters of the objects and properties in the scene observed?[13]

Campbell considers a similar example in his book *Reference and Consciousness* and comments that:

> It is just a mistake to suppose that the Relational View is undermined by the fact that the idiosyncrasies of the perceiver may affect phenomenal content.

(2002, p. 119)

But why is this a mistake? If phenomenal content may be affected by the idiosyncrasies of the perceiver then doesn't it follow straightforwardly that the qualitative character of sensory experience can't *just* be constituted by the qualitative characters of the objects and properties in the scene observed? Campbell's main concern is to argue that the fact that there are various idiosyncratic factors affecting the nature of someone's experience does not vindicate representationalism but even if he is right about this it doesn't follow that such examples are not a problem for the relational view. In any case, there are related phenomena such as optical illusions which do apparently support representationalism. As McLaughlin observes, in cases of visual illusion the object looks some way it isn't, and it is natural, if not unavoidable, to think that 'this involves the visual experience representing the object as being some way that it isn't' (2010, p. 260).

Even if such considerations are put to one side it is not clear that the relational view helps with the puzzle. The crux of the matter is whether the constitutive thesis helps us to see how experience can play a role in explaining our grasp of the conception of objects as mind-independent. Suppose that Campbell is right that the conception of objects as mechanisms for transferring causal influence from place to place is the conception of objects as mind-independent. What exactly is the force of the 'because' in the suggestion that it is because the qualitative character of experience is the qualitative character of the object perceived that experience can play a role in explaining our grasp of this conception? On a relational view sensory experience certainly brings objects into view but representationalists also think that sensory experience brings objects into view. Representationalists don't think that sensory experience brings objects into view in a way that implies that the constitutive thesis is correct but why must we suppose that experience

---

[13] One response to this question might be to argue that in such cases there is a difference in the point of view from which the chart is observed. This threatens to make the notion of 'point of view' so elastic as to be explanatorily useless.

brings objects into view in this specific sense in order to capture the explanatory role of experience? Suppose that, instead of thinking that the qualitative character of sensory experience *is* the qualitative character of the object perceived, we take it that the qualitative character of sensory experience is an effect of the qualitative character of the object perceived, together with the idiosyncrasies of the perceiver. Why, exactly, would this prevent one from allowing that sensory experience plays a role in explaining our grasp of the conception of objects as mind-independent?

Much the same question can be raised about the role of relationism in relation to more overtly epistemic versions of Berkeley's Puzzle, that is, versions of the puzzle which turn on a commitment to experientialism about justification or experientialism about knowledge. Why must sensory experience bring objects and their qualitative characters into the subjective lives of perceivers in the particular manner envisaged by the relational view if it is to justify patterns of inference that reflect our conception of objects as mind-independent? And why must we accept the constitutive thesis in order to find it intelligible that sensory experience plays a role in providing one with knowledge of one's surroundings? There is nothing wrong with the idea that there is a role for sensory experience in providing us with knowledge of what is going on in our surroundings but it is hard to believe that one can only make sense of this idea in terms of the constitutive thesis.

It remains to be seen whether the relational view has the resources to deal with these and other objections. I don't think that it does and that is why I am sceptical about Campbell's response to Berkeley's Puzzle. Clearly there is much more to be said about all this but what if I am right to be sceptical about the relationist response to the puzzle? The alternative which I will be recommending is the representationalist response. In brief, this says that experience can play an explanatory and justificatory role in relation to concepts of mind-independent things because it represents such things. As we have seen, Campbell gives short shrift to versions of representationalism which regard representational content as conceptual content. He is more respectful of versions of representationalism which appeal to the possibility of non-conceptual representational content but ultimately rejects them too. So the next question is: how should a representationalist handle Campbell's objections?

I will have much more to say about this later on in this book but here is a preview: in his book *Sense and Content* Peacocke claims that 'only those with the concept of a sphere can have an experience as of a sphere in front of them' (1983, p. 7). Suppose that this is taken to be an implication of the view that representational content is conceptual. Peacocke's claim is, no doubt, objectionable on a number of grounds but is it a consequence of Peacocke's view that sensory experience can play no role in explaining our grasp of the concept of a sphere, or concepts more generally? Perhaps the worry is this: if one *already* has to have the concept of a sphere in order to have an experience as of a sphere then this concept cannot be acquired from experience. In general, concepts cannot be acquired from experiences which presuppose them.

The problem with this line of reasoning is that it takes experientialism to be a thesis about the acquisition of concepts but this is not what was intended. Experientialism about understanding is not the thesis that concepts are derived from experience.[14] It is the thesis that sensory experience has a role to play in explaining our understanding of concepts. And then the question is whether there is any reason to think that sensory experience cannot play this role if its representational content is conceptual. If there is a reason for thinking this it is not yet apparent what that reason is. It also doesn't follow in any obvious way from the fact that the representational content of sensory experience is conceptual that it can play no role in justifying patterns of inference that reflect the conception of objects as mind-independent or in providing us with knowledge of the objects and properties around us.

What about Campbell's objections to representationalist responses to the puzzle which assume that the representational content of sensory experience is non-conceptual? Are they any more effective? The redundancy objection accuses the representationalist of allowing the fact that sensory experience is conscious to do no work in explaining our grasp of concepts of mind-independent objects. This objection assumes that the phenomenal character of sensory experience is entirely separate from its representational content but in fact there is no need for representationalists to see things in this way.[15] The alternative is to suppose that representations of mind-independent objects and properties are grounded in conscious, sensational aspects of experience in the sense that these aspects of sensory experience determine its representational content.[16] The conscious character of experience is, in this way, tied to its representational content, and subtracting its conscious character would amount to subtracting its representational content. On this account, representationalism can hardly be accused of making the fact that

---

[14] This is clear from Campbell's response to Georges Rey. See Rey 2005 and Campbell 2005.

[15] When I say that there is no need for representationalists to see things this way I'm not denying that many of them do see things this way. If, as many representationalists suppose, the representational content of sensory experience is solely a function of its causal role then consciousness may well be redundant in the way that Campbell thinks. However, this conclusion won't necessarily be unwelcome to 'causal role' representationalists. They might instead regard their view as undermining Campbell's optimistic assumptions about the epistemic value of consciousness.

[16] This alternative is closely connected to the so-called 'phenomenal intentional research programme'. See Kriegel 2013. There is much more in Chapter 8 and my Epilogue about how the notion of phenomenal intentionality helps representationalism to tackle the redundancy objection.

sensory experience is conscious redundant when it comes to explaining our grasp of concepts of objects.

When Campbell discusses a proposal along these lines, he objects that 'representations that derive their meanings from their connection to sensation can only relate to how things are with sensations' (p. 48). However, this is only plausible if, in line with sensationism, sensations are assumed to be non-representational. If sensations can represent mind-independent objects it is implausible that representations that derive their meanings from connections to sensations can only relate to how things are with sensations. This form of representationalism would only be in trouble if there are compelling reasons for thinking that sensations are incapable of representing mind-independent objects and properties. Perhaps there are such reasons but it is not yet clear what they are.

How, in that case, should representationalism respond to the possibility of perception without consciousness? The first thing to say is that just because the representational content of sensory experience isn't separate from its phenomenal character it doesn't follow that there couldn't be representational perceptual states without phenomenal character. We might, however, wonder whether such states can have the same representational content as sensory experience. For example, the representationalist should insist that perceptual states which lack phenomenal character couldn't represent colours and shapes in the way that sensory experience represents colours and shapes. So it is not plausible, in general, that consciousness makes no difference to one's representational capacities. The specific question which the redundancy problem brings into focus is whether unconscious perceptual states could display the world as objective in anything like the way that full-blown sensory experience can display the world as objective. This issue remains unresolved but the capacity of unconscious states to represent objects *as* mind-independent should not be taken for granted.

Furthermore, even if there is an attenuated sense in which, as Campbell claims, mere perceptual states without consciousness could display the world as objective, the question is whether the representationalist *can* find a role for sensory experience in grounding our grasp of concepts of mind-independent objects.[17] The discussion up to this point suggests that the representationalist can indeed find such a role for experience since he is not *committed* to regarding consciousness per se as epiphenomenal. By the representationalist's lights, it is the representational content of conscious experience which has a role in explaining *our* grasp of concepts of objects, not the representational content of perceptual states that can occur without any sort of consciousness. On this account, consciousness is not

---

[17]   See my Epilogue for much more on this.

epiphenomenal and there is no question of the representationalist being forced to admit that sensory experience can be doing no work in explaining our grasp of concepts.

These doubts about the redundancy problem for representationalism will be discussed at length later on in this book, in the concluding chapter. In that chapter I will also give a negative assessment of the supposed justification problem for representationalism. I question the reality of this problem on the grounds that it underestimates the differences between conceptual and non-conceptual representational contents. Non-conceptual contents don't have patterns of use 'quite like those that we have for conceptual contents' (p. 47). It seems, then, that representationalism is in better shape than Campbell suggests and that his own relational view is in worse shape. It is worth pointing out, however, that there is one key respect in which my discussion has followed Campbell's agenda. For by and large I have not questioned experientialism and have concentrated on trying to show that experientialism and representationalism are compatible. But should we be experientialists in the first place? That is the question with which I want to conclude this preliminary discussion.

What does it mean to say that sensory experience has a role to play in explaining our grasp of concepts? What exactly *is* the role of sensory experience in this regard, and is it an essential role? We have seen that the claim is not that concepts are derived from experience so what exactly is someone who endorses experientialism about understanding committed to? The problem is that experientialism only seems really plausible for a relatively narrow range of concepts. For example, it is hard (but not impossible) to disagree with the suggestion that colour experience is in some way fundamental to our grasp of colour concepts and that is why, as Campbell insists, someone who is entirely colour-blind from birth cannot understand colour predicates as we ordinarily understand them. But what about a concept like *gold*? Is experience of gold fundamental to our grasp of this concept, and should we say that someone who has never encountered gold cannot fully grasp this concept or know what gold is? These claims sound much less plausible than the equivalent claims about colour concepts. It is much easier to see how one could, in the absence of any experience of gold, have a perfectly good 'theoretical' grasp of the concept. When presented with a piece of fool's gold, one might be able to reason as follows: gold has the atomic number 79; this lump of metal doesn't have the atomic number 79; so this lump of metal isn't gold. One does not need to have encountered gold in order to be justified in reasoning in this way.

Such mundane examples bring out the obvious limitations of experientialism about understanding, justification, and knowledge. When it comes to more 'theoretical' concepts, its limitations are even more obvious. Do we really want to have to say that sensory experience has a role to play in explaining our grasp of the concept of marriage? Perhaps it is true that one must have sensory experience in order to have any concepts and that there is no concept our grasp of which is not, to this extent, at least indirectly underpinned by sensory experience. But it seemed at the outset that experientialism was making a much more specific point about the way that our grasp of concepts is grounded in sensory experience. The problem is that once we see that there are theoretical concepts which fall outside the purview of experientialism, concepts our grasp of which consists in grasp of the appropriate theory, we are then confronted with the possibility that the concept of a mind-independent object is just such a concept. For, as Campbell puts it:

> It may look as though we could give a comprehensive characterization of how one has the conception of objects as mind-independent without bringing in one's experience of objects at all. For you could give a theoretical characterization of the causal dependencies here, and how the subject grasps them, without mentioning the subject's experience of objects. So this way of explaining what it is to have the conception of objects as mind-independent may seem to lose any role for the subject's experience of objects. (p. 30)

I believe that the threat to his position which Campbell acknowledges in this passage is a serious one, and that there are many concepts our grasp of which is not in any substantive sense grounded in experience. If the concept of a mind-independent object is one of them then the relational view is an unsuccessful attempt to satisfy experientialist requirements on grasp of the concept of a mind-independent object which are themselves questionable.

Here then, is my plan: in the next chapter my focus will be on experientialism, both in general and in relation to the concept of a mind-independent object. My question will be whether experientialism is sufficiently clear and plausible for Berkeley's Puzzle to get off the ground. In Chapter 7 I will develop my criticisms of the relational view: to the extent that there is any truth in the form of experientialism to which Campbell and Berkeley are committed, the relational view fails to explain how sensory experience grounds our conception of mind-independent objects and properties. In the final chapter I will again suspend disbelief about experientialism and argue that representationalism is in the best position to explain how our concepts, including the concept of a mind-independent object, are explained and justified by experience.

In the end, then, my view is that Berkeley's Puzzle has a relatively simple solution. As always with such things, the solution is to question its underlying assumptions. Campbell is impressed by Berkeley because he endorses his experientialism and his antipathy towards representationalism. Philosophers who are more sceptical about experientialism and less sceptical than either Campbell or Berkeley about representationalism have little to fear from the Puzzle. What the Puzzle teaches us is what can go wrong if we tie concepts too closely to experience or refuse to think of experience as representational. To this extent, at least, there is much to be learned from Berkeley.

6

Experientialism

Quassim Cassam

Berkeley's question is: given that our understanding of concepts of ordinary objects and their properties is grounded in sensory experience, how is it possible for such concepts to be of mind-independent objects and properties? His answer is that this is not possible and that the only concepts of objects that are available to us are concepts of mind-dependent objects. A different version of Berkeley's question is: given that our knowledge of our surroundings is grounded in sensory experience, how is it possible for us to have knowledge of mind-independent objects and their properties? Again, Berkeley's answer is that this is not possible and that we can only have knowledge of mind-dependent objects and properties.

To say that our understanding of concepts of ordinary objects and their properties is grounded in sensory experience is to be committed to what I have called *experientialism about understanding*. To say that our knowledge of our surroundings is grounded in sensory experience is to be committed to *experientialism about knowledge*. Berkeley endorses both forms of experientialism and so does Campbell. He describes his 'straightforward solution' to Berkeley's Puzzle as one that accepts 'both (a) our grasp of concepts of ordinary objects is grounded in our experience of those objects, and (b) we have the conception of mind-independent objects' (p. 27). In terms of knowledge, the straightforward solution says that our knowledge of ordinary objects and their properties is grounded in experience and that we can and do still have knowledge of mind-independent objects and properties. The issue between Campbell and Berkeley is whether experientialism is compatible with realism. Berkeley thinks that it is not. Campbell thinks that it is, as long as one has a relational view of experience. The third option on the table is representationalism, according to which experientialism is compatible with realism as long as one has a representational view of sensory experience.

Before looking in greater depth at relationalist and representationalist solutions to the puzzle there is an obvious prior question: should one be an experientialist in the first place? If not, then the puzzle doesn't even get off the ground. But it is hard to determine the merits, or otherwise, of experientialism without having a much clearer idea of what it amounts to. What does it mean to say that our concepts or our knowledge are 'grounded' in experience? What is the nature of this grounding relation?

On an *empiricist* reading of experientialism about understanding, the thesis is that our concepts of objects and their properties are ultimately derived from experience. On this reading, experientialism about understanding is equivalent to a form of concept empiricism, and opponents of concept empiricism see Berkeley's Puzzle as a *reductio* of this doctrine.[1] On a different reading of experientialism about understanding, the sense in which our grasp of concepts of ordinary objects and their properties is *grounded* in sensory experience is that it *depends essentially* on sensory experience. To put it another way, the claim is that sensory experience has an essential role to play in explaining our grasp of concepts of ordinary objects and their properties. Call this the *essential role* interpretation of experientialism about understanding.

There isn't much doubt that the latter is the correct reading of what Campbell has in mind. In an exchange with Georges Rey he explicitly distances himself from concept empiricism.[2] And in the present work he repeatedly makes it clear that his concern is with what is essential to our *understanding* of concepts rather than with questions about the *acquisition* of concepts. The question to which experientialism about understanding is a response is: 'does our grasp of concepts of the objects and properties around us essentially depend on sensory experience?' (p. 4). An experientialist about understanding is someone who thinks that the answer to this question is *yes*, and that it makes no difference whether these concepts are derived from experience or innate.

On a *foundationalist* reading of experientialism about knowledge, the specific sense in which our knowledge of our surroundings is grounded in sensory experience is that 'sensory experience is the foundation of all our knowledge of the world' (p. 14). On an *essential role* reading, the thesis is that sensory experience plays an essential role both in our propositional knowledge that things are thus and so in our surroundings and also in our non-propositional knowledge of the objects and properties around us. On the face of it, one could think that sensory experience plays an *essential* role in our knowledge of the world without thinking

---

[1] See, for example, Rey 2005.
[2] Campbell 2005. That is why I prefer to label Campbell's position 'experientialism'.

that it plays a *foundational* role. So the foundationalist and essential role readings of experientialism about knowledge are different.

There are passages in which Campbell seems to want to endorse foundationalism. He certainly takes Berkeley to be a foundationalist, and adds that 'we ordinarily think of sensory experience as the foundation of our knowledge of our surroundings' (p. 2). The sense in which this is so is that sensory experience is 'the *fundamental* way in which we acquire knowledge of our surroundings' (p. 77). In other passages, however, Campbell is more non-committal. He claims that 'sensory experience does seem to play an essential role in our knowledge of our surroundings' (p. 8) but does not commit himself to the view that sensory experience is foundational.

Having distinguished between the various different senses in which one might be an experientialist we can now ask whether experientialism, in any of these senses, is a defensible doctrine. One way of approaching this question would be to think about what it would take for one *not* to be an experientialist. To put it another way, the question is: what is the position to which experientialism is opposed?

By Campbell's lights, opposition to experientialism comes from what he calls *cognitive epiphenomenalism*. The questions which, according to Campbell, define the debate between experientialism and cognitive epiphenomenalism are:

(a) Does sensory awareness play *any* role in our knowing that things are thus and so?

(b) Does sensory awareness play *any* role in our understanding of concepts of the world around us?

Cognitive epiphenomenalism is the view that the answer to both of these questions is *no*. To be a cognitive epiphenomenalist one would have to think that there is no propositional knowledge in which sensory awareness plays a role, and no concepts—not even colour concepts—our grasp of which depends in some important way on sensory awareness. As Campbell implies, this makes cognitive epiphenomenalism extremely hard to swallow.[3] If the choice is between cognitive epiphenomenalism and experientialism then the latter wins by default, at least on an essential role interpretation of experientialism.

In reality, of course, matters are less clear cut. With regard to experientialism about understanding, the issue is not whether sensory awareness plays *any* role in our grasp of *any* concepts but whether it plays an *essential* role in our grasp of those concepts which are most directly relevant to Berkeley's Puzzle,

---

[3] Needless to say, this doesn't mean that there aren't philosophers who have somehow managed to swallow it.

concepts of mind-independent objects and properties. Campbell contends that in order to grasp such concepts one must have 'the conception of concrete objects as mind-independent' (p. 29). On this basis, the crucial question is whether sensory experience plays an essential role in our grasp of this conception and, if so, what its role is. We can define *anti-experientialism about understanding* specifically as the view that sensory experience has no such essential role. The question whether there is anything wrong with anti-experientialism in this sense cannot be answered by pointing out that there obviously are some concepts—colour concepts might be an example—a proper grasp of which requires sensory experience. This is not something which anti-experientialism needs to deny.

Just as anti-experientialism about understanding needn't deny that there are *some* concepts which it would not be possible for us to understand without sensory experience, so anti-experientialism about knowledge needn't deny that there is *some* knowledge in which sensory experience plays an essential role. The anti-experientialist's suggestion is, rather, that some of our propositional and non-propositional knowledge of our surroundings does not essentially depend on sensory experience in the manner envisaged by experientialism, and that the extent to which sensory experience and knowledge of mind-independent objects and properties can be pulled apart casts doubt on Berkeley's Puzzle. There is no commitment in any of this to cognitive epiphenomenalism, to the view that sensory experience plays no role in any of our knowledge.

Even if experientialism about understanding and knowledge turn out to be defensible the relational view faces further questions. One is whether, assuming that sensory experience plays an essential role in our knowledge and understanding, this view can explain *how* sensory experience grounds our knowledge and understanding of mind-independent reality. Consider this passage, which introduces some of the fundamentals of experientialism:

[W]e ordinarily think of sensory experience as the foundation of our knowledge of our surroundings. What role is there for sensory experience in providing us with knowledge of what is going on around us?

...

Before physics, you might have thought that the qualitative character of sensory experience is actually constituted by the qualitative character of the world. When you encounter the beach ball on the beach, for example ... [t]he beach ball and the sky are constituents of your experience, and their qualitative characters constitute the qualitative character of your experience. That is how experience can be providing you with knowledge of your surroundings. It does so both in providing you with propositional knowledge of how things stand around you, and, more fundamentally, by providing you with some understanding of the concepts of the various objects and properties around you. That's the natural picture. (Ch. 1)

The thesis that the qualitative character of sensory experience is constituted by the qualitative character of the world is what I referred to in the last chapter as the *constitutive thesis* (CT). This thesis is seen by Campbell as distinctive of the relational view of experience. Now we have the idea that: (i) a key role of sensory experience is to provide us with knowledge of our surroundings and with some understanding of concepts of objects, and (ii) experience can play this role *because* its qualitative character is constituted by the qualitative character of the world ('That is how experience can be providing you with knowledge of your surroundings'). So the proposal is that CT explains *how* sensory experience can fulfil what experientialism regards as its cognitive role, that is, how sensory experience is able to ground our knowledge and understanding of reality.

One way of putting pressure on the relational view without rejecting experientialism would be to question this proposal. There are stronger and weaker versions of this objection. The stronger version says that if we conceive of sensory experience in the way that the relational view conceives of it then we have no hope of explaining how sensory experience can fulfil its cognitive role; far from facilitating a satisfactory understanding of how sensory experience grounds our knowledge and concepts, the relational view gets in the way of our developing such an understanding. The weaker objection accepts that this view can make sense of the cognitive role of experience but insists that it is far from unique in this regard, and that other views, including representationalism, are no less well placed to do this. So, quite apart from any independent worries one may have about CT, including the worry that it is undermined by physics, there is no reason to prefer the relational view to representationalism *even from the perspective of experientialism*.

A simple example might help to make the point. I know as I write these words that my wife is home. I know this because I can see her right in front of me, on the sofa in our living room, reading a newspaper. My knowledge that my wife is at home looks like a fairly simple piece of perceptual knowledge, that is, knowledge that is grounded in sensory experience. If I say that I know that my wife is at home because I can see that she is at home I would not be using 'see' metaphorically. And yet, when we think about *how* sensory experience supplies me with knowledge of my wife's whereabouts we run up against a range of factors which the relational view seems, at least on the face of it, not to take into account. Two key factors are *recognition* and *belief*. Even if my wife is, as the relational view insists, a constituent of my sensory experience this wouldn't do me much good, cognitively or epistemically speaking, if I did not recognize her as my wife or did not believe that the sofa she is sitting on is in our home. This doesn't make my knowledge inferential, at least not in any sense which implies that it isn't perceptual. The point is, rather, that the knowledge that sensory experience makes available to us depends on what the perceiver brings to the experience and not just on the objects of experience and the point of view from which they are experienced.

One way of putting this would be to say that what I come to know when I see my wife at home depends on more than my sensory experience but even this wouldn't be right. To see why not, imagine that the scene which I am viewing were to be viewed by a total stranger. The objects and properties the stranger sees are the very same as the ones that I see, and we can suppose that there is no difference in the point of view from which the scene is observed. If, as the relational view claims, the qualitative character of experience is constituted by the qualitative character of the world then one would expect the qualitative character of the stranger's experience to be the same as the qualitative character of my experience, the only difference between us being that only I am in a position to conclude that my wife is at home. This is implausible. Unlike the stranger's experience of an unfamiliar person in an unfamiliar place, my sensory experience is infused by my recognition that the person I am looking at is my wife and by my belief that this is our home. To say this is to say, at the very least, that my sensory experience wouldn't have the phenomenal character that it has in the absence of this element of recognition and belief. The stranger and I experience the same objects from the same point of view but have sensory experiences with different qualitative characters.

One way to deal with this might to be to suggest that Campbell needs to distinguish the sensory core of perceptual experience and its interpretational shell. When two people look at the same objects from the same point of view, they have experiences with the same sensory core, even though their whole experiences are different because of differences in recognition or interpretation. On this account it is the sensory core of one's experience rather than the whole experience that is constituted by the qualitative characters of the objects and properties in the scene observed. One difficulty with this is to see how to separate out what belongs to the sensory core from what belongs to the interpretational shell. Furthermore, even if the core can be distinguished from the shell, there would still be the problem of understanding how sensory experience, without its interpretational shell, can be providing us with knowledge of our surroundings. Suppose there is a strict sense of 'sensory experience' in which my sensory experience is no different from the sensory experience of a total stranger. In that case, given that I'm the only one who knows that my wife is home, it can't just be my sensory experience that explains how I know. The effect of insisting that the interpretive or recognitional element of sensory experience doesn't belong to its sensory core is to make it harder to understand the epistemological or cognitive value of the sensory core of sensory experience.[4]

---

[4] I thank OUP's readers for the suggestion that Campbell needs, and implicitly relies on, a distinction between 'core' and 'shell', or between a person's 'whole experience' and their 'sensory experience'. For my part, I don't think these distinctions get Campbell anywhere.

These observations are a problem both for CT itself as well as for the proposal that sensory experience provides us with knowledge of our surroundings *because* its qualitative character is constituted by the qualitative character of the objects and properties in the experienced scene. In the last chapter I pointed out that the qualitative character of one's visual experience can be influenced by something as mundane as one's eyesight. Now we see that, even for people who are no different in this respect there are likely be significant differences in their sensory experience, depending on whether they recognize what they see, their background beliefs, and, indeed, their emotional response to what they can see. These differences are cognitively as well as phenomenologically relevant because one's beliefs and recognitional capacities have a bearing on what one can *know* on the basis of one's sensory experience, as well as on what one's sensory experience is like. On a view of the qualitative character of sensory experience which does justice to the subject's contribution to sensory experience, there is no doubt that sensory experience has a significant role in providing us with knowledge of the world but this is no longer a relational view. On a relational view, with its focus on the scene observed and point of view, sensory experience cannot easily play the cognitive role which it clearly does play.

There is obviously much more to be said about this but it is hard to avoid the suspicion that the relational view is an overreaction to theories which exaggerate the contribution of the subject and underestimate the contribution of the object in determining the qualitative character of sensory experience. In effect, the relational view makes the opposite mistake; it underestimates the contribution of the subject and exaggerates the contribution of the object. If this diagnosis is correct then the relational view and experientialism are not, in fact, made for one another; approaches which underestimate the role of recognition and belief in sensory experience are less well placed to explain its cognitive value than approaches that do not. For the purposes of this chapter, however, the important question is whether doing justice to the subject's contribution to sensory experience creates problems for experientialism itself, and this brings us back to the central question here: is experientialism any good?

Here, then, is the plan for the rest of this chapter: I will start by taking a closer look at experientialism about understanding, and at the range of concepts a proper grasp of which depends essentially on sensory experience. While there is undoubtedly something right about experientialism I will suggest that it is guilty of exaggerating, in a number of instances, the dependence of understanding on experience. Especially when it comes to concepts of objects which embed the conception of objects as mind-independent we can clearly see the force of anti-experientialism. There are also problems with experientialism about knowledge, at least on a foundationalist reading, and these problems are related to the points I have just been making about belief and recognition. I will conclude by discussing some potential objections to experientialism about knowledge on the essential role reading. I don't think, in the end, that the most serious objections to Campbell's approach to Berkeley's Puzzle are objections to his experientialism but I do want to suggest that experientialism, in its various forms, is far more contentious than his discussion implies.

When Campbell wants to make experientialism about understanding look plausible he usually brings in colour concepts. He thinks that to ask whether sensory experience plays an essential role in our *understanding* of, say, the concept of scarlet is to ask whether sensory experience plays an essential role in our *knowledge* of scarlet, in our non-propositional knowledge of the colour property itself. To have such knowledge is to know 'which property scarlet is' (p. 77). More generally, grasp of colour concepts requires knowledge of what colour properties are, and 'this knowledge can be provided only by experience of the colours' (p. 77). Someone who is entirely colour-blind from birth would lack knowledge of the colours and so cannot understand colour predicates as we understand them. Such a person would be deficient in his grasp of colour concepts.

But how representative are colour concepts of concepts more generally? Campbell's discussion assumes that they are representative and that sensory experience plays an essential role in our understanding of shape and sortal concepts. Just as knowledge of what scarlet is depends on the relevant colour experience so knowledge of shape properties 'seems to depend on experiencing them' (p. 78), and knowledge of what an apple is depends on experience of apples. These claims are far less plausible than the parallel claim about colour concepts and colour properties. Take a concept like *hexagon*. One doesn't need to have encountered a hexagon in order to know that a hexagon is a plane figure with six straight sides and angles or to understand the causal significance of an object's being hexagonal. To know or understand these things just is to have the concept *hexagon*. There is no essential role for experience. The same goes for the concept *apple*. One doesn't need to have seen or eaten an apple in order to know what an apple is, any more than one needs to have seen or otherwise experienced a dinosaur in order to know what a dinosaur is, or to have encountered gold in order to know what gold is. In all of these cases, one can have an intellectual or 'theoretical' grasp of the concept. Sensory experience may add something but doesn't play anything recognizable as an essential role.

Campbell considers a proposal along these lines in relation to shape concepts. He writes:

You might make a long list of causal expectations that a subject ordinarily has of an object, given the facts about its shape, conditional on the other properties of the object. You might argue that grasp of these causal conditions is part of what it is to have the concept of shape.

Indeed, following Shoemaker (1984), you might argue that this is *all* there is to grasp of a shape concept. (p. 65)

Campbell responds that 'this is not all there is to grasp of a shape concept' and that 'one must also have the capacity to access the shape of the object when one encounters the object in experience' (p. 65). 'Access' is a technical notion for Campbell; it is a matter of the subject making it explicit, perhaps by means of verbal report, which properties an object has. If, on encountering something hexagonal, one were incapable of making its shape explicit one would not qualify as having a grasp of the concept *hexagon*.

Does this show that sensory experience plays an essential role in our grasp of shape concepts? Not exactly. All it shows is that someone with the concept *hexagon* must be able to make the corresponding property explicit *if and when* they encounter it in experience; it does not show that an actual experiential encounter with the property is necessary for grasp of the concept. This is, perhaps, a minor point. One might count as grasping the concept *hexagon* in virtue of knowing that a hexagon is a plane figure with six straight sides and angles, but this assumes that one has the concept *straight side*. Maybe sensory experience plays an essential role in our grasp of basic spatial concepts and is therefore indirectly implicated in our grasp of more shape complex concepts like *hexagon*. The deeper point is that grasp of a concept is a matter of degree. In the case of many concepts, sensory experience undoubtedly enriches one's understanding. Someone who has come across the corresponding property in experience may have a *fuller* grasp of the concept, but this is not to say that experience plays an essential role in grasp of the concept if the implication is that without sensory experience one would lack any understanding of the concept. Concepts like *scarlet, hexagon, apple*, and *gold* can all be grasped, to varying degrees, by a subject who has never had sensory experience of the corresponding properties. The question is *how well* one can grasp a concept in the absence of sensory experience, and the answer will vary according to the type of concept. In the case of colour concepts the answer might be 'not very well'. In the case of natural kind concepts the answer is 'pretty well'. Shape concepts are an intermediate case. For the purposes of capturing these important differences experientialism about understanding looks like a fairly blunt instrument.

Berkeley's Puzzle turns on whether sensory experience plays an essential role in our grasp of concepts of mind-independent objects and properties. For Campbell, grasp of such concepts requires the conception of objects as mind-independent, and experience is essential for grasp of this conception. So we now have two questions:

(a) What is it for one to have the conception of an object as mind-independent?
(b) Is sensory experience essential for grasp of this conception?

Here is Campbell's answer to (a):

How is it that we can conceive of the unity of an object without conceiving of its relation to a mind? ... [O]ur conception of the unity of an ordinary concrete object is the conception of a causal unity. To have the conception of concrete objects as mind-independent is to have some understanding of their identity conditions; and those identity conditions have to do with the causal dependence of the way the object is later on the way the object was earlier. When we characterize the identity of the object in this way, we do not need to bring in its relation to a mind. That is how we have the conception of the object as mind-independent. (p. 29)

In relation to (b), anti-experientialism is the view that sensory experience is not essential for grasp of the conception of objects as mind-independent. Instead, as Campbell puts it on behalf of the anti-experientialist, 'All our understanding of objects as causal unities could be, as it were, theoretical, rather than being grounded in sensory experience' (p. 30). The challenge for experientialism is to explain what is wrong with this proposal.

Campbell's response to this challenge turns on a distinction between two ways of thinking about causal connections. We think of causal connections as a matter of there being counterfactual connections between two variables but we also think in terms of mechanisms by means of which counterfactual connections exist. For example:

Suppose we consider any finding established by a randomized control trial, such as a role for vitamin E in the prevention of heart disease. The trial might establish that interventions on the level of vitamin E in a patient will make a difference to the risk of heart disease. But there is a further, compelling question: What is the mechanism by which vitamin E affects the risk of heart disease? The answer 'There is no mechanism' would seem barely intelligible to most researchers... For us the key point is that a prototypical case of a mechanism is provided by our ordinary conception of an ordinary medium-sized object transmitting causal influence from place to place. (pp. 30–1)

The last point is the basis of Campbell's answer to (b): sensory experience brings objects into view and thereby confronts us with the mechanism for transmitting influence. The conception of objects as mechanisms for transmitting causal influence is what underpins the conception of objects as mind-independent, and sensory experience plays an essential role in sustaining the conception of objects as mechanisms: 'In the absence of experience of objects, it is difficult to see how we could have such a conception at all' (p. 32).

Is this plausible? Looking at the vitamin E example again, researchers who think that there has to be a mechanism by which vitamin E affects heart disease may have in mind a number of possibilities but they are unlikely to think of the mechanism as one which sensory experience brings into view. Surely we do not perceive the means by which vitamin E affects heart disease. An underlying mechanism is hypothesized but an underlying mechanism is precisely not something with which there is sensory confrontation. So it is certainly not true, in general, that ordinary perception confronts us with the mechanisms that link intervention and upshot. Campbell's idea is, no doubt, that the case in which perception does confront us with a mechanism is the basic case and that non-sensory cases are somehow derivative. Such claims are, however, extremely difficult to make out. Why couldn't there be a thinker for whom mechanisms are *always* below the surface rather than visible, one whose grasp of the concept of a mechanism is purely theoretical rather than sensory? Nothing that Campbell says demonstrates that such a thing is not possible.

Aside from these worries about (b) there are also worries about (a). Indeed, if what Campbell says in response to (a) is dubious then (b) may become irrelevant. The issue with (a) is this: suppose that, like Berkeley, one thinks of ordinary objects as collections of sensations. On the face of it this does not preclude one from thinking that the way an object is at one time depends causally on the way it was earlier. For x and y to be the same object it isn't necessary that they are the same collection of sensations. It is enough that they are suitably related, and being suitably related may just be a matter of causal dependence. A more difficult question is whether someone who thinks of objects as collections of sensations can still think of them as mechanisms for transferring causal influence. In Campbell's example, I sharpen knife A, take it over to the chopping board, and use it to chop tomatoes. The chopping goes faster and better than it would have done if I hadn't sharpened the knife, or sharpened a different knife B. In this case, 'the movement of the knife itself [is] the mechanism for the transmission of influence' (p. 32), but this is something which an idealist can accept. The 'movement' of objects can be the mechanism for the transmission of influence even if objects are collections of sensations or ultimately mind-dependent in some other more subtle sense. The implication is that one is going to have to go beyond the various considerations to which Campbell appeals if the aim is to explain what it is for one to have the conception of an object as mind-independent. The core notion of a mind-independent object is the notion of an object that can exist unperceived, and we are still missing a plausible story about what it is for one to have this notion.

We might turn, at this point, to Gareth Evans's discussion in his paper 'Things Without the Mind'. Evans proposes that what underpins the conception of objects as mind-independent is grasp of a theory of perception:

Now, the idea of unperceived existence, or rather the idea of existence now perceived, now unperceived, is not an idea that can stand on its own, stand without any surrounding theory. How is it possible that phenomena *of the very same kind as* those of which [someone] has experience should occur in the absence of any experience? Such phenomena are evidently perceptible; why should they not be perceived? To answer this question, some rudimentary theory, or form of a theory of perception is required.

(1980, pp. 261–2)

The theory that Evans has in mind builds on the idea that perception has spatial and temporal enabling conditions: to perceive what is there to be perceived one must be in the right place at the right time. One can then explain why perceptible phenomena are not actually perceived by reference to the possibility of there being no appropriately positioned perceiver.

On this account, the case for thinking that sensory experience plays as essential role in our grasp of the conception of objects as mind-independent is that it plays an essential role in our grasp of the enabling conditions of perception. Without sensory experience how is one supposed to have the concept of perception, or be able to get one's mind around a theory of perception? Indeed, one might think that what is required is not just sensory experience but sensory experience with spatial content: one's sensory experience represents objects and other perceptible things as standing in spatial relations to oneself and *thereby* makes it possible for one to conceive of one's sensory experience as governed by spatial enabling conditions. In the absence of spatial experience one would lack any real understanding of perception and its spatial enabling conditions; one's grasp of such conditions would be purely formal.

This may be the best that can be done to meet the challenge of anti-experientialism about understanding. As always, there remains the worry that a purely formal understanding of the enabling conditions of perception is not the same as no understanding. Experientialism about understanding represents grasp of concepts as something that depends essentially on the thinker having the right kind of sensory experience but grasp of a concept is always a matter of degree and most, if not all, concepts have a component which can be grasped in the absence of sensory experience, or at least in the absence of sensory experience of the corresponding property. That is why experientialism about understanding keeps running into trouble, especially in relation to our more abstract concepts. To talk about the essential dependence on sensory experience of concepts of mind-independent objects, or the concept of a mind-independent object, is always to lay oneself open to the response that all one needs is grasp of a surrounding theory, and that this has little to do with sensory experience. If the response to this objection is that, in the case of many concepts, sensory experience is required for *full* understanding then we will find ourselves drawn into a fruitless debate about what does and doesn't constitute a full understanding of a concept, and why understanding in this sense matters.

None of this is to endorse anti-experientialism about understanding or to say that there is nothing to experientialism. No doubt it is plausible that to conceive of a thinker—God perhaps—with no sensory experience is to conceive of a thinker with no concepts. Concepts are, at least to this extent, grounded in sensory experience. To assume, with Campbell, that our grasp of concepts of ordinary objects is grounded in experience isn't to assume something false or unreasonable but much turns on the specifics and extent of the supposed dependence. Experientialism about understanding, in the unqualified form that underpins Berkeley's Puzzle, is an unsubtle doctrine, and the necessary qualifications and reservations threaten to deprive the puzzle of some of its power. We can still ask how it is possible for concepts of mind-independent objects to be grounded in experience but reflection on this question is unlikely to yield a knock-down argument for the relational view of experience.

Does experientialism about knowledge fare any better? On a foundationalist reading the idea is that sensory experience is the foundation of all our knowledge of the world. There is more than one way of understanding this. For example, there is the view that sensory experience gives us knowledge of our surroundings without dependence on anything else. On this account, sensory experience is foundational in the sense that it is independently authoritative. Interestingly, this makes Locke a foundationalist and Descartes an opponent of foundationalism. For Locke, the deliverances of the senses may be confirmed by concurrent reasons but perceptual knowledge does not depend for its epistemological credentials on the knower's possession of such reasons. For Descartes, in contrast, sensory experience lacks independent authority and only gives us knowledge of our surroundings when supplemented by reason or reasoning, including the reasoning that assures us that our senses aren't deceiving us.

Whatever we end up thinking about the disagreement between Locke and Descartes, one thing that seems reasonably clear is that foundationalism has little going for it if it is the view that sensory experience gives us knowledge without dependence on *anything* else. In the example of my knowledge that my wife is home there is clearly dependence on other things: belief and recognition. The usual response to this line of thinking is to insist on a distinction between *sources* and *enabling conditions* of knowledge; sensory experience is the source of my knowledge that my wife is at home, whereas my capacity to recognize her when I see her is a mere enabling condition. Yet the distinction between enabling conditions and sources is not clear-cut, and the dependence of perceptual knowledge on recognition and belief is still a problem for the view that sensory experience is epistemologically autonomous.

Perhaps, in that case, it is better to construe foundationalism as the view that sensory experience is the *fundamental* way in which we acquire knowledge of our surroundings, even if it isn't epistemologically autonomous. Is this right? Compare knowing that my wife is at home on the basis of sensory experience *versus* knowing that she is at home because I have been told by a reliable witness that she is at home. In what sense is the sensory route to knowledge more 'fundamental' than the testimonial route? Maybe the thought is that sensory experience *generates* knowledge, whereas testimony only *transmits* knowledge. Even this can be, and indeed has been, disputed, but the prevalence of knowledge by testimony is not the only potential problem for the view that sensory experience is the fundamental way in which we acquire knowledge of our surroundings.[5] Scientific knowledge is another potential threat. The insights which science delivers often result from experimentation and theory building in which sensory experience plays, at best, a modest role. In what sense, then, is sensory experience the most fundamental way in which we acquire knowledge of our surroundings?

Fortunately, there is no need to continue this discussion here because experientialism about knowledge is not committed to foundationalism. What it is committed to is the thesis that sensory experience plays an essential role in our knowledge of our surroundings, whether or not it is foundational. It explains our knowledge that things are thus and so as well as our knowledge of the objects and properties around us. For example, 'mere subliminal exposure to any quantity of apples... would not provide you with any insight into what apples are' (p. 78). Similarly, 'a capacity for correct, blindsight-style guessing as to the colours of things would not be enough for knowledge of what the colours are' (p. 77). It is experience that provides us with this knowledge, just as it is experience which provides us with much of our propositional knowledge.

These claims are plausible, though there are some concerns which they don't address. One might wonder to what extent even sensory experience provides one with any genuine insight into the nature of natural kinds. It isn't sensory experience, in any straightforward sense, that tells one that gold has the atomic number 79. Moreover, this insight into the nature of gold might be available to someone who has only ever had subliminal exposure, or even no exposure, to gold. There is also BonJour's example of a clairvoyant who has a hunch that the president is in New York, and whose hunches about the president's location are always correct because they are the product of a reliable mechanism.[6] A certain kind of reliabilist might want to argue that this kind of reliability is sufficient for propositional knowledge and that sensory experience, at least in such cases, is inessential.

---

[5] Jennifer Lackey is someone who thinks that testimony can generate knowledge. See Lackey 1999.
[6] See BonJour 1980.

One thing the experientialist can say in response is that the possibility of a subject who knows where the president is in this way does not show that sensory experience does not play an essential role in *our* knowledge of our surroundings. We are not clairvoyant. More to the point, it is also a mistake to conclude from cases such as BonJour's that, epistemologically speaking, sensory experience makes no difference. As M. R. Ayers convincingly argues, the clairvoyant only knows the president's whereabouts in a secondary or derivative sense. In what Ayers calls 'primary knowledge' one knows *how* one knows what one knows, and this is what the clairvoyant lacks.[7] Sensory experience is relevant to primary knowledge because it accounts for the perspicuity of some such knowledge. When one has sensory experience that P it is not a mystery how one knows that P. Sensory experience plays an essential role in our knowledge of our surroundings because it plays an essential role in making it the case that our knowledge is, unlike the 'knowledge' available to a clairvoyant or blindsight patient, primary rather than secondary.

This defence of experientialism about knowledge does not vindicate everything that Campbell says about the authority of perceptual experience. He makes much of J. L. Austin's example of someone wondering whether there is a pig in the vicinity. If I am the person doing the wondering and then come across a pig in a clearing, the pig has a decisive influence on my beliefs. In Campbell's words:

> It's not just that it is one factor among many causally determining my belief. In this case, where I see it in good light, walk all around it, and so on, the pig itself suspends all other factors from having an impact on whether I believe there's a pig there...The experiential encounter with the pig is not just one consideration among many affecting whether I think there's a pig there. Once it comes into play, it is the *only* factor specifically affecting what I believe on this point. (p. 79)

It is not just that sensory experience is, in fact, decisive in this way; it is also the case that this decisive impact is normatively correct. It is this normative point which Campbell expresses by saying that 'perceptual experiences are *authoritative* in the formation of beliefs about one's surroundings' (p. 80).

Campbell rightly emphasizes that perception without conscious awareness lacks this kind of authority but is wrong to represent the pig example as undermining Quine's view that experience never plays a decisive role in causing belief. Campbell's basic objection to this view is that the architecture of our beliefs requires that sensory experience should sometimes be decisive in the formation of belief, to keep us 'anchored in reality' (p. 83). For that to work, 'it must be that the probability that things are so, given the evidence of perceptual experience, is 1' (p. 81). This is to assume a kind of infallibilism about knowledge which Quine

---

[7] Ayers 1991, pp. 139–44.

and many others would reject. Much of our knowledge is based on considerations which are less than decisive. In addition, it is easy to think of examples in which there is little or no inclination to think that sensory experience is authoritative in the way than Campbell suggests. If I wonder whether anyone in the room is wearing a gold ring and see a gold ring on your finger I am unlikely to regard my sensory experience as settling the question; there are plenty of rings that look like they are made of gold but that aren't. My experience is, indeed, one factor determining my belief that you are wearing a gold ring but is hardly decisive. It lacks the epistemological credentials of the judgement of a competent jeweller, and an epistemologically responsible subject is alive to the possibility that things might not actually be as they seem. On this issue, Quine's picture of experience as liable to be overwhelmed by wider considerations is closer to the truth than the picture of experience as exerting a decisive influence on the formation of belief.

None of this is an objection to the core idea of experientialism about knowledge. The epistemological package which Campbell recommends contains several separable elements. There is the claim that sensory experience plays an essential role in our knowledge of our surroundings, the claim that it plays a foundational role, and the claim that it is decisive in the formation of beliefs. Only the first of these claims is defensible, so it is fortunate that one can endorse this claim without endorsing the others. The thesis that sensory experience plays an essential role in human knowledge is, though at odds with cognitive epiphenomenalism, still relatively modest. Its relative modesty makes it easy to swallow but creates problems for Campbell on other fronts. For given the relative modesty of experientialism about knowledge it seems somewhat unlikely that it entails a relational view of experience. The next chapter will vindicate this suspicion.

It remains to say a brief word about experientialism about justification. This is the view that sensory experience has a part to play in justifying patterns of reasoning or inference that reflect our conception of objects as mind-independent. As Campbell puts it:

Suppose, for instance, that you consider some exercise of reasoning that uses the conception of sameness of object over time. Then, I am suggesting, what validates the correctness of the use of that pattern of reasoning is that the object is identified by your experience of it; and your experience of it is experience of a mind-independent object that is indeed the same over time. (p. 34)

In assessing this proposal there are two cases to consider. There is the case in which 'we have the right to take it, on the basis of observation, without further argument, that we are experiencing one and the same mind-independent object again' (p. 28). Sometimes, however, 'we do need some auxiliary argument before we can take it that we have one and the same thing again' (p. 28). It is only in such cases that reasoning or inference is used to establish the identity of the object. For example, suppose that you visit your old school and find your initials still carved on a desk. Here 'You have the right to take it that it's the same desk; the initials wouldn't be there now if it wasn't for your industry all those years ago' (p. 28).

What gives one the right to take it that it is the same desk? While sensory experience has a role most of the work is done by inference to the best explanation and memory: I remember carving my initials on a desk, and the best explanation of what I can now see is that this is the same desk. The judgement that it is the same desk is the conclusion of an inference but the inference is not justified by one's sensory experience of the desk. The role of sensory experience is to supply one of the premises of the inference ('This desk has my initials carved on it') rather than to justify the inference itself. The inference reflects a view of the world which is partly grounded in sensory experience but it is implausible that what validates the *pattern of inference* is that the object is identified by one's sensory experience of it.

Perhaps, in that case, a distinction needs to be drawn between inferences which *establish* sameness of object and inferences which *exploit* sameness of object. In these terms, Campbell's proposal is that perceptual experiences justify the use of patterns of inference that exploit the sameness of object, as long as the experiences in question relate to a single object in suitably related ways. Suppose I am standing in front of a desk and judge, on the basis of sensory experience, that 'That desk has my initials carved into it.' Then I judge, on the same basis, that 'That desk has your initials carved into it.' If I conclude that there is a desk which has both our initials carved into it then my inference has the following form:

a is F.
a is G.
Something is both F and G.

Are inferences of this form valid? One might think (but see below) that such an inference is only valid if the same thing is being referred to in each of the premises. However, we have already seen that sensory experience need not be what establishes sameness of reference. In the case in which sameness of reference is established in some other way, it is not sensory experience which validates the pattern of inference. Indeed, even in the case in which sensory experience makes it manifest that the same thing is being referred to one might quibble with the notion that sensory experience validates the inference. If a = b then it follows immediately that there is something that is both F and G, even if the thing in question is not an object of sensory experience at all. To this extent, at least, sensory experience is a red herring.

A final observation: Campbell claims that for one's perceptual experiences to justify the use of patterns of inference that exploit the sameness of object it is necessary, though not sufficient, that those experiences 'do in fact relate to a single object' (p. 35). Is this really necessary? Suppose it looks for all the world as though one has encountered the same object but there has been a switch. In this case, it is arguable that one is still justified in concluding that there is something that is both F and G. This would be a false but justified belief. If this is right, then a distinction may need to be drawn between the validity of the inference and the legitimacy, in some weaker sense, of concluding that there is something that is both F and G. Experientialism about justification blurs this distinction and also exaggerates the role of sensory experience in relation to questions of justification. Sensory experience is far from the only thing capable of justifying the inferences which exploit or establish sameness of object.

These reservations about experientialism in its various forms make Berkeley's Puzzle less pressing but are clearly not the end of the matter. For all its limitations, there obviously is *something* to the idea that our knowledge and understanding of mind-independent objects are, in some suitably qualified sense, grounded in sensory experience. To the extent that this is so the question still arises: how is it possible for sensory experience to ground our knowledge and understanding of mind-independent reality? Campbell's answer is clear: we can only understand how sensory experience can ground our knowledge and understanding if we have a relational view of experience. The time has come to explain why this is a mistake.

7

The Relational View of Experience

Quassim Cassam

I have three questions in this chapter:

1. What is the relational view of experience?
2. Is the relational view any good?
3. Does the relational view provide a solution to Berkeley's Puzzle?

A good answer to 1 should aim to identify those features of the relational view that distinguish it from its rivals. Its main rival is representationalism so we should be looking for a clear understanding of the differences between these approaches. As will become apparent, this is less straightforward than it sounds.

As far as 2 is concerned, the discussion so far suggests that the two best arguments in favour of the relational view are that it:

(a) accounts for the qualitative or phenomenal character of sensory experience;
(b) explains how sensory experience is able to fulfil its cognitive or epistemic role.

Indeed, Campbell's suggestion is not just that the relational view does these things but that it is uniquely well placed to do these things.

In relation to (a), the qualitative character of a sensory experience is what it is like to have that experience. The relational view is committed to the following constitutive thesis:

(CT) The qualitative character of sensory experience is constituted by the qualitative character of the objects and properties of the scene observed.

We have already seen in earlier chapters that (CT) faces some potentially serious objections. It would obviously count against the relational view and in favour of a negative response to 2 if these objections lead us to conclude that (CT) is indefensible. If (CT) is no good then that is a serious problem for the relational view.

In relation to (b), to talk about the cognitive or epistemic role of sensory experience is to talk about two things: the role of sensory experience in grounding our understanding of concepts of objects and its role in grounding our knowledge of our surroundings. I argued in the last chapter that the relational view, with its commitment to experientialism, exaggerates the dependence of knowledge and understanding on sensory experience. For present purposes we can bracket this concern. The issue here is whether, even on the assumption that experientialism is basically right, the relational view can explain how sensory experience makes it possible for us to think or know about our surroundings. If it turns out that the relational view does not convincingly explain how sensory experience is able to do its cognitive or epistemic work then this would be a major objection to this view.

With regard to 3, solving Berkeley's Puzzle is essentially a matter of reconciling two claims which Berkeley thinks are irreconcilable. Here are the claims:

Our understanding of concepts of objects is grounded in sensory experience of objects.
Our concepts of objects are concepts of mind-independent objects.

Campbell argues that these claims can be reconciled if and only if we have a relational view of experience. So one question is whether the relational view is at least *a* way of reconciling these claims, that is, a way of making it intelligible that they can both be true. If so, then a further question is whether adopting the relational view is the *only* way to explain how concepts of mind-independent objects can be grounded in sensory experience.

It should be apparent that 2 and 3 are related. Explaining how sensory experience is able to fulfil its cognitive role is, at least in part, a matter of explaining how it can ground concepts of mind-independent objects. If the relational view fails in this regard then it has no solution to Berkeley's Puzzle, and this would be one reason for rejecting this view. Nevertheless, it is helpful to keep 2 and 3 separate because there are questions about the relational view's account of the cognitive role of sensory experience that have little to do with the quality of its response to Berkeley's Puzzle. If the relational view fails to solve the puzzle that is one reason, but not the only reason, for concluding that this view is no good.

Here is the plan for this chapter: I will start by discussing Campbell's account of the relational view, and trying to identify those features of this view which distinguish it from representationalism. Next, I will turn to (a) and argue that there are decisive objections to the relational view's account of the qualitative character of experience. I will also argue that the relational view fails in relation to (b): it doesn't satisfactorily explain how sensory experience fulfils what experientialism regards as its cognitive role. Most significantly for present purposes, the relational view does not satisfactorily explain how it is possible for our grasp of concepts of mind-independent objects, or our knowledge of such objects, to be grounded in sensory experience. If I'm right about this then the relational view fails to reconcile the two propositions which Berkeley regards as irreconcilable, and so does not provide a solution to Berkeley's Puzzle. The puzzle has a solution, but the solution which I will be defending in the next chapter is a representation-alist solution.

So let's begin with 1: what is the relational view of experience and how does it differ from representational approaches? Not surprisingly, given its title, the core of the relational view is the proposal that sensory experience is 'a matter of our being *related* in the right kind of way to the objects and properties around us' (p. 27). Specifically, sensory experience is a three-place relation holding between the observer, the scene observed, and the point of view from which the scene is observed. Furthermore, the qualitative character of one's sensory experience is constituted by the qualitative character of the objects and properties of the scene observed. This is the familiar constitutive thesis which Campbell describes as 'distinctive of the relational view of experience' (p. 33). However, account also needs to be taken of the fact that 'there is not only the scene you are observing; there is the *way* in which you are observing it,' and that 'We cannot say simply that the perceptual experience consists in one's being related to various objects and properties around one, without saying *how* the experience relates one to those objects and properties' (p. 51). The notion of a way of being related to an object or property is, in turn, to be explicated by reference to what Campbell describes as the 'attentional structure' of the experiential relation, that is, the way in which the objects and properties in the scene contribute to the causal structure of the perceiver's experience.

The relational view also sees external objects as *constituents* of sensory experience. The relational view is, in this sense, both a form of direct realism and externalism. It holds that when all goes well sensory experience gives us unmediated access to external objects and properties, and that the identity of a sensory experience is determined by the identity of the objects and properties to which it relates one. Sensory experience of an external object brings the object itself into view and thereby brings its qualitative character into the subjective life of the perceiver. This won't be true, Campbell argues, on analyses on which there is a distinction between the qualitative character of the experience and the qualitative character of the object.

What does Campbell's opposition to representationalism come to? Brian McLaughlin points out that representationalism and the relational view do agree about some things. On McLaughlin's account, which focuses on the visual case, representationalism holds that:

[O]ne visually perceptually experiences an object by having a visual experience with a representational content and the object's bearing an appropriate causal connection to that visual experience.

(2010, p. 246)

On this view, visually perceptually experiencing an object is indeed a *relation* that a perceiver bears to the object, the relation of seeing. This leaves it open that while the object is the *cause* of the visual experience it is a *constituent* of relational experience of visually perceiving it. The latter brings the object itself into view, and into the subjective life of the perceiver. This is something which representationalism would only be forced to deny if it is committed to indirect realism, on which the objects of perceptual experience are images of objects, but representationalism has no such commitment. It holds that one perceives an object by having an experience with representational content but that what one perceives is the object itself, not an image of the object.

We come closer to the heart of the disagreement between representationalism and the relational view if we compare their differing accounts of the qualitative character of sensory experience. Representationalists think that sensory experiences have representational content and that we must think of sensory experiences in this way if we are to do justice to the fact that they have veridicality or accuracy conditions. A sensory experience is veridical just if the world is as it represents it to be. Some representationalists are also committed to the following *representational thesis*:

(RT) The qualitative character of a sensory experience is constituted by its representational content.

Representationalists who endorse (RT) think that the qualitative character of experience is exhausted by its representational content. Such representationalists may take a dim view of (CT). The qualitative character of sensory experience cannot be constituted by the qualitative character of the objects and properties in the scene observed since the objects may not have the properties they are experienced as having. In such cases the representational content of an experience is not satisfied, and the point of (RT) is that the qualitative character of sensory experience is a function of the properties that objects to which it relates are represented as having, not the properties they actually have.

Plainly, (RT) can be correct only if sensory experiences have representational content. Campbell once argued that, on the relational view, 'it makes no sense to ask how the subject is representing what he sees' (2002b, p. 260). Although he doesn't repeat this claim in his chapters for the present volume, he does question whether 'perceptual experience is always a matter of having veridical representations of one's surroundings' (p. 85). A perceptual experience is a veridical sensory experience. Denying that perceptual experience is *always* a matter of having veridical representations of one's surroundings is different from denying that it is *ever* a matter of having such representations. Nevertheless, on the assumption that Campbell still believes that perceptual experiences don't have representational content, he must regard (RT) as misguided. It can't be true, in general, that the phenomenal character of sensory experience is its representational content if there are sensory experiences that do not have this kind of content. A quite different approach is needed, and (CT) is the relational view's alternative to (RT).

One way of summarizing all this would be to say that the basic difference between the relational view and representationalism is that the relational view endorses (CT) but rejects (RT), whereas representationalism endorses (RT) but rejects (CT). This isn't far from the truth but is not quite right as it stands. To begin with, not all representationalists think that the qualitative character of sensory experience is exhausted by its representational content.[1] Such representationalists will want to qualify (RT). In addition, representationalists might even be prepared to accept (CT) in relation to veridical experiences, ones which represent objects as possessing properties which they actually have. At any rate, it won't make much difference in such cases whether we say that the qualitative character of a sensory experience is constituted by its representational content or by the nature of the objects and properties perceived.

The relational view's attitude towards (RT) is also less straightforward than one might think. Even if the qualitative character of perceptual experiences can't be constituted by their representational content (because they don't have representational content), not all sensory experiences are perceptual. For example, hallucinations have qualitative character but their qualitative character cannot be constituted by the qualitative character of the objects perceived. *Ex hypothesi* there are no such objects. Perhaps, in that case, the relational view should concede that hallucinatory experiences have representational content, and that their representational content is their phenomenal character. This would leave the relational view with what McLaughlin calls a 'disjunctive notion' (2010, p. 246) of the qualitative character of experience. On the disjunctive account, the qualitative character of a perceptual experience is a scene, whereas the qualitative character of a hallucinatory experience is a representational content. If the relational view rejects this proposal it is not clear what alternative account of the qualitative character of hallucinatory experiences it has to offer.

---

[1] See, for example, Peacocke 1983, which talks about sensory experience having sensational properties as well as representational content.

Despite these hints of a limited rapprochement between representationalism and the relational view, it would be a mistake to conclude that these two approaches can somehow be reconciled. A position which claims that the qualitative character of sensory experience is its representational content cannot possibly be reconciled with one which says that perceptual experiences don't have representational content. Even if the object of a sensory experience actually has the properties it appears to have, it is one thing to say that the object itself and its properties constitute the qualitative character of the experience and quite another to say that the qualitative character of the experience is constituted by its supposed representational content. The fact that the relational view *might* end up saying the same thing as representationalism about the special case of hallucinatory experiences does not mean that they agree about more fundamental matters.

The next question is: is the relational view any good? This divides into two sub-questions:

(i)   Does the relational view account for the qualitative or phenomenal character of sensory experience?
(ii) Does the relational view explain how sensory experience is able to fulfil its cognitive or epistemic role?

The key to (a) is (CT). If (CT) is no good then the relational view can't seriously claim to have a convincing story about the qualitative character of experience. In the last two chapters I have already briefly discussed some objections to (CT). Now would be a good time to bring these objections together and look at them in more detail.

The first is the *problem of idiosyncratic perception*. I gave the example of two people having their eyes tested by looking at the same eye chart from the same distance and angle. There is no difference in the qualitative character of the scenes observed by the individuals—they are one and the same scene—yet the letters look blurry to one but not the other. This is a difference in the qualitative character of their sensory experiences that is not matched by a difference in the qualitative characters of the objects and properties in the scene observed. How, then, can it be true, as (CT) claims, that the latter constitute the qualitative character of an individual's sensory experience? If, as Campbell concedes, phenomenal content may be affected by the idiosyncrasies of the perceiver, it seems that (CT) cannot be right as it stands. Peculiarities of one's perceptual apparatus cannot fail to have a bearing on what one's sensory experience is like.

Another problem for (CT) is what I propose to call the *problem of infusion*. Suppose I can see my wife sitting in front of me. I recognize her as my wife and thereby know that the person sitting in front of me is my wife. Recognizing my wife is a cognitive achievement, and the issue is how this achievement relates to the qualitative character of my visual experience. Here are two views:

α. The qualitative character of my experience would be just the same whether or not I recognize my wife. My recognition of her is, in this sense, separate from and external to my visual experience of her. The purely perceptual experience is one thing, and how I interpret it is another.[2]

β. The qualitative character of my experience will be different depending on whether I recognize the person sitting in front of me as my wife. My recognition of her is, in this sense, internal to my visual experience of her. My experience is not 'purely perceptual' if this means that it does not incorporate a component of recognition.

I take it that β is much more plausible than α. Borrowing some terminology from Strawson, we might say that my visual experience is *irradiated by*, or *infused with*, my recognition of the person sitting in front of me as my wife.[3] What it's like for me to see her is very different from what it would be like for someone who has no idea who she is to see her. I don't *interpret* my experience as an experience of my wife; its being an experience of my wife is built into its qualitative character.[4]

Recognizing my wife as my wife is closely related to believing that she is my wife, and I can only have the belief that she is my wife if I have the concept *wife*. This suggests that the infusion of sensory experience by recognitional capacities is closely related to its infusion by conceptual capacities. Clearly, not all recognition is conceptual. Our cat doesn't have the concept *wife* but he still recognizes my wife when he sees her. Unlike me, he does not recognize her *as* my wife or, arguably, as anything else. However, this has no bearing on whether recognitional or conceptual capacities are operative in mature human perceptual experience. They are operative in the way that β tries to describe, and their being so operative is part and parcel of what accounts for the qualitative character of our perceptual experience. This is something which (CT) seems to take no account of, and this is another respect in which it fails to deliver a convincing, well rounded picture of the phenomenal character of experience. It fails in this regard because, as pointed out in Chapter 6, it underestimates the contribution of the subject and exaggerates the

---

[2] This notion of the 'purely perceptual experience' corresponds to the idea, discussed above, that Campbell is implicitly relying on a distinction between the sensory core of perceptual experience and its interpretational shell.

[3] This terminology is from Strawson 1974.

[4] This might be disputed, but it doesn't strengthen Campbell's hand to point out how hard it is in practice to draw a clear distinction between what is and isn't built into the qualitative character of experience or its sensory core.

contribution of the object in determining the qualitative character of experience. The problem of idiosyncratic perception is one vivid illustration of this point, and the problem of infusion is another.

The next challenge faced by (CT) is the *problem of illusion*. In a visual illusion, an object or scene looks some way that it isn't. So, for example, in the Müller–Lyer illusion two lines of equal length look unequal in length; one line looks longer than the other even though there is in fact no difference in length. If the qualitative character of sensory experience is constituted by the qualitative character of the objects and properties of the scene observed, and the two lines are in reality exactly equal in length, how are we to explain the fact that one line looks longer? This difference in apparent length is built into the qualitative character of a normal perceiver's experience of the illusion, and representationalists argue that in order to accommodate this phenomenon 'we have to posit that the visual perceptual experience has a representational content' (McLaughlin 2010, pp. 261–2). On this account, the subjective character of experience is given by a false representational content.

Of these objections to (CT) the last is the easiest to deal with. After all, the Müller–Lyer illusion is not a case in which there is a difference in the qualitative character of one's sensory experience of two qualitatively identical objects. The two lines are the same length but they are not qualitatively identical. The hashes attached to the two lines are different and that is why the lines appear unequal in length.[5] This simple explanation of the difference in the qualitative character of one's sensory experience of the two lines is consistent with (CT) and doesn't require one to endorse the view that perceptual experiences have representational content. But (CT) still has to explain how there can be a difference in the qualitative character of two individuals' sensory experiences of *one and the same object*, as a result of differences in eyesight or familiarity with the object. Since these differences in the qualitative character of sensory experience are clearly due to differences between the subjects of experience rather than differences between the objects, (CT) still has some explaining to do. It still has to explain whether and how it proposes to acknowledge the role of the perceiver in determining the qualitative character of experience.

The obvious move at this point for Campbell would be to draw attention to an aspect of the relational view which I have so far only mentioned in passing. As I have represented it so far, (CT) is simply the thesis that the qualitative character

---

[5] For more on the role of the misleading hashes in generating the illusion see Brewer 2011, especially Chapter 5. Despite their obvious relevance I have refrained from discussing Brewer's views here in order to keep the discussion as sharply focused on Campbell as possible.

of sensory experience is constituted by the qualitative character of the objects and properties of the scene observed. However, this is only part of the story. Specifically, Campbell argues that account needs to be taken of the fact that 'there is the point of view from which the scene is being observed, and there may be adverbial modification of the type of experience in question' (p. 33). The qualitative character of the experience is only constituted by the qualitative character of the objects and properties of the scene observed *once these other parameters have been set*. That is why the relational view regards sensory experience not as a two-place relation but rather as a three-place relation between the observer, the scene observed, and the point of view from which the scene is observed.

To see the force of this, consider the case in which you are presented with an array of variously coloured blobs, and in which all there is to separate a figure 5 from its background are the colours of the various blobs. Suppose that you see the figure 5 against its background. What Campbell calls a simple 'Moorean analysis' would describe the situation by saying that 'you are related by the two-place relation of consciousness to the figure 5, and to the properties of colour, location, and shape' (p. 66). In contrast, the relational view tries to do justice to the fact that the colour and location of the 5, but not its shape, are causally responsible for the object being 'selected' or singled out at all. In place of the simple Moorean analysis the relational view tries to give a more informative analysis of the situation by 'distinguishing between the kinds of causal roles played by the properties of colour and location on the one hand, and shape on the other' (p. 66). This is what Campbell says he is trying to capture with his talk of the 'point of view' from which a scene is observed. So 'the correct way to formulate a relational account of perceptual experience is to think of the relation as holding between a thinker and an array of visible properties at various locations, available for use in the selection of objects as figure from ground' (pp. 64–5).

Does any of this help to explain how, from the perspective of (CT), there can be major differences in the qualitative character of two individuals' sensory experiences of one and the same object? The first thing to say is that the example of the figure 5 being singled out on the basis of its colour and location rather than its shape does not look a convincing illustration of the way in which one's point of view affects the phenomenal character of one's sensory experience. For example, the phenomenal or qualitative character of your visual experience of the cup from which I am drinking is different from the qualitative character of my visual experience of the cup, given that we are looking at it from difference angles. In this case, we have different points of view on, and qualitatively different sensory experiences of, the same object, but this is not a difference in the properties that we, or our visual systems, use to single it out.

In the case of the same letter on an eye chart looking blurry to one person but not another, there is no difference in properties that are causally responsible for the letter being singled out by the two perceivers and no difference in their spatio-temporal perspectives on the letter. In neither sense is there a difference in 'point of view', yet there is a difference in the qualitative character of their sensory experiences. Similarly, the fact that what it's like for me to see my wife is different from what it's like for a complete stranger to see her seems to have little to do with any difference in our spatio-temporal perspectives or the properties that we use to single her out. If I recognize my wife and you don't then there is perhaps a sense in which our metaphorical 'points of view' are different, but this is presumably not the notion of point of view which Campbell has in mind when he claims that sensory experience is a three-place relation between the observer, the point of view from which the scene is observed, and the scene observed.

As well as arguing that sensory experience is, in this sense, a three-place rather than a two-place relation, Campbell also makes the closely related claim that there is a *way* in which an external scene is given through perception. According to the relational view, we can't simply say that a perceptual experience consists in one's being related to various objects and properties around one without saying *how* the experience relates one to those objects and properties. Does this help? Can we not say, for example, that in the example of the eye chart the same letter is given to two people in different ways, or that differences in familiarity with an object amount to differences in the way in which the object is given to two perceivers in sensory experience?

Much depends on how we are to understand the notion of a 'way' in which objects and properties are given to a perceiver. Campbell points out that there is a distinction between two ways in which a perceived property can function in relation to a region: it may be used to *select* the object or region—where selection is 'what makes the object or region visible in the first place' (p. 54)—or it may be *accessed* as a property of that object or region. Access is 'a matter of the subject making it explicit, in one way or another, just which manifold properties the object or region has' (p. 54). Suppose that what makes an object visible in the first place is its colour rather than its shape. Then, whether or not its colour is accessed or accessible by the subject, we can say that the 'way' in which the object is given to the subject is 'characterized' by its colour rather than its shape (p. 67). This is what Campbell calls the 'attentional structure' of the perceiver's experience, that is, the way in which 'objects and properties in the scene contribute to the causal structure of the perceiver's experience' (p. 51).

On the face of it there is little here that helps to explain what is going on in cases of idiosyncratic perception or infusion. When two individuals see the same letter

in the same eye chart from the same position there is no difference in the properties that make the letter visible to them. There is, in this sense, no difference in the
'way' the letter is given or in the attentional structure of their experience of the
same 'object' and yet there is a difference in the phenomenal character of their
experience. If I recognize my wife and you don't, and our visual experiences are
qualitatively different as a result, this isn't because different properties are causally
responsible for her being singled out. There is, in this sense, no difference in the
way in which she is given and yet there is a difference in the phenomenal character
of our experiences. So Campbell's notion of a way in which an object is given to a
perceiver does not provide a solution to the problem of idiosyncratic perception
or of infusion. This is hardly surprising because we have already seen that the idea
that sensory experience is a three-place relation does not solve these problems,
and the considerations which lead Campbell to insist that sensory experience is a
three-place relation are the same as those which underpin the idea that there must
be a way in which objects and properties are given to a perceiver.

This is as much as I want to say in response to question (i): does the relational
view account for the qualitative character of sensory experience? I turn to (ii), the
question whether the relational view explains how sensory experience is able to
fulfil its cognitive role. What is the cognitive role of sensory experience? I have
argued that Campbell is an 'essential role' experientialist. On this interpretation,
experientialism says that sensory experience plays an essential role in explaining our grasp of concepts of ordinary objects, our non-propositional knowledge
of the objects and properties around us, and our propositional knowledge of our
surroundings. In practice, these claims are closely related. For Campbell identifies grasp of the concept of, say, scarlet, with knowledge of what scarlet is, and
to know what scarlet is to have non-propositional knowledge of a property; on
this approach, our understanding of concepts consists in our non-propositional
knowledge of the objects and properties around us (p. 77).

I have argued that grasp of concepts is a matter of degree, and that there are
numerous concepts, such as *apple* and *gold*, which can be more or less adequately
grasped by a thinker who has never had sensory experience of the corresponding
properties. Clearly, we also have propositional knowledge which does not depend
in any obvious way on sensory experience. We should reject cognitive epiphenomenalism, the view that sensory experience has no essential role in *any* of our
propositional or non-propositional knowledge, but we should also reject versions
of experientialism which make the opposite mistake of exaggerating the cognitive
role of sensory experience. With this is mind, the question whether the relational
view explains how sensory experience is able to fulfil its cognitive role should be
understood as the question whether the relational view explains how sensory

experience is able to fulfil its *actual* cognitive role rather than what more extreme forms of experientialism conceive of as its cognitive role.

It's no surprise that Campbell focuses on colour concepts in his discussion since it is easier to be an essential role experientialist about, say, the concept of scarlet than about the concept of an apple. Still, it is worth asking whether sensory experience really does play an essential role in our grasp of colour concepts and whether, if it does, the relational view is in a better position to explain this fact than representationalism. Campbell's idea is this: grasp of colour concepts requires 'knowledge of what the colours are', and knowledge of the colours can be provided 'only by experience of the colours' (p. 77). Why accept this conception of the role of sensory experience in providing us with knowledge of the colours? The most straightforward argument proceeds from what Mark Johnston calls 'Revelation'.[6] This is the thesis that it is built into the nature of colour properties that sensory experience, and only sensory experience, can reveal their true nature. Campbell defends a form of Revelation in his paper 'A Simple View of Colour', and Revelation seems to be what underpins his suggestion that 'you wouldn't know what scarlet is, in the absence of experience of it' (p. 77).[7] Sensory experience plays an essential role in sustaining our grasp of colour concepts because it plays an essential role in making the nature of colour properties transparent to us.

Even if we set aside doubts about the assumption that grasp of colour concepts requires insight into the nature of colour itself, this argument is only as good as the arguments for Revelation. Convincing arguments for this thesis are hard to find. We could try something like this: it is in the nature of sensory states such as pain that only sensory experience can provide us with knowledge of what they are. Given that colours are sensory states it follows that only sensory experience can provide us with knowledge of what they are. But why think that colours are sensory states? Locke made much of the supposed analogies between colour and pain but his discussion overlooks significant disanalogies, most notably the fact that pains but not colours are presented as being internal to one's own body. Colour, unlike pain, can exist unperceived, and colours seem to be out there in the world, in a way that genuine sensations do not. These and other such considerations call into question any attempt to base Revelation on the assumption that colours are sensory states.

These somewhat abstract doubts about Revelation can be made a little more concrete by imagining someone born blind who learns to use colour words correctly and grows up to be a colour scientist. Such a person has never experienced colour but do we want to say that he lacks knowledge of what the colours are? There are two extremes which we should avoid. At one extreme is the idea that

---

[6] Johnston 1992.   [7] 'A Simple View of Colour' is Campbell 1993.

colour experience makes no difference, and that when it comes to knowledge of the colours or grasp of colour concepts someone with no colour vision need be no worse off than someone with colour vision. At the opposite extreme is the view that without colour experience one has no idea what the colours are and cannot understand colour predicates in anything like the way we ordinarily understand them. The truth is somewhere in the middle: colour experience clearly makes a difference and provides one with a better grasp of colour concepts but someone with no colour experience can still have some insight into the colours. Grasp of colour concepts, like grasp of concepts generally, is a matter of degree.

There is obviously a lot more to be said about the merits, or otherwise, of Campbell's experientialism about colour concepts but there is no need to come to a definitive conclusion about this issue. For even if we grant Campbell his conception of the essential role of sensory experience in grounding our grasp of colour concepts this doesn't help the relational view of experience. The problem is that there is an obvious gap between Campbell's *explanandum*—the role of sensory experience in sustaining our grasp of colour concepts—and his *explanans*—the relational view of experience. Just because knowledge of the colours can only be provided by sensory experience, why is that a reason for thinking that sensory experience is a three-place relation, or that the qualitative character of sensory experience is constituted by the qualitative character of the objects and properties of the scene observed? How, exactly, does the relational view help to make it intelligible that knowledge of the colours can only be provided by sensory experience?

The force of these questions can be brought out by asking why a representationalist couldn't agree that sensory experience has an essential role in grounding our grasp of colour concepts. Perhaps the worry is that, on a representationalist view of experience, our sensory access to objects and their colour properties is indirect, and that what is required if sensory experience is to ground our concepts is direct sensory access to objects and their properties. But we have already seen that representationalism need not conceive of perception as indirect and it is not clear, in any case, why sensory experience couldn't ground our grasp of concepts if it is indirect. A different concern might be that sensory experience cannot play an essential role in sustaining our grasp of colour concepts if one already needs to have colour concepts in order to have sensory experiences of colour. But this is, at best, only an objection to versions of representationalism which regard the representational content of sensory experience as a form of conceptual content. If sensory experience is representational, but its representational content is non-conceptual, there is no obvious reason why it could not ground our grasp of concepts.

These considerations apply with even greater force to concepts other than colour concepts. Campbell remarks at one point that 'mere subliminal exposure to any quantity of apples ... would not provide you with any insight into what apples are' (p. 78). This is true but it does not at all follow that sensory experience of apples is necessary for grasp of the concept *apple* or insight into what apples are. One no more needs to have seen or tasted an apple in order to know what an apple is than one needs to have encountered a dinosaur in order to know what a dinosaur is. Perhaps sensory experience *enriches* our grasp of natural kind concepts but the relational view is no better at explaining this fact than its rivals. The specific features of this view which distinguish it from, say, representationalism, do not in any way enhance its ability to make sense of the enriching role of sensory experience in relation to natural kind concepts.

What about the essential role of sensory experience in explaining or grounding our propositional knowledge of our surroundings? When I discussed this issue in the last chapter I conceded that sensory experience does make a difference. If I know that the cup from which I am drinking coffee is chipped because I can see that it is chipped it isn't a mystery to me *how* I know. My knowledge is, in Ayers's sense, primary rather than secondary, and I know how I know that the cup is chipped because my sensory experience makes it evident to me that the cup is chipped.[8] In contrast, the clairvoyant who knows the president's whereabouts on the basis of gut instinct rather than sensory experience does not know how he knows. His knowledge is secondary knowledge. But none of this constitutes an argument for the relational view of experience. Sensory experience can be the basis of my primary knowledge that the cup is chipped even if it is false that the qualitative character of my sensory experience is constituted by the qualitative character of the cup. If I'm colour-blind the qualitative character of my experience might be different from the qualitative character of the cup but I can still see, and thereby know, that the cup is chipped.

To sum up, the answer to (ii) is that the relational view doesn't satisfactorily explain how sensory experience is able to fulfil its cognitive or epistemic role. We don't have to be relationalists in order to do justice to the cognitive role of experience, and in any case there are questions about the relational view's understanding of this role. This leaves us with one final question to consider: does the relational view provides us with a solution to Berkeley's Puzzle?

We have seen that solving Berkeley's Puzzle is a matter of reconciling the following claims:

Our grasp of concepts of objects is grounded in sensory experience of objects.
Our concepts of objects are concepts of mind-independent objects.

---

[8] For the distinction between primary and secondary knowledge see Ayers 1991, pp. 139–44.

Berkeley thinks there is a problem here because he thinks that both of the follow-ing claims are true:

Grasp of concepts of mind-independent objects requires the conception of objects as mind-independent.
    Sensory experience can't ground the conception of objects as mind-independent and so can't ground our grasp of concepts of mind-independent objects.

Campbell thinks that only the first of these claims is true. He argues that sen-sory experience of objects can and does ground the conception of objects as mind-independent but that only the relational view can explain how this is possible.

My position is that the relational view is not well placed, and certainly not uniquely well placed, to explain how sensory experience can ground the concep-tion of objects as mind-independent. This is another aspect of this view's failure to explain how sensory experience is able to fulfil what it takes to be its cognitive role. A consequence of this failure is that the relational view does not solve Berkeley's Puzzle. If the puzzle is genuine then we need to look elsewhere for a solution. I say 'if the puzzle is genuine' because, as we saw in Chapter 6, there are also questions about the experientialism to which Berkeley and Campbell both subscribe and which is the basis of the puzzle. Although the main purpose of this chapter is to look into the relational view's response to the puzzle on the assumption that experiential-ism is correct, what I have described as anti-experientialism about understanding remains on the table. On this account, the fundamental mistake is to suppose that sensory experience plays an essential role in our grasp of the conception of objects as mind-independent. The anti-experientialist thinks that it is possible to have a purely intellectual or theoretical grasp of this conception, in which case there is no puzzle, at least no puzzle of the kind that exercises Berkeley and Campbell.

We can start to untangle these complex issues by once again going over what it would be to have the conception of objects of perception as mind-independent. Campbell tackles Berkeley on the assumption that to have this conception is to have the conception of objects as mechanisms for transferring causal influence from place to place. We have already seen that this can't be right. Even idealists who think of objects as collections of sensations, or as mind-dependent in a more subtle way, can regard the 'movement of objects' as a mechanism for the trans-mission of causal influence. The core notion of a mind-independent object is of something which can exist unperceived but the conception of objects as mecha-nisms for transferring causal influence doesn't amount to the conception of them as mind-independent in this sense.

If Campbell's account of mind-independence is rejected, what is the alterna-tive? In Chapter 6 I briefly discussed Evans's proposal that the idea of existence now perceived, now unperceived, cannot stand on its own without a surrounding theory, and that what is required is specifically a theory of perception. A theory of perception of the requisite sort will explain why one might fail to perceive what is there to be perceived. So, for example, it will explain why, given that there is currently a table in my study, it isn't being perceived by me or anyone else. One obvious explanation is that the table is not being perceived because there are no perceivers in the vicinity of my study. More generally, once we have the idea that there are spatial and temporal enabling conditions of perception there is nothing puzzling about the thought that an object that is capable of being perceived isn't actually being perceived. It only needs to be pointed out that nobody is in the right place at the right time.

However, this cannot be the whole story. As Berkeley noticed, it doesn't follow from the fact that I would see my table if I were in my study that the table is still there when I am not perceiving it. An alternative supposition is that I would see the table if I were in my study because there is a divine intention to give me sensory experiences appropriate to seeing the table whenever I go into my study. On this supposition the table doesn't actually exist when it isn't actually being perceived. It would exist if it were being perceived, but that is a different matter; its unperceived existence is hypothetical rather than actual. However implausible this sounds, the issue is whether Berkeley has identified a way for one to acknowledge that there are spatio-temporal enabling conditions of perception but without having to regard objects as mind-independent. Berkeley thinks he has and he is right. So if the intention is to explain how objects of perception can exist unperceived then it isn't going to be enough to point out that perception has spatio-temporal enabling conditions.

What more is needed? It is important not to lose sight of the fact that, contrary to what Berkeley thought, we ordinarily regard things like tables as *material* objects, as occupying regions of space and as having other primary qualities such as shape. If I think of the table in my study in this way I assume that I would perceive it if I were to go to my study. However, I take it that what makes this conditional true is the fact that the table is a persisting thing which occupies a region of space in my study. If this is how I see things then I am conceiving of the table as mind-independent. In contrast, a bare conditional linking what I perceive with my spatio-temporal location doesn't settle the question whether objects of perception can exist unperceived, and so leaves an opening for idealism. The point at which Berkeleyan idealism is no longer an option is the point at which one regards oneself as living in a *material* world.

It doesn't follow from this that I can only conceive of something as mind-independent if I conceive of it as a material object. For example, sounds can exist without being heard and are in this sense mind-independent but they aren't material objects. Yet sounds are not wholly separate from goings-on in the material world. As Evans puts it:

We can think of sounds as perceptible phenomena, phenomena that are independent of us, and that can exist unperceived, because we have the resources for thinking of the abiding stuff in whose changes the truth of the proposition that there is a sound can be regarded as consisting.

(1980, p. 278)

The abiding stuff in question is matter, and the resulting conception of mind-independence is what might be labelled a *materialist* conception. This says that we can't grasp the idea of the same thing existing both experienced and unexperienced 'without ideas corresponding to our ideas of the primary properties of matter' (Evans 1980, p. 278). One's theory of perception tells one what one has to do in order to perceive what is there to be perceived, but what allows one to conclude that what is there to be perceived can exist unperceived is the conception of the world as material. In a given case, what is there to be perceived might not be a material object, but without the idea that objects of perception are grounded in material reality one's conception of what is perceivable won't be the conception of what is genuinely there anyway.

We now begin to see the full force of anti-experientialism about understanding. The threat to experientialism is that 'we could give a comprehensive characterization of how one has the conception of objects as mind-independent without bringing in one's experience of objects at all' (p. 30). Materialism doesn't make this worry go away. The issue is whether someone who has never encountered primary qualities in experience could still have a purely intellectual grasp of concepts of such qualities and, by implication, a purely intellectual grasp of the possibility of existence unperceived. Evans brings this issue into focus with his account of primary qualities. In order to grasp concepts of such qualities:

one must master a set of interconnected principles which make up an elementary theory—of primitive mechanics—into which these properties fit, and which alone gives them sense. One must grasp the idea of a unitary spatial framework in which oneself and the bodies of which one has experience have a place, and through which they move continuously. One must learn of the conservation of matter in different shapes, of the identity of matter perceived from different points of view and through different modalities, and of the persistence of matter through gaps in observation. One must learn how bodies compete for occupancy of positions in space, and of the resistance one body may afford to the motion of another. And so on.

(1980, p. 269)

But if the primary qualities are, in this sense, theoretical, why is sensory experience necessary in order to grasp them? Why couldn't one's understanding of such theoretical properties be purely theoretical? Much the same question can be raised about the supposition that sensory experience is needed in order to understand that perception has spatio-temporal enabling conditions. Again, the question is why this is something that couldn't be understood in purely intellectual or theoretical terms.

Although essential role experientialism doesn't have a completely convincing answer to these questions, it can continue to insist that in the absence of sensory experience it would only be possible for one to have a somewhat attenuated grasp of the interconnected principles of a primitive mechanics. Without sensory experience of bodies one might to some extent be able to understand *that* bodies compete for the occupancy of positions in space, but not *how* or *why* they do so. Sensory experience gives mechanical principles a kind of intelligibility they would otherwise lack. As for shape concepts, the experientialist's claim is not that one needs to have perceived, say, a hexagon in order to grasp the concept of a *hexagon* but that sensory experience plays an essential role in explaining one's grasp of more basic spatial concepts, or possibly even one's understanding of what it is for something to have shape in the first place.

It is also not implausible that sensory experience plays an important role in relation to one's grasp of the enabling conditions of perception. The idea that there are such conditions, and that they have to do with space and time, isn't just an abstract theoretical construct; it is firmly grounded in sensory experience. As I trace a path through the world, things come into view as I move closer to them and recede from view as I move away. The link between what I can see and where I am is built into the content of sensory experience, as is the connection between perception and spatial orientation. As I face the tree in the quad I can see it in front of me. As I turn to the right I can still see the tree but only out of the corner of my eye. I turn further and now the tree disappears from view. Sensory experience, with its egocentric spatial content, makes it evident both *that* and *how* what one perceives is determined by one's spatio-temporal location and orientation. Without this evidence, one might still be able to make some sense of the idea that there is a relation of dependence of perception on location but this dependence would be much less obvious than it actually is.

What is the relevance of this discussion for Berkeley's Puzzle? The question I have been discussing is whether sensory experience is *essential* for grasp of concepts of primary qualities, but the question raised by the puzzle is whether sensory experience *can* ground the conception of objects as mind-independent.[9] The points I have just been making are relevant because, whether or not they would

---

[9] These are two different questions. I discuss the significance of this in my Epilogue.

convince a committed anti-experientialist, they point to ways in which, at least on a materialist conception of mind-independence, sensory experience *can* play such a grounding role: we grasp the idea of mind-independence by grasping a theory of perception, together with ideas of the primary qualities of matter. And the sense in which experience can ground the conception of objects as mind-independent is that it can ground, in the ways that I have been describing, both our theory of perception and our ideas of primary qualities. If sensory experience makes it intelligible to us that perception has spatio-temporal enabling conditions, and that at least some objects of perception have primary qualities, it thereby also makes it intelligible to us that the things we perceive can exist unperceived. And if sensory experience can make this intelligible to us then the puzzle is effectively dissolved.

The remaining question is this: in conceiving of sensory experience as grounding the conception of objects as mind-independent how must we be thinking of sensory experience? Must we have a relational view, as Campbell claims? Here are two reasons why not. First, the grounding role of experience *can* be satisfactorily explained on a representational view of experience. Second, the grounding role of experience *can't* be satisfactorily explained on a relational view of experience. Either way, the relational view isn't uniquely well placed to solve Berkeley's Puzzle and shouldn't be adopted on the basis that only it can solve the puzzle. In reality the relational view is in a worse position to solve the puzzle than its main rival.

It's easy to see why representationalists think that they have a ready-made solution to the puzzle. Their view is that sensory experience grounds our concepts of mind-independent objects because it represents objects *as* mind-independent, and does so in a way that does not presuppose our grasp of such concepts. The notion that some of the things we perceive are persisting space occupiers is built into the non-conceptual representational content of sensory experience, and this makes it possible for sensory experience to play a role in explaining our grasp of concepts of persisting spatial objects. The same point can be made by reference to the idea that there are spatio-temporal enabling conditions of perception. I have argued that this idea is firmly grounded in sensory experience in the sense that the link between what I can see and where I am is built into the content of sensory experience. The content at issue here is representational content. Sensory experience makes it evident that what one perceives depends in part on where one is by *representing* objects as spatially related to one's sense organs.

Campbell has many objections to representationalism and these will be discussed in the next chapter. Still, it is worth making the point here that representationalism has at least a *prima facie* solution to Berkeley's Puzzle. What about the relational view? Suppose we have sensory experiences of objects that are mind-independent either in virtue of having primary qualities or in virtue of being mechanisms for transferring causal influence. On the relational view, do our sensory experiences represent objects as having primary qualities or as being mechanisms for transferring causal influence? If so, there is no substantial disagreement with representationalism. If not, it needs to be explained how the relational view can still regard sensory experience as grounding our conception of objects as mind-independent. What exactly is the relational view's alternative to the representational conception of the grounding relation?

The problem is this: even if sensory experience is a matter of being directly related to mind-independent objects and properties around us, it does not follow that it plays any role in explaining our grasp of the conception of objects as mind-independent. For sensory experience to be playing any such role it must register the mind-independence of objects, where this is either a matter of registering the fact that they have primary qualities or their role as mechanisms for transferring causal influence. If registering these things isn't a matter of representing objects as being a certain way then what exactly is it? How else is the mind-independence of objects supposed to show up in sensory experience? We can still take the objects to which sensory experience relates us to be mind-independent even if it doesn't represent them as such, but then it is unclear in what sense it is sensory experience that is making it possible for us to conceive of objects as mind-independent.

Relationalists may say in response that there is no reason why, on their view, sensory experience can't register the mind-independence of objects. It is, after all, Campbell's view that 'the qualitative character of our experiences of primary qualities is actually constituted by the primary qualities of the objects themselves that we encounter' (p. 14). If the objects we encounter are mind-independent in virtue of having primary qualities, and it is also the case that their primary qualities constitute the qualitative character of our sensory experiences, it follows that our sensory experiences *do* 'register' the mind-independence of objects. They register the mind-independence of objects not by representing them as mind-independent but by having their qualitative character constituted by the qualitative character of objects that are mind-independent.

What does it mean to say that the qualitative character of our experiences of primary qualities is constituted by the primary qualities of objects? If I'm looking at something square how can the qualitative character of my experience *be* the qualitative character of the object if, as is presumably the case, the experience has no shape? This question underestimates how radical the relational view is. Like G. E. Moore, Campbell thinks there is a confusion in talk of the qualitative character of experience if this is taken to imply that there is an array of qualitative characteristics—'qualia'—of experience itself. In ordinary perceptual experience, 'there are only the qualitative characteristics of the objects in our surroundings'

(p. 23). Experience doesn't have its own qualitative characteristics over and above the qualitative characteristics of objects. So when Campbell says that the qualitative character of my sensory experience of the shape of an object is constituted by the shape itself he is not saying that the experience has its own qualitative character that is separate from but somehow determined by the object's qualitative character. What he is saying is that the object itself is a *constituent* of the experience and that its qualitative character just *is* the qualitative character of the object. On this account, the qualitative character of experience 'has nothing particularly to do with perception or experience; it is simply the qualitative character of the world' (p. 18).

I objected previously that the relational view's constitutive thesis exaggerates the contribution of the object to determining the qualitative character of experience. It might now seem that this objection is misplaced: there can only be an exaggeration here if experience has qualitative characteristics in its own right and this is just what Campbell is denying. But the question is whether this denial is plausible, and I contend that it is not. If, in an eye test, a particular letter looks blurry to me then I am having a sensory experience whose qualitative character is different from the qualitative character of the object; the letter isn't blurry. In this case the qualitative character of experience is plainly not simply the qualitative character of the world.

More to the point for present purposes, the idea that in ordinary perceptual experience there are only the qualitative characteristics of the objects in our surroundings doesn't help with Berkeley's Puzzle. The idea is, presumably, that in sense experience we are simply presented with these characteristics and that our being so presented somehow enables us to conceive of objects as mind-independent. How is this supposed to work, especially given that an object's mind-independence isn't one of its qualitative characteristics? We can get a sense of the difficulty by looking at Charles Travis's view of perception, which is similar in some respects to the relational view. For Travis, perception is a source of unmediated awareness which 'simply places our surroundings in view; affords us awareness of them' (2004, p. 65). Perception, on this view, is not representational, and there is no commitment in perception to our surroundings being one way or another. The senses themselves are silent, and when they bring our surroundings into view it is '*for us* to make of what is in our view what we can, or do' (2004, p. 64, my emphasis).

This implies that when we judge that the objects which perception brings into view are mind-independent we aren't simply endorsing what sensory experience tells us. Sensory experience doesn't tell us anything about the world; it simply gives us the world, and leaves it to us to draw our own conclusions about its nature. The conception of objects of experience as mind-independent is our take on the world, our cognitive response to what we perceive, but if we aren't endorsing what sensory experience tells us when we conceive of the world in this way then it's not clear in what sense this conception is grounded in sensory experience. In this picture, it isn't sensory experience which explains our conception of objects as mind-independent, and our grasp of this conception will need to be explained in some other way, if it can be explained at all.

This is presumably not a conclusion which Campbell would welcome since it amounts to a rejection of experientialism. He wants our concepts of objects to be grounded in sensory experience but he doesn't want to tell a representation-alist story about how this is possible. The alternative is to think of our concepts of objects as grounded in the objects themselves, with sensory experience only entering the picture in a supporting role, as something which simply brings objects into view and whose qualitative character is the qualitative character of the objects. But objects like tables are silent as to their own ontological status; they don't tell us that they are either mind-dependent or mind-independent, and being mind-independent is not one of their qualitative characteristics. Given that the table in my study is silent as to its own ontological status it would seem to follow that the conception of it as mind-independent *can't* be grounded in sensory experience *if* the cognitive role of my sensory experience is confined to bringing the table into view without representing it as being any particular way. Sensory experience is as silent on the relational view as it is on Travis's view.

What this shows is that the relational view is inherently unstable since it wants to combine experientialism with the denial that sensory experience has anything to say in its own right about the mind-independence of objects of experience. The problem is that sensory experience can't be what grounds the conception of objects as mind-independent if what Campbell says about the nature of sensory experience is correct. If the qualitative character of experience has nothing to do with *experience* then so much the worse for experientialism. The way to be an experientialist is to be a representationalist rather than a relationalist but Campbell rejects representationalism. So our next question is: are Campbell's objections to representationalism any good?

8

Representationalism

Quassim Cassam

I have argued that Campbell's supposedly 'straightforward' response to Berkeley's Puzzle is neither straightforward nor a solution to the puzzle. The puzzle is to understand how it could be both that our grasp of concepts of ordinary objects is grounded in our experience of those objects and that we have the conception of mind-independent objects. Berkeley finds this puzzling because he can't see how sensory experience could play any part in explaining or grounding our conception of objects of experience as mind-independent. I have claimed that even if sensory experience is, as the relational view maintains, a matter of our being directly related to mind-independent objects that still doesn't explain how our grasp of the conception of mind-independent objects can be grounded in sensory experience. A different approach is needed, one that makes more of the idea that the mind-independence of objects of experience shows up in, or is registered by, sensory experience.

This is the point at which the representational view of sensory experience begins to look like a promising alternative to the relational view. For representationalism, the mind-independence of the objects to which we are related by sensory experience does indeed show up in sensory experience. Sensory experience registers the mind-independence of objects by representing them as mind-independent. It is because, and only because, sensory experience represents objects as mind-independent that it is able to ground our conception of objects as mind-independent. There is absolutely no mystery here: representationalism has what looks like a ready-made solution to Berkeley's Puzzle because it takes the idea that the objects of sensory experience are mind-independent to be built into the representational content of at least some sensory experiences.

Obviously, a representationalist who responds to Berkeley's Puzzle in this way still has to explain what it is for sensory experience to represent objects as mind-independent. Suppose it turns out that in order for our sensory experience to represent objects as mind-independent we already need to have the conception of objects as mind-independent. In that case, how can sensory experience really be what grounds our grasp of this conception? Or is it possible for sensory experience to represent objects as mind-independent in a way that doesn't presuppose a grasp of concepts of mind-independent objects, or the conception of objects as mind-independent? These are questions which representationalism is going to have to answer but they do not detract from the main point: representationalism has what looks like a straightforward solution to Berkeley's Puzzle.

So why does Campbell reject this solution? He argues that representationalism 'offers little prospect of explaining how sensory experience can ground our concepts of mind-independent objects' (p. 47). He has three arguments for this pessimistic view of the prospects for representationalism:

1. One way of being a representationalist 'is to say that the content of experience is conceptual, of the same kind that we exercise in ordinary thinking and judging' (p. 45). On this account we 'could not regard our grasp of concepts as being explained by the role of sensory experience' because 'sensory experience is simply an exercise of our grasp of concepts, one among many of the ways in which we exercise our grasp of concepts' (p. 45).

2. Experientialism is the view that our understanding of concepts of ordinary objects and their properties is grounded in our sensory experience of these objects and their properties. The grounding relation is a justificatory as well as an explanatory relation: sensory experience plays some role in validating ways of thinking that 'reflect the mind-independence we usually take physical things to have' (pp. 33–4). On a representational view of sensory experience we have no idea what role sensory experience might have in such a validation.

3. Sensory experience is a form of phenomenal or sensory awareness, and sensory awareness 'is what happens when … there is something it is like to perceive' (p. 40). To ask how sensory experience can ground concepts of mind-independent objects is therefore to ask how phenomenal awareness or phenomenal consciousness can ground such concepts. But all we get from representationalism is an account of how the representational content of sensory experience enables it to ground our concepts; the phenomenal character of sensory experience is doing no work in representationalism's response to the puzzle, so it offers no answer to the question whether 'phenomenal consciousness plays any role in our having a conception of the world around us, and if so, what that role might be' (p. 40).

Since 1 amounts to the objection that conceptualist representationalism is incompatible with experientialism I'll call it the *incompatibility problem* for conceptualist representationalism. 2 is a succinct statement of what I have called the *justification*

problem for representationalism. Finally, 3 is the *redundancy problem* for representationalism because it implies that the fact that sensory experience is conscious is
redundant relative to the project of explaining our grasp of concepts.

In my view, representationalism in its best form has responses to all of these
problems and nothing that Campbell says proves otherwise. I'm going to proceed
as follows in defence of this. First I will give an account of representationalism
and distinguish two different forms of this doctrine. Next, I will explain in greater
detail how representationalism deals with Berkeley's Puzzle. The two key questions in this context are:

(a) What would it be for sensory experience to represent objects as mind-
    independent?
(b) How does the fact that sensory experience has this representational content
    enable it to play a role, as required by experientialism, in grounding and
    explaining our grasp of the conception of mind-independent objects?

Finally, in the third part of this chapter, I will return to the issues of incompatibility, justification, and redundancy. The third of these issues raises questions about
how representationalism conceives of the relationship between the representational content of sensory experience and its phenomenal character. Campbell
assumes that they are entirely separate and this is what gives rise to the redundancy problem. Representationalists should respond by insisting on a much closer
link between the representational and the phenomenal.

The key idea of representationalism is that sensory experiences have representational content, that is, they represent the perceiver's environment as being a certain way.[1] To say that experiences represent the perceiver's environment as being
a certain way is to say that they can be evaluated as correct or incorrect. So, for
example, the sense in which my current visual experience represents the cup from
which I am drinking coffee as chipped is that my experience is correct or veridical
only if my coffee cup is chipped. If my experience would be veridical regardless of
whether the cup is chipped then it isn't an experience which represents the cup as
chipped, and I cannot be said to be experiencing the cup as chipped.

An important question for representationalism is whether the representational
content of experience is conceptual or non-conceptual. Two key issues here are:

i. Are the representational contents of experience composed of propositions,
   concepts, or senses?

[1] Peacocke describes the representational content of perception as 'the conditions it represents to
its subject as holding in the world' (2001b, p. 609). He also describes representational content as 'content that is evaluable as correct or as incorrect' (2001a, p. 240).

ii. Is the representational content of experience characterizable only in terms of concepts which the subject himself possesses?

Conceptualist representationalists think that the answer to one or both of these questions is 'yes', and that the representational content of sensory experience is to this extent conceptual. *Non-conceptualist* representationalists think that the answer to one or both of these questions is 'no', and that the representational content of experience is to this extent non-conceptual.[2] Underlying this disagreement is a disagreement over whether the representational content of sensory experience is the content of a possible judgement. Conceptualist representationalists think it is, and that it follows from this that the content of sensory experience isn't a special kind of content. It is just the kind of content which beliefs and judgements have. Non-conceptualist representationalists disagree, and that is why they respond as they do to i and ii.

Now consider my current visual experience of a tree. The tree is a mind-independent object so a natural question is: does my experience represent the tree as mind-independent? Many representationalists would say that it does. According to Susanna Siegel, for example, 'the objects we seem to see are presented to us as subject-independent' (2006, p. 356). What Siegel calls subject-independence is what I call mind-independence; it is 'the independence of a thing's *existence* from the experience that the subject has in seeing it' (2006, p. 357). Siegel talks about objects being 'presented' in visual experience as subject-independent, but what she is talking about is the representational content of sensory experience.

Others go further and insist that we usually experience objects like trees not just as mind-independent objects but as mind-independent *material* objects, as bounded space occupiers. On this account there are contents of thoughts and experiences 'which require for their truth that the objective material world be a certain way' (Peacocke 1989, p. 7), and the representational content of my current visual experience of a tree is one such content. If what I am aware of is a hologram rather than a material object then my experience is not veridical, and this is a reflection of the fact that my sensory experience represents the tree as a material object. My experience isn't neutral as to the ontological status of the tree and is veridical only if the object I am experiencing is mind-independent and material.

In what sense does my sensory experience represent the tree as mind-independent? This takes us back to a question I raised earlier: what would

---

[2] Byrne 2004 gives a useful account of different conceptions of conceptual and non-conceptual content.

it even be for sensory experience to represent a mind-independent object *as* mind-independent? An unpromising answer to this question is supplied by conceptualist representationalists who hold that ordinary sensory experience is 'permeated' by concepts of mind-independent objects, and that this is the sense in which it represents objects as mind-independent.[3] This is unpromising in part because it makes it difficult to see how the sensory experiences of non-human animals could represent mind-independent objects, on the assumption that many such animals don't have concepts of mind-independent objects or the conception of objects as mind-independent. Their sensory experiences can't be permeated by concepts they don't have. We could deny that non-human animals experience objects as mind-independent but that would be absurd.[4]

A better approach would be to argue as follows: a mind-independent object is one that is there anyway, that can persist beyond the course of a subject's experience of it. When such objects are experienced they are experienced *as* persisting, and this is at least part of what it is for them to be experienced as mind-independent. The challenge, then, is to make sense of the idea that objects can be represented in experience *as* persisting, *as* there anyway, without the subject needing to have the concept of mind-independence. An example might help. As I walk towards the tree in the quad I experience it as coming into view. But experiencing the tree as coming into *view* is not the same as experiencing it as coming into *existence*. To experience the tree as coming into view is to experience it as something that was there already, and as coming into view because I am moving closer. As I keep walking, the tree eventually recedes until at some point I can no longer see it. To experience the tree as receding from view is not to experience it as diminishing in size. Receding is not the same as ceasing to exist, and the experience of an object gradually disappearing from view is not the experience of it gradually ceasing to exist. My experience represents the tree as *persisting* as my location changes and I move away. To the extent that my sensory experience represents the tree as a persisting thing it represents it as mind-independent, but the experience of objects as coming into view or as disappearing from view is not confined to creatures with concepts.

A closely related way of thinking about the representation of mind-independence in sensory experience is in terms of what Tyler Burge calls 'perceptual constancies'. These are 'capacities to represent a given particular, property, relation, or kind as the same, despite significant differences in registration of proximal stimulation' (2009, p. 318). For example, 'we can see an entity as being of a specific size while taking

---

[3] This is P. F. Strawson's version of conceptualist representationalism. See Strawson 2011.

[4] I agree with Peacocke when he says that 'a mental state can have a content that concerns the objective world without the subject who enjoys that state having a conception of objectivity' and that 'this possibility is realized in the case of the perceptual state of lower animals' (2001b, p. 614).

up more or less of the visual field' (2009, p. 318). As I walk towards the tree in the quad it takes up more of my visual field but does not appear to change in size. The sensory representation of the tree as the same despite changes in the registration of proximal stimulation does not presuppose my possession of concepts but nevertheless amounts to the mental representation of the tree as mind-independent. Like the representation of the tree's persistence, the representation of constancy is the representation of the tree's existence as independent of sensory experience.

Not everything that is mind-independent is a material object. The shadow cast by the tree exists independently of being experienced but is not a material object. In contrast the tree is a material object, and my sensory experience of the tree is the sensory experience of it not just as mind-independent but as a mind-independent *material* object. In what sense? Locke held that what makes an object a material object is that it has 'primary qualities' such as shape and solidity. The tree in the quad has primary qualities and the fact that it has primary qualities is evident in my sensory experience. My sensory experience represents the tree as shaped, located, and solid, and thereby represents it as a material object. It doesn't follow that what I am experiencing is a material object rather than, say, a hologram, but my experience is veridical only if it is material.

As an aside, it might be worth saying something about the role of self-awareness in this account. There is a view, associated with P. F. Strawson, that for sensory experiences to represent objects as mind-independent their subject must conceive of himself as in the mind-independent world as an object among others.[5] As Campbell says:

Strawson would have taken it absolutely for granted that there is no saying what it would be for a subject to have objective representations, unless we appeal to the subject's having the conception of itself in a mind-independent world. The idea is that whatever we appeal to as a determinant of content, if we do not appeal to the subject's own conception of the mind-independent world, we will not be able to explain what *makes* the subject's perceptual representations into representations of a mind-independent world.

(Campbell 2011, p. 274)

The account I have been arguing for does not endorse this view. It explains what makes the subject's perceptual representations into representations of a mind-independent world without appeal to the subject's having the conception of himself in a mind-independent world, since this conception is not required for the representation of objects as constant or persisting or as possessing primary qualities. The self-awareness which is required is much more primitive. For example,

---

[5] See Strawson 1966.

when I experience the tree in the quad as gradually coming into view I have a sense of my own movement and changing location, and this might be thought of as a form of self-awareness. However, this basic self-awareness doesn't require the *conception* of oneself in a mind-independent world. Animals which presumably have neither the conception of a mind-independent world nor the conception of themselves in such a world can still be aware of mind-independent objects and be aware of them *as* mind-independent.

Suppose that the discussion so far is along the right lines: sensory experience can and does represent objects as mind-independent by representing them as constant, persisting, and material.[6] The next thing that needs explaining is how this enables sensory experience to do the very thing Berkeley thinks can't be done, namely, ground the *conception* of the objects of sensory experience as mind-independent. The key is to understand what 'ground' means in this context, and this takes us back to the discussion of experientialism in Chapter 6. One version of experientialism is experientialism about understanding. This says that:

Our understanding of concepts of ordinary objects and their properties is grounded in our sensory experience of those objects and properties.

According to Campbell the sense in which this is so is that sensory experience plays an essential role in explaining our grasp of concepts of ordinary objects and their properties. I called this 'essential role' experientialism, and pointed out that it is much more plausible in relation to some concepts than others.

The present question is not whether it is plausible that sensory experience plays an essential role in relation to our grasp of the conception of objects as mind-independent but whether, on the assumption that it is plausible, representationalism can explain how sensory experience can play this role. On the face of it nothing could be simpler. To conceive of the tree in the quad as mind-independent is to conceive of it as existing independently of my or any other subject's experience of it. To do that is to conceive of it as constant and persisting, but I have argued that my sensory experience represents the tree as constant and persisting. It's not just an abstract theory or hypothesis that the tree is mind-independent, it is also how my sensory experience represents the tree.

So the proposal is this: sensory experience of objects as mind-independent can play an essential role in grounding our grasp of the conception of objects as mind-independent because it gives concrete reality to this conception and ensures

---

[6] There is obviously much more to be said about all this. For example, there is also the idea that experiences of objectivity require the imagining of alternative perspectives. See Church 2013 for an exploration of this idea, and Strawson 1974 for an influential account of the role of imagination in perception of objects.

that our understanding of the idea that objects like trees are mind-independent isn't purely formal. In Kant's terminology, the conception of objects as mind-independent would be empty and insubstantial without the experiential backing of sensory experiences which *display* their mind-independence in just that way that representationalism speaks about.[7] If sensory experience didn't represent objects as mind-independent it would be quite mysterious what it adds to our grasp of the conception of objects as mind-independent, or why it should be essential for grasp of this conception. The fact that sensory experience is a relation to objects that are in fact mind-independent is neither here nor there unless the mind-independence of objects actually shows up in sensory experience, as is quite clearly the case on a representational but not on a relational view of sensory experience.

A worry that one might have about the story so far is that it underestimates what is involved in conceiving of an object as there anyway. Conceiving of the tree in the quad as there anyway is a matter of conceiving of it as there before I came into sensory contact with it, and as potentially continuing to exist even when I am no longer experiencing it. As noted in a previous chapter, there are those who think that these are ideas that can't stand on their own, without any surrounding theory. According to Evans the requisite theory is a theory of the spatio-temporal enabling conditions of perception: if one is to perceive what is there to be perceived one must be in the right place at the right time. With this simple theory in place it is now easy to explain in these terms why the tree in the quad, which is there to be perceived, is not actually perceived at various times: it isn't perceived because no one is in the right place at the right time.

On this account, it is still possible, on a representational view of sensory experience, to understand how sensory experience can play an essential role in grounding our grasp of the conception of objects as mind-independent. It plays this role because it plays an essential role in grounding our understanding of the enabling conditions of perception. Take the idea that what one can experience is determined in part by one's spatial location. Sensory experience is able to ground this idea because it represents objects and other perceptible things as standing in spatial relations to the perceiver. As the tree in the quad comes into view it isn't a mystery to me why I can now see something I couldn't see before; my sensory experience represents the tree as coming into view *because* my location is changing. In other words, my sensory experience makes it evident to me *that* what I can perceive depends in part on where I am, and it also makes it evident *how* perception and location are related. If sensory experience lacked spatial representational

---

[7] See the section called 'Schematism of the Pure Concepts of Understanding' in Kant 1932.

content one would lack any real understanding of perception and its spatial enabling conditions; one's understanding of such conditions and the conception of
mind-independence which they underpin would be empty and formal.

The discussion so far has focused on experientialism about understanding. The
issue in this context is whether representationalism can account for the essential
role of sensory experience in grounding our understanding of the conception of
objects as mind-independent. This form of experientialism is closely related to
experientialism about knowledge and about justification. The former says that
sensory experience plays an essential role in grounding our knowledge of our surroundings. The latter says that sensory experience plays an essential role in justifying our concepts of objects and the conception of reality which our concepts
embed. It is clear from the way we reason that we do in fact think of objects as
mind-independent, and experientialism about justification claims that sensory
experience contributes to the justification of such patterns of reasoning.

Can sensory experience do these things on a representationalist view? It's hard
to see what the problem is. To say that sensory experience plays an essential role
in our knowledge of our surroundings is to imply that at least some of what we
know about the world around us must be based on sensory experience. So a natural question is: what must sensory experience be like for this to be the case? That
depends on how we understand the 'based on' relation. In fact there are many different ways of understanding this relation but the central case in which knowledge of the world is based on sensory experience is not only consistent with, but
calls for, a representational view of sensory experience. This is the case in which
I believe that P (where P is some proposition about mind-independent reality),
and my belief amounts to knowledge at least in part because my sensory experience gives me a reason to believe that P. So, for example, my experience of the tree
in the quad gives me a reason to believe that there is a tree in the quad, and thereby
helps to make it the case that I know, on the basis of sensory experience, that there
is a tree in the quad. However, my sensory experience gives me reason to believe
that there is a tree in the quad precisely because it *represents* a tree and *represents*
it as being in the quad. This is the representational content of my sensory experience, and the view I am defending is that the way to make sense of the epistemic
role of sensory experience is by reference to the idea that sensory experience has
representational content.

This brings us neatly to experientialism about justification. What does it mean to
say that sensory experience plays a role in 'justifying a concept'? The most straightforward view is that what sensory experience can justify is the *application* of (some)
concepts. To apply the concept *tree* to the tree in the quad is to judge that it's a tree.
On what basis do I do that? On the basis that it has various characteristics that

I take to be characteristic of trees. I know that it has these characteristics because my sensory experience represents it as having them. I am justified in applying the concept *tree* in this case because my sensory experience represents a trunk, leaves, branches, and so on, and represents them as belonging to a single thing. There are, of course, other ways of being justified in judging that that thing is a tree—you might tell me that it is a tree—but to the extent that it is sensory experience that does the justifying it is able to do this because of its representational content.

When Campbell discusses the justificatory role of sensory experience he concentrates on its role in validating ways of thinking or patterns of reasoning that reflect our conception of objects as mind-independent. What are these patterns of reasoning and how can sensory experience help to validate them? Here is an example from Campbell:

> We reason in ways that reflect our conception of objects as mind-independent... We engage in reasoning to establish object identity that proceeds by arguing that the later object is the way it is only because the earlier object was the way it was; therefore they are identical. Suppose, for example, that you visit your old schoolroom and find your initials still carved on a desk. You have the right to take it that it's the same desk; the initials wouldn't be there now if it wasn't for your industry all those years ago. (p. 28)

The reasoning in this example reflects 'a conception of the object as having its identity constituted in a way that is independent of its relation to any mind'. The question is whether, on a representational view, perceptual experience could provide us with any justification for reasoning in this way.

This is not a difficult question. The conclusion that the desk I can now see is the very desk at which I sat at school is the product of inference to the best explanation. The role of sensory experience isn't directly to validate the inference but to validate the view of objects which the inference exploits. The inference exploits the conception of objects like desks as mind-independent, and the role of sensory experience is to validate that conception. How? By representing objects *as* mind-independent. I have already explained how sensory experience does that. It is because sensory experience represents objects like desks as mind-independent, as having their identities constituted in a way that is independent of its relation to any mind, that it validates the background conception of objects which I rely on when I infer that *this* desk, the one I can see, is *that* desk, the one I remember.

To sum up: Campbell's objection to representationalism is that it offers little prospect of explaining how sensory experience can ground our concepts of mind-independent objects. In reality, representationalism offers every prospect of explaining how sensory experience can do this. Whether we think of grounding by reference to experientialism about understanding, knowledge, or justification, the proposal that sensory experiences represent objects as mind-independent makes it possible for representationalism to explain how sensory experience anchors a conception of objects which Berkeley thought couldn't possibly be grounded in experience. If any solution to Berkeley's Puzzle deserves to be called 'straightforward', it is the one suggested by representationalism. In that case, why is Campbell so pessimistic about the prospects for a representationalist solution to Berkeley's Puzzle? This brings us, finally, to the three problems he thinks that the representationalist response faces, the problems of incompatibility, redundancy, and justification.

The worry about incompatibility is this: if we think of the representational content of sensory experience as conceptual then we could not regard our grasp of concepts as explained by the role of sensory experience, or as grounded in sensory experience. The implications are that conceptualist representationalism is incompatible with experientialism, and that this is a problem for conceptualist representationalism rather than for experientialism. Of course, conceptualist representationalists might not see things this way. They might say that if there is an incompatibility then so much the worse for experientialism. However, a prior question is whether it's true that experientialism and conceptualist representationalism are irreconcilable. Campbell's point is that we can't see our concepts as being grounded in sensory experience *if* sensory experience is simply an exercise of our grasp of concepts but this is only relevant if this is how conceptualist representationalists think of sensory experience. They do not. For example, McDowell is an influential conceptualist representationalist who rejects the idea that sensory experience, which is a form of what he calls 'receptivity', is an exercise of our grasp of concepts. He proposes that conceptual capacities are 'drawn on *in* receptivity', but adds that 'it sounds off key in this connection to speak of *exercising* conceptual capacities at all' (1996, p. 10). To exercise a concept, as one does when one judges that things are thus and so, is to be active, but sensory experience is passive. In sensory experience one finds oneself 'passively saddled with conceptual contents' (1996, p. 31), and it's not clear why or how it is supposed to follow from this that sensory experience can't play an essential role in grounding or explaining our grasp of concepts, the very concepts that are drawn on in receptivity. Why couldn't it be, as Kant believed, that sensory experience presupposes conceptual capacities, *and* that conceptual capacities presuppose sensory experience?

Just as there are worries about the compatibility of conceptualist representationalism and experientialism that are based on a misunderstanding of conceptualist representationalism so there are worries about the compatibility of the two doctrines that turn out to be based on a misunderstanding of experientialism. The most common misunderstanding is to interpret experientialism as equivalent to concept empiricism, to the view that our concepts are derived from sensory experience. It's not difficult to see why this might lead one to conclude that experientialists can't be conceptualist representationalists. The thought is this: our concepts can only be derived from sensory experience if our having sensory experience is prior to our having any concepts, and this implies that the sensory experiences from which our concepts are derived must have non-conceptual representational contents. If all sensory experience is already permeated by concepts, as conceptualist representationalism supposes, then it would be incoherent to suppose that it is also the *source* of our concepts.[8]

This argument does not show that experientialism is incompatible with conceptualist representationalism. It doesn't show this because experientialism isn't committed to concept empiricism. Experientialism is a view about our grasp of concepts. It is not a view about our acquisition of concepts. It does not say, or imply, that it must be possible for us to have sensory experience before we have any concepts. What it says is that sensory experience plays an essential role in explaining our grasp of concepts. This could be the case even if our concepts are innate. It could also be the case if the representational content of sensory experience is conceptual. As we have seen, there is no reason why the sensory experiences which underpin our grasp of, say, concepts of mind-independent objects, couldn't be ones that draw on concepts of mind-independent objects. The relation between grasp of such concepts and sensory experience could be one of mutual dependence, in which case there is no reason for conceptualist representationalism and experientialism to disagree; sensory experience can play an essential role in grounding or explaining our grasp of the very concepts by which sensory experience is permeated.

With regard to the justification problem, in one sense I have already dealt with this problem: sensory experience can play a role in validating ways of thinking that reflect the mind-independence of objects because it represents objects as mind-independent. So what is Campbell's worry? This is what he says:

If we are interested in the validation of the patterns of reasoning that reflect our grasp of objects as mind-independent, how could an appeal to non-conceptual content help? There will presumably be some patterns of use governing non-conceptual contents…Perhaps what it comes to that non-conceptual contents 'display the world as objective' is that they are governed by patterns of use quite like those that we have for conceptual contents relating to mind-independent objects. Perhaps the suggestion is that the patterns of inference governing conceptual contents actually are justified by their relations to the similar patterns of use governing non-conceptual contents. But then we have simply pushed the problem back to the validation of the patterns of use governing non-conceptual contents. We

---

[8]   See Patton 2006 for further discussion.

have no idea how such a validation might be given and still less do we have any idea what role sensory experience might play in such a validation. (pp. 46–7)

It's hard to avoid the impression that the problem which Campbell detects in this passage is entirely the result of modelling the non-conceptual on the conceptual. Concepts like *tree*, or terms referring to ordinary physical objects, have 'patterns of use'. Specifically, they figure in patterns of inference which reflect the conception of objects as mind-independent. The role of sensory experiences is to validate such patterns of inference but they don't have patterns of use 'like those we have for conceptual contents'. This would make their contents conceptual or at least quasi-conceptual, and this is precisely what non-conceptualist representationalism denies. On this approach, there is no parallel between the way in which sensory experiences represent objects as mind-independent and the way that conceptual contents represent objects as mind-independent.

I have already explained the sense in which sensory experiences represent objects as mind-independent. When my sensory experience of the tree in the quad represents it as mind-independent by representing it as existing unperceived there is nothing recognizable as a pattern of use, and nothing which requires its own validation as Campbell's discussion suggests. Nothing validates my sensory experience in the way that my sensory experience validates my conception of the world. To ask what role sensory experience might play in the validation of patterns of use governing non-conceptual contents is to fail to do justice to the notion of non-conceptual content as most non-conceptualist representationalists conceive of it. We have no idea what role sensory experience might play in such a validation because we have no idea how sensory experience can justify its own non-conceptual content.

That leaves the redundancy problem, which Campbell presents as a problem for non-conceptualist representationalism. The question is: can this form of representationalism allow that phenomenal consciousness plays any role in our having a conception of the world around us? Campbell thinks not. He argues that that non-conceptualist representationalism ends up making phenomenal consciousness and, by implication, also sensory experience redundant in relation to our grasp of concepts. If this is right then representationalism faces a dilemma: if it goes conceptualist then it runs into the incompatibility problem. If it goes non-conceptualist then it faces the redundancy problem. I've already argued that the first horn of this dilemma is spurious. The second horn is no less spurious, but this will take a little more time to show.

Here is a succinct statement of the redundancy problem for the non-conceptualist representationalism:

[A]ny kind of non-conceptual content that could be ascribed to sensory experience could also, in principle, be ascribed to perceptual states in the absence of sensory experience. This means that…[w]e do not have here a way in which the [non-conceptualist] representationalist can acknowledge the explanatory role of experience. From the point of view of understanding our grasp of concepts of mind-independent objects, on this analysis we would be just as well off with perceptual states that had this capacity to 'display the world as objective', even if those perceptual states were not themselves conscious states. (p. 46)

The key to this objection is the relationship between sensory experience and phenomenal consciousness. Let's say that sensory experience is phenomenally conscious to the extent that it has phenomenal character, that is, to the extent that there is something it is like to have it. Without phenomenal character sensory experience wouldn't be sensory *experience*. However, representationalists think that sensory experiences also have representational content, so an important question is: how is the representational content of sensory experience related to its phenomenal character? It is this question which brings to light the redundancy problem for non-conceptualist representationalism.

Campbell takes it that non-conceptualist representationalism is committed to the view that the phenomenal and representational or intentional aspects of mentality are separate from one another. This is sometimes called *separatism*.[9] Separatists think that 'Representation is one thing, and awareness is another' (p. 76). Sensory experiences include perceptual experiences, and separatism says that to have such an experience is to be in a perceptual state that just happens to be conscious. Although the perceptual state represents the world as being a certain way, the fact that the state is conscious, and so amounts to a perceptual *experience*, has no bearing on its representational content. Consciousness, on this view, is a kind of glow that perceptual experiences have. However, this glow can be subtracted from a perceptual experience without affecting its representational content. A perceptual experience without phenomenal consciousness is a 'mere' perceptual state, and such states are no less capable of representing mind-independent objects than perceptual experiences. They constitute the representational core of perceptual experiences, which only represent mind-independent objects because mere perceptual states represent mind-independent objects.

If representationalism is committed to separatism then Campbell is right that it leaves no room for sensory experience to play an essential role in our having a conception of the world around us. *Sensory experience* can only be playing an essential role in explaining or grounding our grasp of concepts of mind-independent

---

[9] According to Horgan and Tienson, separatism 'treats phenomenal aspects of mentality and intentional aspects of mentality as mutually independent, and thus separable' (2002, p. 520).

objects if *phenomenal consciousness* is playing such a role but phenomenal consciousness would be doing no work in the representationalist's story if separatism is correct. This is the problem of redundancy: the fact that sensory experiences represent mind-independent objects has little to do with the fact that they are conscious, and therefore little to do with the fact that they are sensory *experiences*. If our grasp of concepts of mind-independent objects can be satisfactorily explained by reference to our being in mere perceptual states which nevertheless represent objects as mind-independent ('display the world as objective') then the only conclusion to be drawn is the one that Campbell draws: when it comes to explaining our grasp of concepts, including concepts of mind-independent objects, sensory experience is redundant because phenomenal consciousness is redundant.

The obvious question to ask at this point is this: why suppose that representationalism is committed to separatism? If separatism leads to the redundancy problem then that is a very good reason for representationalists not to be separatists, and the most promising versions of non-conceptualist representationalism do not endorse separatism. For example, opposition to separatism is a key element of the so-called 'phenomenal intentionality research programme'.[10] The idea behind this programme is that intentional states, including sensory experiences, have their representational or intentional contents 'by virtue of their phenomenology' (Horgan and Tienson 2002, p. 520). Subtract the phenomenal character of a sensory experience and you also subtract, or at least significantly alter, its representational content. It's not true on this account that any kind of non-conceptual content that could be ascribed to sensory experience can also be ascribed to mere perceptual states in the absence of sensory experience. To the extent that sensory experiences represent objects as mind-independent, and thereby ground our grasp of concepts of mind-independent objects, they do so by virtue of their phenomenal character. The clear implication is that phenomenal consciousness plays a crucial role in our having a conception of the world around us, and that we would not be as well off with perceptual states that aren't conscious.

The challenge facing representationalists who want to argue in this way is to explain how sensory experiences can have their intentional contents by virtue of their phenomenal features. In particular it needs to be explained how the fact that sensory experiences represent mind-independent objects can have anything to do with their phenomenal character given that there are actual cases of perceptual representation without awareness. Blindsight is a case in point. Blindsight patients are able to respond to visual stimuli without consciously perceiving them. They 'perceive environmental conditions' but 'consciousness is missing'

---

[10]   See Kriegel 2013 for an overview.

(Burge 2010, p. 374). If such patients represent the conditions they perceive as mind-independent, there is no question of their perceptual intentionality being phenomenal; their ability to represent objects has no phenomenological basis. In that case, why suppose that ordinary sensory experiences represent objects 'by virtue of their phenomenology'?

More generally, there is a natural way of thinking about the phenomenal which makes it hard to see how the phenomenal and the intentional could interpenetrate as the phenomenal intentionality programme requires. On this way of thinking, phenomenal features of sensory experience are sensations, and this is a problem for the notion of phenomenal intentionality because sensations are not representational in their own right. They can function as signs of their regular causes but aren't intrinsically representational; *in themselves*, sensations do not represent the world as being a certain way. And then the obvious question is: if sensations aren't intrinsically representational how can they possibly ground the representational content of sensory experiences?

There are a number of things of things a representationalist can say in response to this question. The two leading options are to argue that:

(I) Sensations are intrinsically representational.
(II) Even if sensations aren't intrinsically representational this doesn't mean that the representational content of sensory experiences cannot be grounded in their phenomenal character.

(I) suggests that representationalism only makes the phenomenal redundant on a conception of sensation which representationalists needn't accept. For sensations to be representational they must have correctness conditions, but they *do* have correctness conditions. For example, a sensation of red is veridical if there is something red causing it. As Ayers observes, bodily sensations represent parts of one's own body and perceptual sensations 'present their objects as being in certain causal and spatial relations to ourselves and our sense organs' (1991, p. 192). There is no question of such sensations lacking intentional content, or of their intentionality being somehow extrinsic rather than intrinsic. Sensations are intrinsically representational, and that is how sensory experiences can have their representational content by virtue of their sensory or phenomenal character.

An example might help: I talked earlier about the sensory experience of the tree in the quad as coming into view and about how the experience of objects as coming into or receding from view contributes to the representation of them as mind-independent. When I experience the tree in the quad as coming into view I experience it as getting closer. To say this is to say that I have the *feeling* or *sensation* that the tree is getting closer. This is a comment about the phenomenal character of my sensory experience, a comment about what it is like to have that experience. Of course, it is also a comment about its representational content, but at least part of the reason that my sensory experience represents the tree as getting closer is that it has a certain phenomenal character. If it didn't feel to me as if the tree in the quad is getting closer, in what sense does my sensory experience nevertheless represent the tree as getting closer? In contrast, if my experience has its representational content by virtue of its phenomenology it is no surprise that it has the representational content which it so plainly has.

In this example the phenomenal character of my sensory experience is assumed to be representational: what the experience is like is specified by how it represents things as being. This implies, plausibly enough, that the sensation of the tree as getting closer has correctness conditions: if it turns out to be a trick of the light, and the tree isn't in fact getting any closer, then how my experience feels is not veridical, and this way of talking about my sensation is in keeping with the idea that sensations have veridicality or correctness conditions. Indeed, the sensation of the tree as getting closer is not just intentional but intrinsically intentional. It is the sensation it is, and has the phenomenal character it has, because it is the sensation or impression of the tree as coming closer rather than, say, a sensation or impression of the tree as receding. My sensory experience has its representational content by virtue of the intrinsic intentionality of my sensation. To put the point in more general terms, the intentionality of sensory experience can be phenomenal because the phenomenal is itself intentional.

Whereas (I) challenges Campbell's assumption that sensations aren't representational, (II) questions the assumption that sensations would have to be intrinsically representational in order for sensory experiences to have their intentional contents by virtue of their phenomenal character. How is that possible? Because sensations that are not themselves representational can still be *structured*, and the intentionality of sensory experience can be accounted for by reference to the structure of sensations. Kant has something like this in mind in the *Critique of Pure Reason*. Sensory experiences are what he calls 'empirical intuitions', and he argues that empirical intuitions have both form and matter. Sensations, which Kant believes are not intrinsically representational, are the matter of empirical intuition. The forms of empirical intuition are the orders or manners in which the sensations that constitute its matter are given to consciousness. Kant famously argues that space and time are the two forms of intuition. The implication is that sensations come to us in spatio-temporal arrays, and that this helps to account for the intentional content of sensory experience.

Sensations can be spatially ordered because they are bodily occurrences, and they are able to represent objects in space at least in part because they are themselves spatially organized.[11]

What is compelling about Kant's discussion is not the particular account he gives of the structure of sensation but the underlying notion that the phenomenal is structured and that the representational content of sensory experience is partly explained by the structure of the phenomenal. Katalin Farkas has something similar in mind in this passage:

> Consider a typical visual experience like surveying the scene in front of you. This kind of experience is overwhelmingly presentational: objects and their properties appear as experience-independent. The scene provides lots of details that you can explore in typical ways: if you turn your head, or approach an object, the quality of the experience changes in very familiar and highly predictable ways, suggesting the presence of an experience-independent state of affairs.

(2013, p. 108)

To talk about phenomenal features of perceptual experiences as 'organised into a systematic, cross-modally coherent and predictable order' is to talk about what Farkas calls the 'structure of experience', and her suggestion is that this structure is 'responsible for the phenomenal appearance of an experience-independent object' (2013, p. 109). The details of Farkas's account of the structure of experience are different from Kant's but the underlying idea is similar: the phenomenal has its own structure, and this opens up the possibility that the intentionality of sensory experience is constituted by its phenomenal features.

There remains the issue of blindsight. Does the possibility of a person responding to visual stimuli without consciously perceiving them support Campbell's idea that phenomenal consciousness can be subtracted from sensory experience without fundamentally affecting its representational content? That depends on whether blindsight patients are in perceptual states which, without being conscious, not only represent mind-independent objects but represent them as possessing the characteristics which ordinary sensory experiences represent them as possessing. It's not clear that they do. From the fact that blindsight patients are responsive to visual stimuli it doesn't follow that they are perceptually representing objects or representing them as mind-independent. At best they are doing these things in an attenuated sense, and can grasp concepts of mind-independent material objects only because they do also have sensory experiences. Sensory experiences not only represent objects but represent them as continuing to exist unperceived, as being

---

[11] See Falkenstein 1995 for more on all this.

of a specific size while taking up more or less of the visual field, as solid, shaped, coloured, and so on. It's not credible that mere perceptual states can do all of these things, and the most straightforward explanation is: mere perceptual states aren't conscious. There is no compelling argument from blindsight that phenomenal consciousness contributes nothing to the representational content of sensory experience. Indeed, the limits to what blindsight patients are able to represent suggest precisely the opposite.

To sum up: Campbell thinks that non-conceptualist representationalism runs into the redundancy problem because it is committed to separatism. In response, I have suggested that representationalists needn't be separatists and that the phenomenal intentionality programme provides a concrete illustration of the possibility of an anti-separatist representationalism. The idea that sensory experiences have their intentional content by virtue of their phenomenology might be attacked on the basis that phenomenal features of sensory experience are sensations, and that sensations are not representational. In reply, I have outlined two ways of responding to this line of attack. If it turns out that neither (I) nor (II) is defensible then there would be a redundancy problem for representationalism, but Campbell doesn't show that (I) and (II) are indefensible. Without a convincing argument against the possibility of sensory experience having its intentional content by virtue of its phenomenology the verdict on the redundancy objection must be: not proven.

Where does this leave Berkeley's Puzzle? At one point in his discussion, Campbell introduces the puzzle in the form of a dilemma. He writes:

If you think of sensory experience as a matter of representing how things are, then it's not obvious how awareness can have a fundamental epistemic role to play, since you can have representations without awareness. (pp. 47–8)

This horn of the dilemma is the redundancy problem for representationalism. The alternative is to think of sensory experience as a matter of having sensations. This makes consciousness the key to sensory experience, but now there is another problem:

If we think of sensory experience as a matter of having sensations, then it's hard to see how sensory experience can be providing knowledge, in the first instance, of anything but those sensations themselves. (p. 47)

This horn of the dilemma is a problem for what Campbell calls 'sensationalism' and for what I referred to in Chapter 5 as 'sensationism'. We might try escaping this dilemma by proposing a hybrid approach according to which 'our representations of the mind-independent world are grounded in sensational aspects of perception'

(p. 48). We can call this hybrid approach *sensationist representationalism*. But now we run into the following version of Berkeley's Puzzle:

(1) There is a distinction between representational and sensational aspects of perceptual experience.

(2) All the representations we can form have the contents they do in virtue of their connections to the sensational aspects of experience.

(3) Representations that derive their meanings from their connections to sensation can only relate to how things are with sensations.

Faced with this argument, the only way out, Campbell argues, is to adopt the relational view of sensory experience.

It should now be clear how we should deal with the dilemma: with respect to the first horn, there is no conflict between thinking that sensory experience is a matter of representing how things are, and thinking that awareness plays a fundamental epistemic role. As we have seen, the manner in which sensory experience represents how things are is grounded in conscious awareness. This implies that consciousness is intentional, as indeed it is. With respect to the second horn, the idea that sensory experience is a matter of having sensations only makes it hard to see how sensory experience can be providing knowledge of anything but sensations on the assumption that sensations don't represent anything beyond themselves. This is what sensationists like Berkeley think, and it is striking how much Campbell concedes to Berkeley on this point. But representationalists should refuse to think of sensations in this way. Indeed, if sensations are themselves representational then it may not make all that much difference to Berkeley's Puzzle whether we say that sensory experience is a matter of representing how the world is or a matter of having sensations, given that sensations represent how the world is. In effect, the representational content of sensory experience is grounded in sensation, and this is the hybrid approach. Sensationist representationalism endorses the phenomenal intentionality programme and is effectively the approach I have been recommending in this chapter. Unlike the relational view, sensationist representationalism has no trouble explaining how our grasp of concepts of mind-independent objects can be explained by the role of sensory experience.

Berkeley's Puzzle is supposed to be a problem for sensationist representationalism but it would be much more accurate to say that sensationist representationalism is a problem for Berkeley's Puzzle, in so far as the puzzle depends on the three claims I have just quoted. What is objectionable about (1) is not the bare notion of a distinction between sensational and representational aspects of sensory experience but Campbell's insistence on interpreting this distinction as implying a commitment to separatism. Without separatism, there is no decisive redundancy objection to representationalism. The problem with (2) is that it is stronger than it needs to be. There is no need to say that *all* the representations we can form have the contents they do in virtue of their connections to sensation. What sensationism representationalism claims is not that there can be no representations that aren't grounded in sensation but that it wouldn't be possible for sensory experience to represent objects as mind-independent, in a way that grounds our grasp of concepts of mind-independent objects, were it not for the role of sensory awareness or phenomenal consciousness. As for (3), only an extremely impoverished conception of sensations could lead one to endorse this claim. If sensations are intentional then it's false that representations that derive their meanings from their links to sensation can only relate to how things are with sensations. They can also relate to how things are with the objects our sensations represent.

The fundamental point is this: sensory experience can explain our grasp of concepts of mind-independent objects because it represents mind-independent objects, and represents them as mind-independent. Sensationist representationalism solves, or dissolves, Berkeley's Puzzle by arguing against Berkeley's conception of sensory experience, and showing how this conception relies on assumptions about the nature of sensory experience that there is no good reason to accept. According to Campbell, the puzzle is to describe the explanatory role of sensory experience 'without being driven to the conclusion that all we can have knowledge of is experiences' (p. 18). The point I have been making in response is that on a representationalist view of sensory experience there is no serious danger of our being driven to this conclusion.

Campbell's Epilogue

The main problem posed by Berkeley's Puzzle is, I think, to explain how it can be that sensory experience, the buzzing, blooming world of conscious perception, grounds our concepts of a mind-independent world. How can sensory experience be providing knowledge of anything but sensory experience itself? In his insightful discussion, Quassim Cassam gives an answer. He says:

As I walk towards the tree in the quad I experience it as coming into view. But experiencing the tree as coming into *view* is not the same as experiencing it coming into *existence*. To experience the tree as coming into view is to experience it as something that was there already, and as coming into view because I am moving closer. As I keep walking, the tree eventually recedes until at some point I can no longer see it. To experience the tree as receding from view is not to experience it as diminishing in size. Receding is not the same as ceasing to exist, and the experience of an object gradually disappearing from view is not the experience of it gradually ceasing to exist. My experience represents the tree as *persisting* as my location changes and I move away. To the extent that my sensory experience represents the tree as a persisting thing it represents it as mind-independent, but the experience of objects as coming into view or as disappearing from view is not confined to creatures with concepts. (P. 162)

So your perception of the tree represents it as stable in size (and so on) through variations in your experience of it; and represents the existence of the tree as independent of your observation of it, in that the thing does not seem to be coming into and going out of existence as it comes into view and goes out of view. There is similarly, presumably, the phenomenon of constancy for colours: we don't, in general, perceive the colours of objects as springing into existence or going out of existence as we observe them, and we often perceive the colours of objects as being stable through changes in illumination that affect their appearance. If ordinary perception represents objects and colours as mind-independent in this sense, isn't that enough to let us answer Berkeley, and to explain how sensory experience can be grounding the conception of a mind-independent world?

Cassam mentions Tyler Burge as holding a similar view to his own:

A closely related way of thinking about the representation of mind-independence in sensory experience is in terms of what Tyler Burge calls 'perceptual constancies'. These are 'capacities to represent a given particular, property, relation, or kind as the same, despite significant differences in registration of proximal stimulation' (2009, p. 318). For example, 'we can see an entity as being of a specific size while taking up more or less of the visual field' (2009, p. 318). As I walk towards the tree in the quad it takes up more of my visual field but does not appear to change in size. The sensory representation of the tree as the same despite changes in the registration of proximal stimulation does not presuppose my possession of concepts but nevertheless amounts to the mental representation of the tree as mind-independent. Like the representation of the tree's persistence, the representation of constancy is the representation of the tree's existence as independent of sensory experience. (Pp. 162–3)

I might mention that a complementary view is also suggested by Susanna Siegel, who says that our visual experiences characteristically represent the mind-independence of objects by representing something like the following complex conditions:

(SI) If S changes her perspective on o, then o will not thereby move...
(PC) If S substantially changes her perspective on o, her visual phenomenology will change as a result of this change.

(2010, pp. 178–9; cf. pp. 182, 189–94)

(PC) emphasizes the other side of the picture: that there will be variation in one's experience of an object as one changes one's perspective on it, even though the object itself does not change. Cassam and Burge emphasize the perceived constancy of the object through variation in perception of it. Siegel emphasizes the variation in perception of the object with variation in the perceiver's situation. But these seem to be complementary emphases in a single picture rather than conflicting views.

This is, evidently, an appealing explanation of how representationalism might try to address Berkeley's Puzzle. There are two problems I want to focus on:

(1) It doesn't explain what work sensory experience does in grounding our concepts of mind-independent objects.
(2) It doesn't characterize the sense in which we ordinarily think of concrete objects as mind-independent.

To see the first problem, notice, on the face of it, you could give an explanation of the role of perception in grounding thought about a mind-independent world that, while similar to Cassam's, gave no explanatory role to sensory experience. Tyler Burge actually advocates this position. As Cassam says, Burge's account of the representation of mind-independence is similar to his own. Yet Burge gives no role to sensory experience. Burge gives the jumping spider as an example of creature that plainly meets his criteria, relating to perceptual constancy, for the representation of a mind-independent reality (2010, pp. 515–16). But establishing that the spider meets those criteria does not require that we show it to be conscious. As Burge puts it, in giving an analysis of what perception is, and explaining its role in cognition, 'I drop the association with consciousness' (2010, p. 368).

The second problem is this. Does Cassam's talk of 'persistence and constancy', whether or not it relates specifically to *conscious* perception, really hit what is central to our conception of objects as mind-independent? Doesn't it merely point out some corollaries of mind-independence rather than addressing the thing itself? The problem here is to specify exactly what it is about the environment that perceptual constancy reveals. Suppose, for example, that you (or someone else, gentle reader) are plagued by an odour of rotting fish in your kitchen. You can't figure out where it is coming from. You can triangulate it. As you move towards some locations the smell gets more intense, as you move away the smell gets less bad. When you escape from the kitchen altogether, the smell, as Cassam says, recedes rather than seeming to go out of existence. When you go back in, it's still there. So far as Cassam's 'persistence and constancy' criteria go, your sense of smell is therefore representing the odour as fully objective. When you see and kick a rock, on Cassam's account, your perception is not representing the thing as any more objectively there than your sense of smell represents the odour of fish as objectively there.

You might feel that this objection is unfair. I said that Cassam's explanation of the sense in which perception represents things as mind-independent doesn't differentiate between perception of odours and perception of rocks. But there is a passage in which he seems to be addressing just this point:

> Not everything that is mind-independent is a material object. The shadow cast by the tree exists independently of being experienced but is not a material object. In contrast the tree is a material object, and my sensory experience of the tree is the sensory experience of it not just as mind-independent but as a mind-independent *material* object. In what sense? Locke held that what makes an object a material object is that it has 'primary qualities' such as shape and solidity. The tree in the quad has primary qualities and the fact that it has primary qualities is evident in my sensory experience. My sensory experience represents the tree as shaped, located, and solid, and thereby represents it as a material object. It doesn't follow that what I am experiencing is a material object rather than, say, a hologram, but my experience is veridical only if it is material. (P. 163)

One reading of Cassam's position is that odours and shadows and rocks and trees are all mind-independent, the former two not possessed of shape and solidity, the latter two possessed of shape and solidity, and all that we have here is a relatively arbitrary distinction between different types of mind-independent object.

I think that the problem here is that there is a more basic notion of mind-independence, that has to do with what we might call the *causal autonomy* of the world. The rocks and mountains around us have lives of their own. They have causal structures that don't depend on their relations to any mind. Suppose a rock falls. The way the fall affects the rock depends, in part, on the internal constitution of the rock itself, what it's made of, and so on. Whether there's a mark on the rock as a result of the fall will depend, in part, on what kind of stuff the rock was made of, how hard it is. If there's a mark on the rock later, that will be, in part, because of how the rock was earlier. If the rock rolls, the mark will now be found at a new location. The rock is the mechanism by which causal influence—such as the effect of the fall on the rock—is transmitted over time. None of this has anything to do with a mind. The things around us have their own causal structures, their own causal lives. If light bounces off a thing and affects a perceiver, the object itself will be largely unaffected. How the object strikes the perceiver will depend on the way the object is itself, and on the perceiver's point of view. But the relation to a mind here, that the object is affecting a mind, may leave the object unchanged. That's the basis of the perception of persistence and constancy that Cassam talks about. It's because the object is unchanged by perception of it that there can be perception of it as unchanging through variation in how and whether it is perceived.

The difference that Cassam points to between shadows and trees seems to me to be a difference principally in the causal structures of the two kinds of things. Shadows are epiphenomena; unlike trees, they do not have any significant internal causal structure. The way the shadow is later does not causally depend on the way the shadow was earlier. The way the shadow is later causally depends only on such factors as how the tree is then and where the sun is then. If doesn't matter how the shadow was earlier. If the shadow earlier had been obliterated by momentarily focusing a spotlight on it, that wouldn't make any difference at all to how the shadow is now. It's because shadows are epiphenomenal in this way that we don't think of them as material objects. Similar points apply to the smell of rotting fish in the kitchen. The smell doesn't have an internal causal structure in the way that a rock does. The way the smell is later doesn't causally depend on the way the smell was earlier. It depends only on how things are with the stuff generating the smell. Smells are epiphenomena; trees and rocks are not.

When Cassam tries to explain the distinction between shadows and trees by focusing on Locke's distinction between primary and secondary qualities, I don't think he means to be giving an arbitrary distinction between mind-independent objects that happen to satisfy one list of properties as opposed to another list of properties. I think he is, in effect, registering another aspect of the causal autonomy of objects, namely that some properties seem to be more central to the causal structures of objects than others. There are two ways in which shape and size, and so on, might be argued to be more central to the causal structure of a rock, say, than is colour:

(1) The causal interwovenness of primary qualities.
(2) The primary qualities of a single object over time constitute a causal progression; the secondary qualities of an object over time constitute an epiphenomenal progression.

Both of these notions need some explanation, and the second, in particular, is open to challenge. To see what I mean by 'interwovenness', suppose that you're shaping a flint into an arrowhead for hunting. You have various desiderata: you want it to fly well, to have significant stopping power on impact, and so on. So you are acting on various characteristics of the flint: its shape, size, weight, and so on. The outcome for each of the desiderata will be the joint product of the combination of shape, size, weight, and so on. No one of these factors alone will determine the stopping power of the arrow, for example. In contrast, the colour of the arrowhead, though you can indeed affect that, will not combine with any of these other properties to yield some significant outcome. In general, colour acts only to affect the perception of the colour of the object, and it largely acts alone.

To illustrate the distinction that I have in mind between epiphenomenal progressions and causal progressions, consider the kind of clock that is projected onto a screen. So on the screen there is a pool of light on which you can see the numbers on the clock and the hands going around them. Now here the positions of the hands on the screen at one time are not caused by the positions of the hands on the screen at an earlier time. They are caused by the working of the machinery in the projection system. So the various positions of the hands on the screen over time are an epiphenomenal, rather than a causal, progression. An epiphenomenal progression is a temporal sequence whose earlier members are not the causes of later members. A causal progression, in contrast, is a temporal sequence whose earlier members are the causes of later members. For example, if you consider the sequence of positions of the hands on an ordinary physical clock, the positions of the hands earlier are among the causes of the positions of the hands later. If you had reached in and changed the positions of the hands earlier, that would have made a difference to the positions of the hands later.

Now a natural thought about the primary qualities of a concrete object, as opposed to its secondary qualities, is that the primary qualities of an object over time constitute a causal progression, whereas the secondary qualities of the object over time constitute a phenomenal progression. One fundamental argument here was given by Locke:

Pound an Almond, and the clear white Colour will be altered into a dirty one, and the sweet Taste into an oily one. What real Alteration can the beating of the Pestle make in any Body, but an Alteration in the Texture of it?

(*Essay*, II/viii/20)

By 'Texture' here Locke means the microphysical constitution of the thing. The style of argument here will be familiar to anyone who knows, for example, popular accounts of Wilder Penfield's electrical stimulation of the temporal lobes. If electrical stimulation of the temporal lobes generates, for example, specific conscious memories, doesn't that show that conscious memories are merely epiphenomena thrown off by the brain? The causal progression over time is a causal progression in the brain; the conscious memories over time are merely an epiphenomenal progression. Similarly, Locke is arguing, since colours are affected by operations such as pounding, which can only be thought to be acting on the underlying microphysics of the almond, the real causal progression over time is a progression at the level of microphysics. The colour of an object over time is merely an epiphenomenal progression.

I think that these lines of thought are what underlie the notion that the primary qualities of a material object matter for its identity in a way that the secondary qualities of the object do not. The unity of an object over time is a causal unity. And the interwoven causal progression constituted by the primary qualities of the object matters for its identity in a way that the epiphenomenal progression constituted by its secondary qualities does not.

I actually think that we should resist this line of thought, at least insofar as it relates to colour. Consider again the case of Penfield's patient. You might acknowledge the possibility of interventions at the brain level that affect someone's conscious memories, but want to hold on to the idea that conscious memories can be causally efficacious. Similarly, you might acknowledge, with Locke, the possibility of interventions at the microphysical level that affect the colour of an object, but hold on to the idea that colour is causally efficacious.

Still, this is not the fundamental problem with giving so much weight to the distinction between primary and secondary qualities in explaining what it is to perceive an object as mind-independent. The real problem is that our experience of objects as mind-independent does not seem to be reducible to our experience of the object as having primary qualities (together with perceptual constancies). As we saw earlier, we think of concrete objects not merely as causally connected, but as the mechanisms by which causal influence is transmitted over time. And what provides us with this conception of physical objects as mechanisms is our experience of the physical objects themselves. One way to see the point here is to reflect on a comparison between the primary qualities of a concrete object and the psychological properties of a person. The psychological properties of a person, such as belief, desire, and memory, will be interwoven in generating the behaviour of that person, as I said the primary qualities of a flint will be interwoven in generating its behaviour. And the psychological states of a person over time will very often constitute a causal, rather than an epiphenomenal, progression. So if the interwoven and causal character of primary qualities is enough for us to have the conception of a concrete physical object, why is grasp of the interwoven and causal character of psychological properties not enough for us to have the conception of the mind as a 'psychological object'? It seems to me to be a datum that we don't have any such conception of 'the mind': that was Hume's point when he said that, on entering into himself, he 'encounter'd only various particular perceptions' (*Treatise* I/iv/6). I think the moral is that we can't explain the notion of a concrete object in terms of the relations among causally significant properties. Rather, the conception of a concrete object, as a mechanism for the transmission of causal influence, is made available to us by sensory experience of objects. Hume's point, that we have no such experience of the mind as a concrete unity, is on this view not a datum in need of explanation. It is, rather, the datum that explains why we do not have the conception of the mind as a concrete unity.

I've said that if we focus on phenomena such as perceptual constancy in trying to explain the sense in which we have sensory experience of mind-independent objects, we achieve only an attenuated conception of mind-independence. We have to be able to characterize the sense in which we experience objects as autonomous causal unities. Is this something that the representationalist about perception could simply acknowledge? The trouble for the representationalist is that it's very difficult to see how to give any account of perceptual experience that recognizes perception of mind-independence in any more full-blooded sense than that provided by perceptual constancy. The problem is a basic one for the representationalist: that representationalism deals only with the aspects of the environment that are visually *accessed* by the subject. The problem is that the phenomena of object perception are best understood at the level of visual *selection*.

The usual formulations of representationalism do not provide any way of dealing with aspects of experience that relate to the level of visual selection, rather than the level of visual access. Consider how the representationalist is to explain the sense in which the representations that they have in mind are *conscious*, or 'personal level', representations. Cassam writes:

> [M]y sensory experience gives me reason to believe that there is a tree in the quad precisely because it *represents* a tree and *represents* it as being in the quad. This is the representational content of my sensory experience, and the view I am defending is that the way to make sense of the epistemic role of sensory experience is by reference to the idea that sensory experience has representational content. (P. 166)

We could put the idea by saying that perceptual representations are taken to be *seemings*: the content of a perceptual representation is a matter of how things seem to the subject. Getting knowledge from visual representation is then just a matter of taking things to be as they seem. The level of visual experience that we are dealing with here is the level of *access*: visual attention has made it explicit that this is a tree and that it's in the quad.

A similar line of thought is developed by Susanna Siegel: 'The sense in which experiences have contents (according to the Content View)...picks up the strand of ordinary usage that takes contents to be things conveyed by sources of information (as when we speak of the contents of a newspaper story)' (2010, p. 28). Something like this notion of content being 'conveyed' to the subject is evidently required if we are to explain what it means to say that representations are 'there in experience'. What does it mean? Siegel says there are three ways content can be 'conveyed':

1. [I]f it would be content of explicit beliefs that are natural to form on the basis of visual experience.
2. [I]f it enables the experience to guide bodily actions. For instance, suppose you see the door but don't form any explicit beliefs about the shape of its doorknob, yet you adjust your grip in advance of touching the doorknob as you reach for it.
3. [A] content is conveyed to the subject by her experience if it is manifest to introspection that it is a content of experience.

(2010, p. 51)

This passage again brings out the sense in which the representationalist deals only with aspects of the visual scene that are *accessed* by the subject. Recall the case we discussed at length in Chapter 3: someone without colour concepts, without colour induction or any ability to sort or match things by colour, who can nonetheless see the figure 5 in a colour-blindness test. Let us stick with our simplifying assumption that the figure 5 is distinguished from its background only by its colour; colour is not being used merely as a guide to form or motion. Such a person has no potential to form beliefs about the colour of the object, no tendency to use colour itself as a guide to action, and no introspective knowledge of the colour aspects of the experience; no *access* to the colour of the 5. Nonetheless, since the 5 is plainly visible to this person, the colour of the thing must be making a difference to visual experience. If there weren't differentiations of colour in the visual experience itself, the 5 wouldn't be consciously visible at all. The 5 is being visually *selected* on the basis of its colour. But the subject isn't capable of accessing the colour of the 5. It's not easy to see how the representationalist might plan to accommodate this kind of phenomenon. The representation of colour must be there in the experience if the colour is to be there in the experience at all; but in what sense is the *representation* of colour 'there in the experience' if it can't be accessed by the subject? On a relationalist picture, as we saw, this kind of case simply illustrates the kind of causal structure there can be in the subject's experiential relations to one and another characteristic of the environment. (I am here, of course, setting aside the still more basic problem, highlighted by Siegel's 'newspaper' example, that the representationalist can't explain the sense in which colour itself is actually there in the experience.)

A similar point might be made about Alex Byrne's argument, on behalf of representationalism, that (roughly) if two perceptions are phenomenally different, there must be a difference in how things *seem* to the subject (Byrne 2001). Suppose you have a subject A looking at an object differentiated from its background only by its colour (not by form or motion). And suppose you have a subject B looking at an object differentiated from its background only by its colour. And suppose that the two situations are exactly the same in every respect, except that the colours of the two objects are different. This hypothesis seems to demand, if the subjects both experience those objects, that the colours of the objects be making a difference to their experiences. Yet the colour vision of those subjects may be entirely instrumental for object perception. The subjects may be quite unable to engage in judgements about colour, or making any other use of visual access to colour. (This need not be something that could be easily rectified: it may be something that is deeply grounded in the brain structure of the species to which those individuals belong, their level of maturity, or just the specifics of those two individual subjects.) So although their colour experiences are different, there may be no difference in how the world *seems* to our two subjects. (The force of this point can be masked if you consider not two different subjects, but a single subject whose experience changes over time (cf. Byrne 2001). Change in colour might indeed be noticed by our subjects, given the pervasive sensitivity of the visual system to flicker; but that is not the same as showing that the objects themselves seem one way rather than another in point of colour.)

The upshot is that there's a dimension of visual experience that is missed by representationalism: the level at which properties are used to select objects from their backgrounds. I have concentrated on a closely specified example to make the point vivid: but of course that distinction is there in the perceptions even of someone who is capable of easily accessing and thinking about the colours of things. Now although visual experience certainly relates to objects, it is arguable that our visual experience of objects is to be understood not at the level of *access*, but at the level of *selection*. In what sense is the object the *unit* of visual attention? To use a helpful analogy from Huang (2010), we can contrast two notions of 'unit'. One has to do with measurement: when you are making explicit the various characteristics of a scene before you, what units do you use in characterizing it? Another has to do with divisibility: when you are visually grabbing an aspect of a perceived scene in order to find out about it, what is the smallest unit that vision generally uses? Objects are plainly the units of vision in this second sense, that what we pull out from a scene is an entire object (thus, for example, it's hard to keep track of just one end of a line, without also keeping track of the other end). But that's not to say that accessing the characteristics of one end of the line automatically gives you access to the characteristics of the other end of the line. I suggested earlier that our experience of objects as mind-independent should be characterized at the level of selection, rather than at the level of access. Thus, to characterize the sense in which we visually experience objects as mind-independent, we should be looking at the way in which vision grabs and keeps track of objects over time. The ways in which vision does this reflect the immanent causal structures of the objects being tracked. We can keep track of objects through radical changes in their qualitative characteristics, through gaps in their observable spatial paths, even through discontinuities in their spatio-temporal paths. When we visually keep track of an object, we are keeping track of it as a causally continuous thing.

Let's go back to the question I raised earlier: Does representationalism explain why the conception of objects as mind-independent requires sensory experience? In addressing this Cassam appeals to the 'phenomenal intentionality research programme', according to which 'intentional states, including sensory experiences, have their representational or intentional contents "by virtue of their phenomenology"', as Horgan and Tienson (2002) put it. As Uriah Kriegel remarks, '[p]erhaps the most important kind of claim made on behalf of phenomenal intentionality is that it is in some way *basic* among forms of intentionality' (2013, p. 13). This echoes the first idea driving Berkeley's Puzzle:

Sensory experience is the foundation of both our knowledge that things are thus and so, and our knowledge of what things and properties are there in our environment.

We can only think about the things and properties around us because our thoughts are grounded in our experiences of the things and properties around us. Recall the second idea driving Berkeley's Puzzle:

Sensory experience can provide knowledge only of sensory experience itself.

Like the relationalist, the phenomenal intentionalist aims to resist this popular idea. In fact, experience provides knowledge of the objects and properties experienced, rather than knowledge of experience itself. To illustrate his point about the dependence of thought of objects as mind-independent on sensory experience, Cassam writes:

When I experience the tree in the quad as coming into view I experience it as getting closer. To say this is to say that I have the *feeling* or *sensation* that the tree is getting closer. This is a comment about the phenomenal character of my sensory experience, a comment about what it is like to have that experience. (Pp. 173–4)

When Cassam talks about 'the *feeling*... that the tree is getting closer', or 'the... *sensation* that the tree is getting closer', he wants to be talking about a representational state, but not one that could occur in the absence of consciousness. The trouble is to understand why not. Why couldn't we, with Burge 'drop the association with consciousness', but still have perceptual representation of object constancy?

As I understand him, Cassam wants to acknowledge not just that it's intuitive that there is a necessary connection between intentionality and sensory experience, but that our ability to think about or represent objects as mind-independent can in some sense be explained in terms of the connection between thought and sensory experience. At this point, it seems to me, there is a lot of pressure on Cassam to endorse the relational view of experience. The whole point of the relational view is to provide a conception of experience as tying one up to the things and properties around one in a way that can ground your abilities to think about those things and properties. If you don't have that conception of sensory experience, how can you say that we can have thoughts about the things and properties around us 'in virtue of' their connection to phenomenology?

Cassam's picture is that sensory experience involves both representation and sensation, and that representation is grounded in sensation. Either we say that sensations are intrinsically representational, or we say that at any rate:

Even if sensations aren't intrinsically representational this doesn't mean that the representational content of sensory experiences cannot be grounded in their phenomenal character. (P. 173)

And Cassam really seems to have in mind some explanatory connection between intentionality, on the one hand, and sensation, or phenomenal character, on the other:

To the extent that sensory experiences represent objects as mind-independent, and thereby ground our grasp of concepts of mind-independent objects, they do so by virtue of their phenomenal character. (P. 172)

Why does Cassam talk about sensation at all? I think it's because he is trying to hold on to internalism about sensory experience: the idea that the qualitative character of sensory experience does not depend constitutively on any relations between the subject and the environment. This means that the 'qualitative character of experience' can't be thought of as constituted by the qualitative character of the environment of the subject. It has to be something internal to the subject. That's what Cassam calls 'sensation'. So, as he says, the minimum that he wants is that representation is grounded in sensation. In particular, representation of objects as mind-independent is grounded in sensation. But here the original problem seems as difficult as ever. But how can representation of mind-independence *depend* on sensation, in this sense? If the sensation is merely 'considered by itself without relation to any external object', in Reid's phrase (*Essays on the Intellectual Powers of Man*, 1785/2002, pp. 150–1), how can it be of the slightest help in forming representations of the mind-independence of external objects? The simplest way to get from the doctrine of phenomenal intentionality to the relational view of experience is to ask: how could the ability to represent the world be *explained* by sensory experience? On the relational view, sensory experiences should be thought of as relations between the subject and the external, qualitative world. Characterizing what it is like to have the experience is, in part, a matter of characterizing the external world that is being experienced. And it is because the intentional states are connected to these relational experiences that we can think about the external, qualitative world at all.

Cassam's Epilogue

The question which representationalism and the relational view are both trying to answer is:

(HP) How is it possible for sensory experience to ground our grasp of concepts of mind-independent objects?

A related question is: how is it possible for sensory experience to provide us with *knowledge* of mind-independent objects? I will focus on (HP), which assumes that we do grasp concepts of such objects, and that sensory experience does play a role in explaining our grasp of them. The problem, as Berkeley sees it, is that there are various factors that make it look impossible for sensory experience to ground our grasp of concepts of mind-independent objects. This is what gives rise to (HP). Like other broadly Kantian 'how-possible' questions, (HP) 'acquires its characteristic philosophical bite by being asked against the background of materials for a line of thought that, if made explicit, would purport to reveal that the question's topic is not actually possible at all' (McDowell 1996, p. xiii).[1]

I argue that representationalism about sensory experience provides a straightforward response to (HP). Campbell's solution to Berkeley's Puzzle draws on his relational view of experience. Campbell is unimpressed by representationalism's response to Berkeley's Puzzle, and in his Epilogue he concentrates on clarifying his objections to representationalism rather than on defending the relational view. He has three main objections to representationalism, and what I want to do here is to respond to each of these objections, before considering the extent to which representationalism can take on board Campbell's insights. The main point I want to insist on, however, is that Campbell's discussion contains no clear, knock-down objection to representationalism as a solution to Berkeley's Puzzle. On a representationalist view of experience, (HP) loses its characteristic philosophical bite because there is nothing to suggest that sensory experience *can't* ground concepts of mind-independent objects.

---

[1] In the terminology of Cassam 2007 this makes 'how-possible' questions 'obstacle-dependent'. The question 'How is X possible?' doesn't arise in a philosophical vacuum. We normally ask this question when there is something that makes X look impossible or problematic.

How should representationalism respond to (HP)? The idea I develop in my chapters is that sensory experience can ground our grasp of concepts of mind-independent objects, and make it possible for us to grasp such concepts, because and to the extent that:

1. Sensory experience represents mind-independent objects, and represents them as mind-independent by representing them as persisting and/or constant.
2. Sensory experience can represent mind-independent objects without the subject needing to have concepts of such objects. The representational content of sensory experience is, in this sense, non-conceptual.
3. Sensory experience has its non-conceptual representational content by virtue of its phenomenology or conscious character. The intentionality of sensory experience is phenomenal intentionality. I will refer to this as the Phenomenal Intentionality Thesis, or PIT for short.[2]

Notice what does *not* follow from this approach to (HP): it doesn't follow that only sensory experiences have representational content. Pictures, neural assemblies, and tree rings can all have representational content, though not in the same way that sensory experiences can have this type of content. It also doesn't follow that sensory experience is *essential* for a grasp of concepts of objects. It's not true, in general, that if X makes Y possible then X is necessary for Y.[3] Catching the Eurostar makes it possible to get from London to Paris but there are many other ways of doing it. In principle, sensory experience might make it possible for us to grasp concepts of objects even if there are other ways in which a grasp of such concepts might be grounded.

This might be an issue for Campbell. He implies that sensory experience grounds our grasp of concepts of objects only if the latter 'depends essentially' on sensory experience, but Berkeley's question is: how is it *possible* for sensory experience to play a role in grounding our grasp of concepts of mind-independent objects? Why should a satisfactory answer to this question have to demonstrate that the explanatory role of experience is an *essential* role? When something is incorrectly thought to be impossible, in the way Berkeley thinks that it is impossible for experience to ground concepts of mind-independent objects, the proper way to deal with this is to show that, and how, what is claimed to be impossible is in fact possible.

---

[2] Key discussions of phenomenal intentionality include Horgan and Tienson 2002 and Loar 2003. See also the essays collected in Kriegel 2003.
[3] See the first two chapters of Cassam 2007 for much more on this.

However, showing how something is possible is not the same as showing that it is necessary. I will come back to this.

Here is a brief summary of Campbell's objections to representationalism, as stated in his Epilogue:

(a) 'It doesn't characterize the sense in which we ordinarily think of concrete objects as mind-independent' (p. 180).

(b) 'It doesn't explain what work sensory experience does in grounding our concepts of mind-independent objects' (p. 180).

(c) It misses a key dimension of visual experience, 'the level at which properties are used to select objects from their backgrounds' (p. 187).

Of these, (b) is the most serious. In my chapters I refer to it as the redundancy objection since it amounts to the objection that representationalism makes sensory experience redundant in relation to our grasp of concepts of objects. PIT was my response to this objection and Campbell's Epilogue is of special interest in this connection because it responds to PIT.

Let's start with (a). Campbell is critical of the notion that mind-independence is just a matter of persistence and constancy. On my account, sensory experience represents objects as mind-independent by representing them as there anyway (persistent) and the same despite variations in experience (constant). Campbell objects that persistence and constancy only provide an 'attenuated conception of mind-independence' (p. 185) because they wrongly imply that even such things as smells and shadows are 'fully objective'. Campbell believes 'there is a more basic notion of mind-independence, that has to do with what we might call the *causal autonomy* of the world' (p. 181). This more basic notion explains why, even though they can be persistent and constant, smells and shadows are mere 'epiphenomena' (p. 182).

Here is a vivid illustration of what Campbell means by 'causal autonomy':

Suppose a rock falls. The way the fall affects the rock depends, in part, on the internal constitution of the rock itself, what it's made of and so on. Whether there's a mark on the rock as a result of the fall will depend, in part, on what kind of stuff the rock was made of, how hard it is. If there's a mark on the rock later, that will be, in part, because of how the rock was earlier... The rock is the mechanism by which causal influence—such as the effect of the fall on the rock—is transmitted... None of this has anything to do with a mind. The things... have their own causal structures, their own causal lives. (pp. 181–2)

Causal autonomy in this sense is what smells lack, and that's why they are epiphenomenal. A smell does not have an internal causal structure in the way that a rock does. The way the rock is later depends on the way it was earlier but the way the smell is later doesn't depend on the way it was earlier. Just talking about persistence and constancy makes it hard to do justice to this fundamental difference between different kinds of 'object'.

Here are three observations about this line of argument.

i. It doesn't amount to an objection to representationalism per se, as distinct from an objection to one aspect of one version of representationalism. The most that it shows is that representationalism needs to give a better account of what it is for objects to be mind-independent and, by implication, a better account of what it is for sensory experience to represent objects as mind-independent. Instead of saying that sensory experience represents objects as mind-independent by representing them as persisting and constant, why can't representationalism say that sensory experience represents objects as mind-independent by representing them as causally autonomous? Unless for some reason sensory experience can't have this content it's the obvious move to make if what Campbell says about mind-independence is correct.

ii. It's false that the 'persistence and constancy' account has to regard smells as 'fully objective'. What it says is that such 'entities' are mind-independent to the extent that they are persistent and constant. Here, *mind-independent* means 'capable of being perceived and of existing unperceived'. Something can be mind-independent in this sense and yet epiphenomenal and therefore not fully objective. This might be true of smells, given that they are secondary qualities. They lack primary qualities, and so aren't material objects. Not everything that is mind-independent is a material object, but the distinction between material and other objects isn't arbitrary since the primary qualities which make an object a material object also causally explain its secondary qualities. Once the 'persistence and constancy' account is modified to take this into account, it can then say what is actually true: rocks and smells are both mind-independent in virtue of being persistent and constant, but the primary qualities of rocks make them more full-bloodedly mind-independent than smells.

iii. Even by Campbell's own lights 'we can't explain the notion of a concrete object in terms of the relations among causally significant properties' (p. 185). The causal autonomy account allows the interwoven psychological states of a person to count as a 'psychological object' but 'we have no such experience of the mind as a concrete unity' (p. 185). At a sufficiently high level of abstraction, rocks, minds, dinner parties, hurricanes, and all manner of 'continuants' can be described as autonomous causal unities, just as they can all be 'persistent'. Yet, ontologically speaking, they are not on a par.

Why not? The key is that we think of concrete objects not merely as causally connected, but as 'the mechanisms by which causal influence is transmitted from place to place' (p. 31). Yet smells are mechanisms in this sense. In the example of the knife and the chopping board (Ch. 2), it is the *movement* of the knife that is the mechanism for the transmission of causal influence from place to place but smells are also capable of moving from place to place. As the smell of rotting fish which causes the kitchen to be evacuated drifts into the living room, it causes the living room to be evacuated too. The drifting of the smell is the mechanism by which the causal influence of the fish is transmitted from one place to another, but smells are epiphenomena. This isn't a basic case because smells aren't ordinary objects: 'a prototypical case of a mechanism is provided by our ordinary conception of an ordinary medium-sized object transmitting causal influence from place to place' (p. 31). To put the point another way: for an object to be mind-independent in the most basic sense it isn't enough that it is a mechanism for the transmission of causal influence from place to place. It also has to be a material object, whose causal influence is grounded in its primary qualities. At this point we have arrived, by a rather circuitous route, at what looks like a kind of synthesis of Campbell's view and mine.

I don't want to make too much of these observations about (a) because, as I've said, I don't believe that it is an objection to representationalism as such. If it's possible to deal with (a) by coming up with a position that synthesizes Campbell's view of mind-independence and mine then so much the better. Matters get much more serious with (b). The primary target of this objection is what might be called 'reductive' representationalism, which accounts for the representational content of sensory experience in causal terms.[4] In my chapters I didn't consider what a reductive representationalist might say in reply to Campbell. Instead I just pointed out that representationalism doesn't have to be reductive and that it can deal with the redundancy objection by going non-reductive and endorsing PIT. I have some thoughts about Campbell's response to non-reductive representationalism but I'd like to begin by considering what a reductive representationalist might say about his arguments.[5] My view is that both forms of representationalism have considerable room for manoeuvre but my main objective is to defend non-reductive

---

[4] A contrast between 'reductive' and 'non-reductive' representationalism is implicit in my Chapter 8. I owe to Howard Robinson the suggestion that the reductive/non-reductive distinction provides a good way of framing the discussion.

[5] What I am here calling 'non-reductive representationalism' is equivalent to what I refer to in Chapter 8 above as 'sensationist representationalism'.

representationalism against the redundancy objection. I still maintain that representationalism in this form has a viable solution to Berkeley's Puzzle.

Reductive representationalism sees what Campbell calls 'sensory experience' as made up of two distinct elements: 'mere' perceptual states, which represent by virtue of their causal relations to the objects and properties they represent, and conscious sensations. The latter account for the phenomenal character of sensory experiences, but they contribute nothing to the representational content of sensory experience, which is a wholly separate matter. This 'separatist' dimension of reductive representationalism explains Campbell's comment that 'on this analysis we would be just as well off with perceptual states that had this capacity to "display the world as objective", even if those perceptual states were not themselves conscious states' (p. 46). The implication is that reductive representationalism does not explain what work sensory experience does in grounding our concepts of mind-independent objects, and so does not solve Berkeley's Puzzle.

A hard-nosed reductive representationalist might not be bothered by this. They might think that the *point* of reductive representationalism is to make it vivid that consciousness is redundant when it comes to explaining our capacity to represent and think about objects, so it isn't an objection to reductive representationalism to point out that it does just that. The issue is whether it's true that consciousness is epistemically significant. Campbell assumes that it is, and asks how it can be true, but his assumption is not beyond dispute. Furthermore—and this is the key point—even if consciousness is explanatorily redundant in just the way that reductive representationalism implies, this doesn't mean that it doesn't have any answer to (HP). Whether sensory experiences have representational content by virtue of their conscious character or their causal role, the fact remains that they *can* represent objects and represent them as mind-independent. As long as this is so, and the representational content of sensory experience is non-conceptual, there is no reason why sensory experience couldn't be what grounds our grasp of concepts of mind-independent objects.

I take it that Campbell would be dissatisfied with this response, but would he be right to be dissatisfied? Remember what the puzzle is supposed to be:

> The main problem posed by Berkeley's Puzzle is, I think, to explain how it can be that sensory experience, the buzzing, blooming world of conscious perception, grounds our concepts of a mind-independent world. How can sensory experience be providing knowledge of anything but sensory experience itself? (p. 179)

Reductive representationalism claims to explain precisely what Campbell says needs to be explained in order to solve Berkeley's Puzzle: the proposal is that sensory experience can ground concepts of a mind-independent world by representing the mind-independent world. What is wrong with this proposal? Here are three things that might be wrong with it:

A. Sensory experiences can't ground concepts of mind-independent objects in this way if they don't have representational content, or don't represent mind-independent objects. This could be because perceptual states don't have representational content or because perceptual states are not components of sensory experiences. Either way, reductive representationalism would be in trouble but there is no indication that Campbell has anything like this in mind. Unlike Charles Travis, he doesn't argue explicitly against the idea that perception is representational, though it might be that some such thought is driving some of Campbell's arguments.

B. Sensory experiences represent mind-independent objects, but not in a way that would enable them to ground concepts of mind-independent objects. Merely having sensory experiences with the appropriate content isn't sufficient for one to grasp concepts of mind-independent objects without the appropriate background cognitive capacities. Again, this is arguable but is not Campbell's point. Having sensory experiences with the appropriate representational content might still be necessary for grasp of concepts even if it isn't sufficient.

C. If reductive representationalism is correct then sensory experiences don't represent in virtue of their conscious character. This means that even if there is a sense in which, in virtue of representing objects as mind-independent, sensory experiences can ground concepts of a mind-independent world, they can't do so *qua* sensory experiences. They can't ground concepts of mind-independent objects *qua* sensory experiences because the conscious element of sensory experiences that makes them sensory *experiences* does no work in grounding our concepts. This also implies that sensory experiences don't play an *essential* role in grounding our concepts: subtract consciousness and we would be left with something less than a sensory experience—a mere perceptual state—that can still ground our concepts. This is the 'subtraction argument' against reductive representationalism. It's an argument against reductive representationalism on the assumption that, as I put it in Chapter 6, 'the sense in which our grasp of concepts of ordinary objects and their properties is *grounded* in sensory experience is that it *depends essentially* on sensory experience'.

Although there isn't much doubt that C is Campbell's argument against reductive representationalism there is plenty of doubt about its cogency. For a start, even if you think that a sensory experience does its representing by virtue of its causal role, or by virtue of embedding a 'perceptual state' that has representational content by virtue of its causal role, it still doesn't follow that consciousness is doing no work in explaining how sensory experiences which represent objects as mind-independent can thereby ground the corresponding concepts. While consciousness might not be contributing anything to the *representational content* of sensory experience it might be contributing in other ways to the explanatory role of experience. Perhaps without consciousness perceptual states could still represent mind-independent objects but not ground concepts of mind-independent objects. Clearly, it needs be explained how consciousness could be playing this role, and it's also true that hard-nosed reductive representationalists might have little interest in arguing in this way. Nevertheless, it needs to be pointed out that the subtraction argument is too quick.

However, the biggest problem with C is that it asks reductive representational-ism to do something that was not a part of the original tender. Reductive represen-tationalism was asked to explain how sensory experience can play a certain role in our thought about the world, and this is exactly what the reductive representation-alist has done. In response, it is being objected that it's not enough for reductive representationalism to show how sensory experience can ground our concepts of a mind-independent world. It also has to explain how sensory experience can do this '*qua* sensory experience'. Where did this requirement come from? Why isn't it enough that sensory experience can ground our concepts? This is related to the point I made above about the difference between explaining how experience can be playing a role in grounding our grasp of concepts and showing that experience is essential for our grasp of concepts. Only the former is required to answer (HP), so even if the subtraction argument really does show that sensory experience isn't essential, why is that a problem? To repeat, explaining how X can do Y—how sensory experience can ground concepts of mind-independent objects—doesn't require you to demonstrate that X is necessary for Y.

The most straightforward way for Campbell to deal with this reaction to C would be to reformulate the puzzle so as to bring out more clearly what is at issue. As Campbell notes at one point, 'we might say that what is driving Berkeley's argu-ment is that idea that perceptual consciousness has an *epistemic* role to play in our cognitive lives' (p. 26), and the real question is how *that* is possible. This is Berkeley's Puzzle: to understand how *consciousness* can ground our concepts of a mind-independent world. As far as this issue is concerned, it is irrelevant that 'mere' perceptual states can represent mind-independent objects. How is the sup-posed fact that perceptual states can represent objects *without* being conscious meant to help us understand the epistemic role of *consciousness*? Faced with this question, there is a straightforward move for representationalism to make, and it is the move I made in my chapters. The obvious move is to insist that consciousness is intrinsically representational, and can ground our concepts of mind-independent objects because *it* can represent mind-independent objects. On this account, sensory experiences have representational content but they don't represent mind-independent objects only by virtue of their causal relations to mind-independent objects. Rather, they have their representational content by virtue of their conscious character. Take that away and you are left with nothing.

The position at which we now have arrived is non-reductive representationalism. What I have just been reiterating is that representationalism can deal with the redundancy objection by endorsing PIT and rejecting the assumption, shared by both Campbell and reductive representationalism, that consciousness cannot be representational in its own right. What does Campbell think is wrong with this approach? In the concluding pages of his Epilogue he quotes me as talking about the feeling or sensation of the tree in the quad as coming into view, where experiencing something as coming into view is not the same as experiencing it as coming into existence. As Campbell notes, what I'm talking about is a representational state that couldn't occur in the absence of consciousness. The trouble, he says, is to understand why not. Why couldn't we drop the association with consciousness but still have the perceptual representation of object constancy? He argues that my picture is one in which representation is grounded in sensation and that this does nothing to solve Berkeley's Puzzle:

[H]ow can representation of mind-independence *depend* on sensation in this sense? If the sensation is merely 'considered by itself without relation to any external object', in Reid's phrase...how can it be of the slightest help in forming representations of the mind-independence of external objects?

Campbell suspects that I only talk about sensation because I am an internalist about sensory experience, committed to the idea that the qualitative character of sensory experience doesn't depend constitutively on any relations between the subject and the environment. (pp. 189–90)

Taking these points in reverse order, my position is not that the qualitative character of sensory experience doesn't depend constitutively on relations between the subject and the object of experience. My view is that it *also* depends on other factors, such as the constitution of the subject. This isn't to deny that relations between the subject and the environment also matter, so the resulting position has both internalist and externalist elements. The appropriate response to Campbell's tendency to underestimate the subject's contribution to the qualitative character of experience isn't to make the opposite mistake of underestimating the object's contribution.

The crux of the matter is what Campbell writes in the passage in which he refers to Reid. Campbell asks how a sensation can be of the slightest help in forming representations of mind-independence. It's easy to read this question as missing the point of PIT: sensations can help us form representations of mind-independence because they are intrinsically representational, and can represent mind-independent objects. However, this proposal only leads to further 'how-possible' questions: how can sensations be representational? How can a mind-dependent sensation represent a mind-independent object? The right response to these questions is to ask what the problem is supposed to be. Why *shouldn't* a sensation be capable of representing something that isn't a sensation? It all depends on where you start. If you start with the assumption that sensations are non-representational the proposal that they can ground our grasp of concepts of mind-independent objects is bound to look pretty mysterious. However, the question the non-reductive representationalist is raising is whether this assumption about the nature of sensation is correct. The point of PIT is not just that sensations are intrinsically representational but also that the intentionality of sensation is 'in some way basic among the forms of intentionality' (Kriegel 2013, p. 13). Against this background there is no reason why a sensation shouldn't be capable of representing something that isn't a sensation. The question, 'How can a sensation be representational?' only arises against background assumptions which non-reductive representationalism rejects.

It appears that we have reached a stand-off. Non-reductive representationalism tackles Berkeley's Puzzle on the basis of a conception of sensation which Campbell repudiates, while Campbell argues against non-reductive representationalism on the basis of assumptions about the nature of sensation which *it* rejects. Where do we go from here? Instead of arguing about whether sensations can themselves be representational—an issue concerning which there isn't much prospect of agreement—it would be far more constructive to focus on Campbell's first objection to non-reductive representationalism in the passage quoted above. In that passage, just before the Reid reference, Campbell asks how the representation of mind-independence can depend on sensation. The point is that *even if* sensations are intrinsically representational, it is a further question whether the supposed representational content of sensation is doing any work in grounding our grasp of concepts of mind-independent objects. This amounts to a kind of redundancy objection to non-reductive representationalism, similar to the redundancy objection to reductive representationalism. The implication is that representationalism in its non-reductive form isn't off the hook just because it sees consciousness as representational. It can be true that consciousness is representational but not true that our being conscious is what explains our grasp of concepts.

How is this latest redundancy objection supposed to go? Campbell's thought seems to be that the representation of mind-independent objects can't depend on sensation because even if it's true that sensations can represent mind-independent objects, it isn't true that *only* sensations can do this. Non-reductive representationalists don't think that representation of objects is the exclusive preserve of consciousness, and must grant that mere perceptual states can also represent objects as mind-independent. But once you accept that, that is, once you accept that even without consciousness the perceptual representation of object constancy is still possible, it starts to look as though consciousness isn't necessary for grasp of concepts of objects. If consciousness is, in this sense, redundant, then Berkeley's Puzzle remains: to understand how consciousness can ground our concepts of a mind-independent world.

It's clear what a non-reductive representationalist should say in response to this. Once again, there is a question about a shift in the rules of engagement. The question is: how can it be that consciousness grounds our grasp of concepts of a mind-independent world? The non-reductive representationalist's answer is: because consciousness, in the form of sensation, can and does represent a mind-independent world. When perceptual sensations represent objects as constant and persisting or, if you prefer, as autonomous causal unities, they thereby represent them as mind-independent and so make it possible for us to grasp what it would be for them to be mind-independent. It doesn't undermine this response to Berkeley's question to point out that mere perceptual states can also represent mind-independent objects. That only shows that the role of consciousness in grounding our grasp of concepts of objects isn't essential, but that is neither here nor there. The issue isn't whether our grasp of concepts of mind-independent objects *must* be grounded in sensation but whether it *can* be so grounded. To *this* question, non-reductive representationalism has a straightforward answer.

In fact, this response to the redundancy objection is in some ways too concessive. The possibility to which this objection draws attention is that representation of objects is possible without consciousness, with blindsight often being cited as a concrete illustration of how this can happen. I have envisaged non-reductive representationalism as questioning the relevance of this possibility but there is also a question about its coherence. Blindsight patients might be responsive to mind-independent objects and register their presence without being conscious of them, but is registering the presence of a mind-independent object the same as representing it as mind-independent? What is missing from blindsight is any conscious awareness of objects as occupying space, as coming into or receding from view. There is no conscious awareness of objects as persisting or constant or as causal unities, and the result is that the representation of objects in blindsight is nothing like the representation of objects in sensation. Only in a very attenuated sense can the blindsighted be said to be representing objects *as* mind-independent in their 'perceptual states', and it can't be assumed that the representation of objects as mind-independent by mere perceptual states without consciousness is sufficient to ground concepts of mind-independent objects. The redundancy argument assumes that consciousness makes no difference to the ability to represent objects as mind-independent but that is precisely the point at issue.

A non-reductive representationalist who argues like this doesn't have to deny that the blindsighted still have concepts of mind-independent objects, but this is easy to explain: their grasp of such concepts is grounded in their normal conscious awareness of objects rather than in episodes of blindsight. Suffering from blindsight doesn't mean *never* having any conscious awareness of objects, and it is only because mind-independence is *normally* represented by us consciously that we can make sense of it sometimes being represented unconsciously, in mere perceptual states. Furthermore, what grounds our concepts of mind-independent objects is the conscious representation of objects, and this makes consciousness anything but redundant. It can't be redundant if it is basic among the forms of intentionality. Subtract consciousness of mind-independence and we would only be left with an empty and formal understanding of the concept of a mind-independent object.

Once the redundancy objection is finally off the agenda, the only remaining option for Campbell is to launch a frontal assault on the idea that sensations can be representational, and this takes us back to the stand-off I described above. The redundancy objection looked like a way for Campbell to argue against non-reductive representationalism without having to deny that sensations are representational. It turns out that the redundancy objection is no such thing and that Campbell cannot acknowledge that sensations are conscious states with intentional content. If sensations can represent mind-independent objects without presupposing concepts of mind-independent objects then there is no reason why our grasp of such concepts can't be grounded in sensation. In the end, Campbell's objection to non-reductive representationalism must come down to an objection to its conception of sensation, but what is needed is a clear and cogent argument against thinking of sensations as representational. In the absence of such an argument, the only possible verdict on the charge that non-reductive representationalism fails to explain how consciousness can ground our concepts of mind-independent objects must be: not proven.

Campbell's third major objection to representationalism is that it misses the level of visual experience at which properties are used to select objects from their backgrounds:

The usual formulations of representationalism do not provide any way of dealing with aspects of visual experience that relate to the level of visual selection rather than the level of visual access. (p. 185)

Campbell explains the distinction between selection and access in Chapter 3. The distinction is between two ways a perceived property can function in relation to an object or region: 'Grabbing the thing out from its background (selection) is one thing, and characterizing it (access) is another' (p. 54). In these terms, a property may be used to select an object or region, or it may be accessed as a property of that object or region. Selection is what makes the object or region visible in the first place, and is possible without access. Imagine being presented with an array of coloured blobs in which all there is to separate a figure of 5 from its background are the colours of the blobs. You can only see the 5 if you have conscious experience of the various colours involved. However, 'although you may have used your conscious experience of [its] colour to select the 5, and then go on to access various properties of the 5, such as its size, shape, and orientation, it seems entirely possible that you could select the 5 on the basis of colour without yet having any capacity to access colour properties' (p. 58).

This is all very plausible: there is a distinction between selection and access, and there can be selection without access. What is not clear is why any of this is a problem for versions of representationalism which view the representational content of sensory experience as non-conceptual. In Campbell's example, the 5 can be selected on the basis of its colour as long as its colour is represented by one's sensory experience, but sensory experience can represent the colour of the 5, and enable its selection, regardless of whether one is able to characterize its colour or, indeed, any other colour properties. This is especially clear given Campbell's tendency to describe access in terms of language. If accessing the colour of the 5 is a matter of giving a 'verbal report of its colour' (p. 59), then few representationalists would want to claim that only accessed or accessible properties can be represented or selected in visual experience. To characterize a property is to *conceptualize* it but the representational content of sensory experience is, I have claimed, non-conceptual. This form of representationalism is designed to deal with aspects of experience which relate to selection rather than access.

Here, as elsewhere in Campbell's discussion, it is hard to avoid the impression that his primary target is 'conceptualist' rather than 'non-conceptualist' representationalism. He does mention the view that sensory experience has non-conceptual representational content, but he models the non-conceptual on the conceptual (see my Ch. 8). If one is serious about the possibility that sensory experience can represent colour or other properties that one is unable to characterize, why would one suppose that the selection/access distinction is a problem for representation-alism? Going by his discussion of Siegel, something like the following worry might be at the back of Campbell's mind: sensory experience can represent the colour of an object only if the '*representation* of colour [is] "there in the experience"'. How can that be if the colour can't be accessed by the subject? Suppose one says that the representation of colour is there in the experience just if, in line with one of Siegel's suggestions, it enables the experience to guide bodily action. But if the represen-tation of colour is doing that then we are back at the level of access. To say that someone has no *access* to the colour is to say, among other things, that they have 'no tendency to use colour itself as a guide to action'.

If this is Campbell's concern, then the representationalist can deal with it by pointing out that this depends on a reinterpretation of the notion of access: the fact that the representation of a given property is serving to guide one's bodily actions has little to do with the idea that one has the capacity to characterize that property. The reason for thinking that a property can be selected without being accessed is that a property can be selected without the subject being able to characterize it. It's an entirely different matter whether a property can be said to be accessed if it doesn't serve to guide one's actions. As far as PIT is concerned, the sense in which a representation shows up in one's experience is that it shows up in, and is deter-mined by, the phenomenal character of one's experience. Having a representation show up in one's experience in *this* sense has nothing to do with whether one can characterize or conceptualize the property. At this level, representation is about phenomenology, not conceptualization.

That's as much as I want to say about Campbell's objections to representational-ism. If, as I have argued, these objections are unsuccessful, where does that leave the relational view of experience? Are there elements of this view that represen-tationalism can or should accommodate? That depends on what one thinks is the basic point of the relational view. In his book *Reference and Consciousness*, Campbell makes it clear that the proposition to which the relational view is trying to do justice is that:

[w]hatever else is true of it, experience of objects has to explain our ability to think about those very objects.

(2002b, p. 114)

Another way of expressing this would be to say that it is experience of objects that puts us in a position to think about them. In these terms, Campbell's point is that experience can put us in a position to think about objects only if it is a simple rela-tion between subjects and objects, that is, only if perceivers can stand in this rela-tion to objects regardless of whether they can think about them. There is no hope of sensory experience explaining our ability to think about objects if it presupposes an ability to think about them.

It's possible to imagine a representationalist disputing Campbell's *explanandum*. Such a representationalist might argue that the experiences of a subject who is being deceived by a malicious demon are sufficient to put them in a position to think about objects even though, *ex hypothesi*, there are no objects for them to think about. On this view, being in a position to think about objects doesn't require actual cognitive contact with objects. However, this is not something a representationalist *has* to say. Representationalism can accept that experience of objects puts us in a position to think about them. As long as the perceptual representation of objects is non-conceptual, thought about objects needn't come into it. On this reading, the tension between representationalism and the relational view is more apparent than real since having representational content doesn't prevent an experience from being a simple relation in the sense that matters.

In reality, of course, there is far more to our being able to think about objects than can be accounted for either by representationalism on its own or by the relational view. Barry Stroud correctly observes that:

We acquire our capacities as masters of propositional thoughts about a mind-independent world only by gradually becoming socialized into a living linguistic practice that enables us to speak and think in those ways.

(2013, p. 10)

The point of the relational view is that these capacities need to be grounded in our sensory experience of the world. The point of the representational view is that the capacity to think about a mind-independent world can only be grounded in sensory experience of the world if sensory experience represents objects as mind-independent. This is how mind-independence shows up in experience, and my claim is that experience represents mind-independent objects not in virtue of our grasp of concepts of mind-independent objects but rather in virtue of the conscious character of experience. This is the heart of the disagreement between Campbell's view and mine. I haven't *proved* that sensations are intrinsically representational, any more than Campbell has proved that they couldn't be. What I am saying is that in the absence of a conclusive argument against the coherence of the notion of phenomenal intentionality, and with a proper understanding of what it takes to answer a 'how-possible' question, there is no compelling reason to believe that representationalism can't solve Berkeley's Puzzle.

References

Aggernaes, A. 1972. 'The Experienced Reality of Hallucinations and Other Psychological Phenomena'. *Acta Psychiatrica Scandinavica* 48, 220–38.

Allport, Alan. 1989. 'Visual Attention'. In Michael I. Posner (ed.), *Foundations of Cognitive Science* (Cambridge, MA: MIT Press), 631–82.

Austin, John Langshaw. 1962. *Sense and Sensibilia*. Oxford: Oxford University Press.

Ayers, Michael R. 1970. 'Substance, Reality, and the Great, Dead Philosophers'. *American Philosophical Quarterly* 7, 38–49.

Ayers, Michael R. 'Introduction'. M. R. Ayers (ed.), *Berkeley: Philosophical Works* London: Everyman 1975.

Ayers, Michael R. 1991. *Locke: Epistemology and Ontology: Volume 1: Epistemology*. London: Routledge.

Barbur, J. L., A. J. Harlow, and G. Plant. 1994. 'Insights Into the Different Exploits of Colour in the Visual Cortex'. *Proceedings of the Royal Society of London, Series B*, 258, 327–34.

Berkeley, George. 1734/1975. *A Treatise Concerning the Principles of Human Knowledge*. Reprinted in M. R. Ayers (ed.), *Berkeley: Philosophical Works*. London: Everyman 1975, 62–127.

Block, Ned. 2010. 'Attention and Mental Paint'. *Philosophical Issues*, 20, 23–63.

BonJour, Lawrence. 1980. 'Externalist Theories of Empirical Knowledge'. *Midwest Studies in Philosophy* 5, 53–73.

Borges, Jorge Luis. 2007. 'Story of the Warrior and the Captive'. In Jorge Luis Borges, *Labyrinths*. New Directions: New York.

Boswell, James 1791/1992. *The Life of Samuel Johnson Ll.D.* Alfred A. Knopf: New York and Toronto.

Bouvier, Seth E. and Stephen A. Engel. 2006. 'Behavioral Deficits and Cortical Damage Loci in Cerebral Achromatopsia'. *Cerebral Cortex* 16, 183–191.

Brewer, Bill. 2011. *Perception and Its Objects*. Oxford: Oxford University Press.

Burge, Tyler. 2009. 'Perceptual Objectivity'. *Philosophical Review* 118, 285–324.

Burge, Tyler. 2010. *Origins of Objectivity*. Oxford: Oxford University Press.

Byrne, Alex. 2004. 'Perception and Conceptual Content'. In E. Sosa and M. Steup (eds), *Contemporary Debates in Epistemology*. Oxford: Blackwell.

Campbell, John. 1993. 'A Simple View of Colour'. In John Haldane and Crispin Wright (eds), *Reality: Representation and Projection*. Oxford: Oxford University Press, 257–68.

Campbell, John. 2002a. 'Berkeley's Puzzle'. In Tamar Szabo Gendler and John O'Leary Hawthorne (eds), *Conceivability and Possibility*. Oxford: Oxford University Press, 127–43.

Campbell, John. 2002b. *Reference and Consciousness*. Oxford: Oxford University Press.

Campbell, John. 2005. 'Reply to Georges Rey'. *Philosophical Studies* 126 145–53.

Campbell, John. 2006. 'Manipulating Colour: Pounding an Almond'. In Tamar Gendler and John Hawthorne (eds), *Perceptual Experience*. Oxford: Oxford University Press.

Campbell, John. 2011. Review Essay on Tyler Burge, *Origins of Objectivity*, *Journal of Philosophy*, 108, 269–85.

Cassam, Quassim. 2007. *The Possibility of Knowledge*. Oxford: Oxford University Press.

Cassam, Quassim. 2011. 'Tackling Berkeley's Puzzle'. In Naomi Eilan, Hemdat Lerman, and Johannes Roessler (eds), *Perception, Causation, and Objectivity*. Oxford: Oxford University Press.

Cavanagh, Patrick, M.-A. Henaff, F. Michel, T. Landis, T. Troscianki and J. Intriligator. 1998. 'Complete Sparing of High-Contrast Color Input to Motion Perception in Cortical Color Blindness'. *Nature Neuroscience*, 1, 242–7.

Church, Jennifer. 2013. *Possibilities of Perception*. Oxford: Oxford University Press.

Cohen, Michael A., Patrick Cavanagh, Marvin M. Chun, and Ken Nakayama. 2012. 'The Attentional Requirements of Consciousness', *Trends in Cognitive Sciences* 16, 411–17.

Davidoff, Jules. 1991. *Cognition Through Color*. Cambridge, Mass.: MIT Press.

Dyer, F. C. 2002. 'The Biology of the Dance Language'. *Annual Reviews of Entomology* 47, 917–49.

Evans, Gareth. 1980. 'Things Without the Mind'. In Zak van Straaten (ed.) *Philosophical Subjects*. Oxford: Oxford University Press.

Falkenstein, Lorne. 1995. *Kant's Intuitionism: A Commentary on the Transcendental Aesthetic*. Toronto: Toronto University Press.

Farkas, Katalin. 2013. 'Constructing a World for the Senses'. In Uriah Kriegel (ed.), *Phenomenal Intentionality*. New York and Oxford: Oxford University Press, 99–115.

Fish, William. 2009. *Perception, Hallucination, and Illusion*. New York: Oxford University Press.

Franklin, Anna. 2006. 'Constraints on Children's Color Term Acquisition'. *Journal of Experimental Child Psychology* 94, 322–7.

Franklin, Anna and Ian R. L. Davies. 2004. 'New Evidence for Infant Colour Categories'. *British Journal of Developmental Psychology* 22, 349–77.

Gallistel, Charles R. 1990. *The Organization of Learning*. Cambridge, Mass.: MIT Press.

George, Rolf. 1981. 'Kant's Sensationism'. *Synthese* 47, 229–55.

Glymour, Clark and David Danks. 2007. 'Reasons as Causes in Bayesian Epistemology'. *Journal of Philosophy* 104, 464–74.

Gould, J. L. 1986. 'The Locale Map of Honey Bees: Do Insects Have Cognitive Maps?' *Science* 232, 861–3.

Gould, J. L. and C. G. Gould. 1988. *The Honey Bee*. New York: W.H. Freeman.

Graham, T. S. and M. Collett 2002. 'Memory Use in Insect Visual Navigation.' *Nature Reviews: Neuroscience* 3, 542–52.

Harman, Gilbert. 1990. 'The Intrinsic Quality of Experience', *Philosophical Perspectives* 4, 31–52.

Heywood, C. A., A. Cowey, and F. Newcombe. 1991. 'Chromatic Discrimination in a Cortically Colour Blind Observer'. *European Journal of Neuroscience* 3, 802–12.

Horgan, Terence and J. Tienson. 2002. 'The Intentionality of Phenomenology and the Phenomenology of Intentionality'. In David Chalmers (ed.), *Philosophy of Mind: Classical and Contemporary Readings*. New York: Oxford University Press.

Huang, Liquiang. 2010. 'What is the Unit of Visual Attention? Object for Selection, but Boolean Map for Access'. *Journal of Experimental Psychology* 139, 162–79.

Huang, Liqiang and Harold Pashler. 2007. 'A Boolean Map Theory of Visual Attention'. *Psychological Review* 114, 599–631.

Jackson, Frank. 2002. 'Epiphenomenal Qualia'. In David Chalmers (ed.), *Philosophy of Mind: Classical and Contemporary Readings*. New York: Oxford University Press.

Jacovides, Michael. 1999. 'Locke's Resemblance Theses'. *Philosophical Review* 108, 461–96.

Johnston, Mark. 1992. 'How to Speak of the Colors'. *Philosophical Studies*, 68, 221–63.

Kant, Immanuel. 1932. *Critique of Pure Reason*, trans. N. Kemp Smith. London: Macmillan.

Kennedy, Matthew. 2010. 'Naïve Realism and Perceptual Experience'. *Proceedings of the Aristotelian Society* 110, 77–109.

Kolterman, R. 1974. 'Periodicity in the Activity and Learning Performance of the Honey Bee'. In L. B. Browne (ed.), *The Experimental Analysis of Insect Behavior*, 218–26. Berlin: Springer.

Kowalski, Kurt, and Herbert Zimiles. 2006. 'The Relation Between Children's Conceptual Functioning with Color and Color Term Acquisition'. *Journal of Experimental Child Psychology* 94, 301–21.

Koyré, Alexandre. 1965. *Newtonian Studies*. Cambridge, Mass.: Harvard University Press.

Kriegel, Uriah. 2013. 'The Phenomenal Intentionality Research Program'. In Uriah Kriegel (ed.), *Phenomenal Intentionality*. Oxford and New York: Oxford University Press.

Kripke, Saul. 1980. *Naming and Necessity*. Cambridge, Mass.: Harvard University Press.

Lackey, Jennifer. 1999. 'Testimonial Knowledge and Transmission'. *Philosophical Quarterly* 49, 471–90.

Lewis, David. 2002. 'What Experience Teaches'. In David Chalmers (ed.), *Philosophy of Mind: Classical and Contemporary Readings*. New York: Oxford University Press.

Loar, Brian. 2003. 'Phenomenal Intentionality as the Basis of Mental Content'. In Martin Hahn and B. Ramberg (eds), *Reflections and Replies: Essays on the Philosophy of Tyler Burge*. Cambridge, Mass.: MIT Press.

Locke, John. 1690/1975. *An Essay Concerning Human Understanding* (ed. P. H. Nidditch). Oxford: Oxford University Press.

Martin, M. G. F. 2004. 'The Limits of Self-Awareness'. *Philosophical Studies* 120, 37–89.

McDowell, John. 1985. 'Values and Secondary Qualities'. In Ted Honderich (ed.), *Morality and Objectivity*. London: Routledge and Kegan Paul.

McDowell, John. 1996. *Mind and World*. Cambridge, Mass.: Harvard University Press.

McLaughlin, Brian. 2010. 'The Representational vs. the Relational View of Visual Experience'. *Royal Institute of Philosophy Supplement* 85 (67), 239–62.

Menzel, Randolf, U. Greggers, A. Smith, S. Berger, R. Brandt, S. Brunke, et al. 2005. 'Honeybees Navigate According to a Map-Like Strategy'. *Proceedings of the National Academy of Sciences*, 102, 3040–5.

Moore, G. E. 1903. 'The Refutation of Idealism'. *Mind* 48, 433–53.

Moore, G. E. 1939. 'Proof of an External World'. *Proceedings of the British Academy* 25, 273–300.

Nagel, Thomas. 2002. 'What is it Like to be a Bat?'. In David Chalmers (ed.), *Philosophy of Mind: Classical and Contemporary Readings*. New York: Oxford University Press.

Oyebode, Femi. 2008. *Sim's Symptoms in the Mind*. Edinburgh: Elsevier.

Patton, Victoria. 2006. *Conceptualism and Concept Acquisition*. Oxford D. Phil. Thesis. Unpublished.

Peacocke, Christopher. 1983. *Sense and Content*. Oxford: Oxford University Press.

Peacocke, Christopher. 1989. *Transcendental Arguments in the Theory of Content*. Oxford: Clarendon Press.

Peacocke, Christopher. 2001a. 'Does Perception Have a Non-Conceptual Content?'. *Journal of Philosophy* 98, 239–64.

Peacocke, Christopher. 2001b. 'Phenomenology and Non-Conceptual Content'. *Phenomenology and Philosophical Research*, 62, 609–15.

Quine, W. V. O. 1953. 'Two Dogmas of Empiricism'. In W. V. O. Quine, *From a Logical Point of View*. Cambridge, Mass.: Harvard University Press.

Reid, Thomas. 1785/2002. *Essays on the Intellectual Powers of Man*. University Park: Pennsylvania State University Press.

Rey, Georges. 2005. 'Explanation, Not Experience: Commentary on John Campbell, *Reference and Consciousness*'. *Philosophical Studies* 126, 131–43.

Rice, Mabel. 1980. *Cognition to Language: Categories, Word Meaning, and Training*. Baltimore, MD: University Park Press.

Russell, Bertrand. 1950/1995. *An Inquiry Into Meaning and Truth*. Abingdon and New York: Routledge.

Sacks, Oliver. 1995. 'The Case of the Colorblind Painter'. In Oliver Sacks, *An Anthropologist on Mars*. New York: Alfred A. Knopf.

Sacks, Oliver. 2012. *Hallucinations*. New York: Alfred A. Knopf.

Shoemaker, Sydney. 1984. 'Properties and Causality'. In Sydney Shoemaker, *Identity, Cause and Mind*. Cambridge: Cambridge University Press.

Siegel, Susanna. 2006. 'Subject and Object in the Contents of Visual Experience'. *Philosophical Review* 115, 355–88.

Siegel, Susanna. 2010. *The Contents of Visual Experience*. Oxford: Oxford University Press.

Simons, Daniel J. and Christopher F. Chabris. 1999. 'Gorillas in Our Midst: Sustained Inattentional Blindness for Dynamic Events'. *Perception* 28, 1059–74.

Strawson, P. F. 1966. *The Bounds of Sense*. London: Methuen.

Strawson, P. F. 1974. 'Imagination and Perception'. In P. F. Strawson, *Freedom and Resentment*. London: Methuen.

Strawson, P. F. 2011. 'Perception and Its Objects'. In P. F. Strawson, *Philosophical Writings*. Oxford: Oxford University Press.

Stroud, Barry. 2013. Contribution to APA Symposium on *Berkeley's Puzzle*. Unpublished.

Travis, Charles. 2004. 'The Silence of the Senses'. *Mind* 113, 57–94.

Tye, Michael. 2013. 'Transparency, Qualia Realism and Representationalism'. *Philosophical Studies*, in press.

Von Frisch, Karl. 1967. *The Dance Language and Orientation of Bees*. Cambridge, Mass.: Harvard University Press.

Wehner, Randolf. 1992. 'Arthropods'. In F. Papi (ed.), *Animal Homing*, 45–144. London: Chapman and Hall.

Wehner, Randolf, B. Michel and P. Antonson. 1996. 'Visual Navigation in Insects: Coupling of Egocentric and Geocentric Information'. *Journal of Experimental Biology* 199, 129–40.

Weiskrantz, L. 1986. *Blindsight: A Case Study and Implications*. Oxford: Oxford University Press.

Weiskrantz, Lawrence. 2007. 'The Case of Blindsight'. In Max Velmans and Susan Schneider (eds), *The Blackwell Companion to Consciousness*. Oxford: Blackwell.

Woodward, James. 2003. *Making Things Happen: A Theory of Causal Explanation*. Oxford: Oxford University Press.

Wundt, Wilhelm. 1898. 'Die Geometrisch-Optischen Täuschungen'. *Abhandlungen der Mathematisch-Physischen Classe der Sächsischen Gesellschaft der Wissenschaften* 24, 53–178.

Index

Printed and bound by CPI Group (UK) Ltd, Croydon, CR0 4YY